Horace Marryat

A Residence in Jutland

The Danish Isles and Copenhagen

Horace Marryat

A Residence in Jutland
The Danish Isles and Copenhagen

ISBN/EAN: 9783743408111

Manufactured in Europe, USA, Canada, Australia, Japa

Cover: Foto ©Andreas Hilbeck / pixelio.de

Manufactured and distributed by brebook publishing software (www.brebook.com)

Horace Marryat

A Residence in Jutland

A RESIDENCE IN JUTLAND,

THE DANISH ISLES, AND COPENHAGEN.

By HORACE MARRYAT.

IN TWO VOLUMES.—Vol. II.

LONDON:
JOHN MURRAY, ALBEMARLE STREET.
1860.

The right of Translation is reserved.

LONDON: PRINTED BY W. CLOWES AND SONS, STAMFORD STREET,
AND CHARING CROSS.

CONTENTS OF VOL. II.

CHAPTER XXVIII.

The five steeples of Kallundborg church — Its castle, the last resting-place of Christian II. — The Nero of the North vindicated — His negociations with Scotland — Death of Prince Valdemar at Refsnæs — Legend of the Holy Anders — Death of Frederic II. — Story of Prince Hagbard and the fair Signe — The Birnam wood stratagem — Sir Eskil Snubbe — The Isles of King Hiarne and Alruna his Queen .. .. PAGE 1

CHAPTER XXIX.

Boller, the place of banishment of Christina Munk — Her regal state — The copper nail in a bed of gold — The eatable snail naturalized by a Frenchman — Coffin of Count Griffenfeld — Præstegaard of a Jutland clergyman — Agnete and the merman — The English Cinque Ports — Legend of the Elder Queen 14

CHAPTER XXX.

Silkeborg — Cap of Bishop Peter — The Jutland lakes — The treasure-seeker — Himmelbjerg, Queen of the Jutland mountains — The fiery beacon — Lovers of Laven Castle — The paper manufactory 26

CHAPTER XXXI.

The fish and the ring — Fortunes of the house of Stubbe — The traitor page — Marsk Stig, the outlaw — Château of Friisenborg — Artificial egg-hatching 38

CHAPTER XXXII.

Siege of Kalø — The lord of Mols — Danish Whittington — The Lady Hilda Trolle — Round church of Thorsager — Château of Rosenholm — Origin of the Rosenkrantz name — Holger the savant — Erik's rebuke of Cromwell — Jutland clergy — Clausholm — Meeting of King Frederic and Anne Reventlow .. .. PAGE 46

CHAPTER XXXIII.

Bruusgaard and the Bruces — Randers' commerce, her gloves and beer — Duel of the Counts — Manors of the Scheel family — A midnight wandering in Jutland 62

CHAPTER XXXIV.

The village of Mariager — Story of Sir Hem and Sir Sem — Poor Mary's well — A black stork — A Jutland plain — Sea of barrows — Wicked Baroness of Lindenborg 71

CHAPTER XXXV.

Aalborg or Eel Castle — Its armes parlantes — Death of King John — Jens Bang and the miser's daughter — The Agger Canal — Skipper Clemens, leader of the Vendel boers — Hog family — Their high and ancient descent — Coat of Jørgen Bille — Great bog of Jutland — Børglum and Bishop Crump — The lady of Asdal and the flitch of bacon 82

CHAPTER XXXVI.

Old manor of Høgholt and its dairy-farm — Two sisters of Jerup — Pontoppidan — Jutland's most northern manor — Lighthouse of Skagen — Storm of flying sand — Wrecks — Melons and sea-nettles — Sweet gale and bog moss — Frederikshavn — The Jutland Dido 103

CHAPTER XXXVII.

Manor of Voergaard — Skipper Clemens and Bishop Crump again — Lady Ingeborg Skeel and the architect — The message of her husband — Her disturbed spirit — Her prison, the Rosodonten — Her Sunday pastime — Her monument — The road-side inns of Queen Margaret — Jutland mode of boiling eggs 117

CHAPTER XXXVIII.

Nørlund Manor — Ellen Marsviin and Ludvig Munk — Meeting of King Christian and the fair Christina — Names of the Jutland nobility — Almshouse of Aalborg — Scottish guard of Christian II. — Prince Niels and his tutor — Duke Knud's suit of scarlet — Mermaid monument at Tiele .. .. PAGE 127

CHAPTER XXXIX.

Pagan city of Viborg — Erik the Lovely and the harper — The Danish Luther — First of the Longobardi — Sir Niels Bugge and the Castle of Hald — Murder of King Erik Glipping — Church of Anscarius — Railway engineer — King Knud's invasion of England — Manor of Krabbesholm — Parson Mads the slanderer — Caps of Fuur Island — Mors, birthplace of Hamlet — His story as told by Saxo .. 136

CHAPTER XL.

County of Thy — Superstitions concerning tombs — Plague of sand — Wicked Queen of England — Draining the Sjørring lake — The pedlar and the geese — Anne Boleyn — The Liimfiorde — Story of Liden Kirsten — Sale of a wreck — Old Abellona and her amber — beads — Loss of life off this coast 155

CHAPTER XLI.

The Agger canal — Food of the peasants — The girl who trod upon bread 174

CHAPTER XLII.

Battle of the Giants — Patriotism of a peasant — Sequel to the story of Hamlet — Protection against flying sand — Magnus Munk and the still — Gipsies the outcasts of society — The dragon and the wizard — Appearance of the Black Pest — Depopulation of the Ale Mose 177

CHAPTER XLIII.

Legend of the English prince and his bed of gold — The luck of Vosborg manor — Little Peter the cow-driver — The industrious Nisses — Long Margaret and her eight murders — Private tutor of Prince George of Denmark — Story of Havelock the Dane — Customs on Christmas-eve — The corporal and his little child 193

a 2

CHAPTER XLIV.

The bells of Thim — Gyldenstierne of Thimgaard — Poorhouse of Ringkjøbing — Old rat of Hee — Threshing to the sound of music
PAGE 210

CHAPTER XLV.

Island of Fanø — Voluminous petticoats and black masks of the peasant women — Their Oriental character and Dutch cleanliness — Queen Thyre wrecked off the Isle of Man — Amber-gathering 218

CHAPTER XLVI.

Ribe Cathedral — The anchorite Bishop — Sacred theatricals — Ribe "ret" — Sumptuary laws — Bridal trousseau of the eighteenth century — Ragged schools of the middle ages — Death of Queen Dagmar — Queen Agnes at Ribehuus — Funeral of Marsk Stig — The robber's bride — Legend of Tovelil — A Tinghuus — The werewolf and the nightmare — The night-raven and the basilisk — Monument to the heroes of Fredericia — Farewell to Jutland 224

CHAPTER XLVII.

The island of Funen — Red cabbage of Sir Niels Bugge — Ploughing ghosts — Odin and Odense — Murder of St. Knud — The traitor Blakke — Funeral of Kirstine Munk — Dormitorium of the Ahlefeldts — The lady who danced herself to death — The pet cats of Mrs. Mouse — King John and his family — The Lear of Odense and his daughters 244

CHAPTER XLVIII.

Funen continued — King Christian II. and the ape — Deathplace of Ellen Marsviin — By-laws of Nyborg — Women to be buried alive — Laws of adulteration — King Hans' invitation to his daughter's christening — Story of Kai Lykke and the Queen — The rival Nisses — St. George killed the dragon in Denmark — Svendborg, the Pig Castle — Guas made archbishop — Island of Thorseng the apanage of Count Valdemar — Portraits of the House of Oldenborg .. 258

CHAPTER XLIX.

The Island of Lyø — Capture of King Valdemar by his treacherous vassal — Kirstine Munk and her children — Horns of Wedellsborg — Marksmen of Middelfart — Snoghøi in Jutland — Brahe, the King of Funen — Island of Thorø, and Balder's stone — Ellen Marsviin married again; turns cattle-dealer — Her game of cards with the king — Island of Langeland and the giant Rud — Sir Otto Krump's defence of Tranekjær .. .. PAGE 275

CHAPTER L.

Island of Lolland — Yule-feast of Olaf Hunger — Wendish families from Rugen — Royal ordinances — Lutheran clergy — Sir Edward the Pedagogue Priest — Shell of the Swedes — Mr. Ursins and our Prince George — Birthplace of Erik Glipping — The Curate of Helsted and the mother's curse — Tale of Sir Otto Rud and King John — Revelations of St. Bridget — The ill-behaved nuns of Maribo — Grave of Eleanor Ulfeld — King Charles "forgets" the loan — Eleanor in captivity and death — The bricked-up lady of Hardenberg .. 291

CHAPTER LI.

Island of Falster — Queen Sophia and the parson's wife — How she rules her household — The lady who could not die — Molesworth's account of swan-shooting — Familiar spirits and other superstitions of the island — Island of Møen — The strong-minded Dorothea — The bathing-place of Liselund — The chalk klints and beauty of the scenery — The Klint King — Bacchanalian harvest-homo .. 312

CHAPTER LII.

The island of Bornholm; its reputation for salmon — A coachman from the diggings — Round churches of Ny and Ole — Church-pushers and hourglasses — The Trolles of Bornholm — Their tricks upon Bondevedde — Their patriotism — How they love butter — The three-legged cat — They man the cliffs to defend the island — Hammershuus, the prison of Corfitz and Eleanor Ulfeld 323

CHAPTER LIII.

Farming in Bornholm — Village beacons — The rock scenery — The White Oven visited at Christmas secure from ghosts — Bornholm gold coined by Christian IV. — Its diamonds in favour with Queen Louisa — Round church of Øster Lars — Fastelavn at Shrovetide — — Forest of Alminde — The birds at the Cross — Tower of Christiansminde — Horse-fair — Font of Aakirkeby 342

CHAPTER LIV.

Return to Zealand — Island of Bogø — King Valdemar and the Hanseatikers — The Goose Tower — Goose carried off by King Erik — Castigation of the fair Cecilia — Herlufsholm the Harrow of Denmark — Old Bridget and the missing title-deeds — The gallant Admiral Trolle — Hvitfeldt the chronicler's Dance of Death .. PAGE 358

CHAPTER LV.

Peter Thott and his høi — The Black Friis of Borreby — The enchanted bell of the Letter-room — Old Valdemar Daa the alchemist — The giant girl and the sandhills — The "Lady of the Morn" the curse of Zealand — Thorvaldsen at Nysø — The convent for noble ladies at Gisselfeld — Peter Oxe the minister of Frederic II. — The ladies of Vemmetofte — A starlight night — Spoliation of the goddess Freia 369

CHAPTER LVI.

The dominions of the Elf King — Hospitality at Store Hedinge — The Trolles and the church of Højerup — Vallø, the Queen of Danish convents — The ancient house of Bille — Lucia the Flower of Denmark — The last of the Rosensparres — Ledreborg, the ancient Leira — Court etiquette of King Ring — Legend of King Skiold, founder of Leira 382

CHAPTER LVII.

Destruction of the Palace of Frederiksborg by fire 393

CONCLUSION 399

ILLUSTRATIONS OF VOL. II.

CHURCH, KALLUNDBORG	*Frontispiece.*
ROUND CHURCH OF OSTER LARS, BORNHOLM	*Title-page.*
ROUND CHURCH, THORSAGER	*Page* 49
SECTIONS AND GROUND-PLANS OF CHURCH, THORSAGER	49
THOR'S HAMMER BECOME A CROSS	51
SKAGEN	107
FEGGEKLIT, ISLAND OF MORS	151
LIDEN KIRSTEN'S GRAVE	162
FIGURE-DRAWINGS OF THE FIFTH CENTURY	181
CATHEDRAL, RIBE	225
SECTIONS OF CHURCH OF OSTER LARS, BORNHOLM	348
STEVNSKLINT AND CHURCH OF HØIERUP	385
FONT AT AAKIRKEBY, BORNHOLM	357

JUTLAND

AND

THE DANISH ISLANDS.

CHAPTER XXVIII.

The five steeples of Kallundborg church — Its castle, the last resting-place of Christian II. — The Nero of the North vindicated — His negociations with Scotland — Death of Prince Valdemar at Refsnæs — Legend of the Holy Anders — Death of Frederic II. — Story of Prince Haglard and the fair Signe — The Birnam wood stratagem — Sir Eskil Snubbe — The Isles of King Hiarne and Alruna his Queen.

KALLUNDBORG.

June 10*th*. — KALLUNDBORG, like many other places in Denmark, has little to boast of beyond its site, historical recollections, and its church, founded by Esbern Snare [*] — one of the most remarkable ecclesiastical buildings in any country. Long before arriving at Kallundborg you see her four lofty octagonal towers rising against the horizon; in former days it boasted, more lofty than the rest, a fifth, springing from the centre of the building. These five steeples were built by Esbern Snare, says tradition, in honour of his family — the highest (about to be rebuilt) [†] to his mother, the lady Inge, and the four surrounding ones

---

[*] In 1171.
[†] The rebuilding of the centre tower has just been completed (1860). We give the church as it now stands.

VOL. II. B

to her four daughters; and because one of the girls was lame, he built one of the steeples less than the other three. Some years since there lived at Kallundborg a churchwarden, a man of taste; the pillars by which the centre tower was supported gave offence to his eyes, so he ordered the columns to be removed, and, deprived of its support, down came clattering the lofty tower, extinguisher and all, about the heads of the congregation. Unfortunately the perpetrator of this barbarism was not buried alive under the ruins.

Of the ancient castle of Kallundborg, also founded by Esbern Snare, on the model of Axelhuus, no remains now exist. It bore an important part in the history of its country, but was thoroughly destroyed by the Swedes in the occupation of 1658. Within its walls were confined first Albert of Sweden by Queen Margaret; then later the widow of Steen Sture, and other Swedish ladies of rank, after the siege of Stockholm in 1520. Christian himself found a resting-place in Kallundborg, when released from the prison of Sønderborg; and here he lived comfortably, well clothed and fed, and was allowed the privileges of the chace; and here too he died at the age of seventy-three,* after passing ten years within its walls. It is related that one day, when out hunting, he suddenly disappeared, to the great alarm of his attendants; and when discovered hiding in a ditch, he laughed at their fears of his escape, for where could he run to, and indeed, who would receive him?

The day he received the news of the death of Christian III. he burst into a flood of tears, exclaiming,

---

* Christian II. died 1559.

"Now my time will not be long:" nor was it, for he did not long survive his cousin.

I am not going to enter into the defence of this monarch, and have Vertot brought up against me, and the "Nero of the North" thrown in my teeth; still, after what I have read in the Danish historians, I am of opinion he has been blackened more than necessary; added to which he had one great crime in the eyes of the sixteenth century—his leaning towards the Reformed faith. The Emperor Charles V., in speaking of him, said, "If our brother-in-law, against our counsel and will, change his religion, so also will we change our affection and support towards him." Another writer declares him "to have been a Protestant at heart, though he dare not profess the faith openly."

Christian was neither flesh nor fowl—Catholic or of the Reformed faith—an object of suspicion to both parties: had it not been for his "grand connexion" the Emperor, he would in all probability have declared himself, and have taken his seat among the Protestant potentates of Europe.

I have already alluded to the volume of King Christian II.'s Correspondence, lately published at Copenhagen, from letters preserved in the archives of Bavaria, dating from the year 1519 to 1531. There are many therein—interesting as regards his negotiations with England and the sister kingdom of Scotland—in which figures a certain Dr. Alexander Kingome, who signs himself your "humblest of Chaplains." Kingome was a Scotchman by birth, and employed as an emissary to procure aid from King Henry VIII. of England. After a time the answer arrived, worded in most elegant Latin. Dr. Kingome was received at Richmond by the King's Grace, at the same time and in the suite of that learned man Sir Thomas More, and in the presence of Cardinal Wolsey, by the splendour of whose retinue he appears to have been greatly struck. Bluff King Hal is sorry, very sorry, that his approaching war with Scotland prevents him from rendering the assistance his brother the King of Denmark requires; his hands are fully occupied: and later the great Cardinal writes a letter himself to explain the reason why his royal master cannot spare the "one ship" he prays for. If our English Sovereign could afford no help to poor harassed Christian, advice costs nothing; so he writes a letter in his own hand, advising him on no account to irritate his people by raising money in the country: he might have as well advised a starving mendicant to live generously.

The negotiations with Scotland proved quite as unsatisfactory as those with her sister kingdom: indeed more so, for the English declined to afford him aid point blank, while the Scotch were everlastingly promising, and intriguing about something, and never performing their promises after all. I find a most civil letter from the Chancellor of Scotland, regretting that the King of Scots is too occupied by his approaching war with England to go to his cousin's assistance; and then come promises and disappointment about help from the exiled Duke of Albany. It is at last settled that Robert Barton, with the well-known Andrew, his brother, is to equip a fleet to come to his aid, in conjunction with Robert Falconer. Then there's a spoke in the wheel—a riot in Edinburgh, and the arrival of an envoy, Magnus Bille, from King Frederic, Christian's uncle, and Falconer proves faithless. King James V., through his secretary

Hepburn, now writes his cousin word to take refuge in Scotland.

Then writes Kingome:—"James Beaton, Archbishop of St. Andrew, would so much like to be made a cardinal; if King Christian could only procure his election through the Pope and his brother-in-law the Emperor, much good might ensue." But Christian's interest is at a low ebb in those quarters; he is suspected of hankering after " Luthers lære ;" and the Regent Margaret has her eyes open and looks somewhat askant; so his faithful spouse Elizabeth writes him word. As soon as matters appear to be coming round, they are all afloat again.

In the year 1526 dies Queen Elizabeth, and she is hardly buried when it is proposed, in a letter from the faithful Kingome, that Christian should, as a "coup d'état," espouse a half-sister of King James V., then only fifteen years of age, daughter of our English Princess Margaret Tudor and her husband the Earl of Angus, whom she married, hated, and tried to get divorced from. But this marriage never came off; and, what is worse, help never came from Scotland.

Christian had, however, on his side, shuffled just as much; for when in earlier days his cousin, the King of Scots, applied to him for aid against the English, he pleaded, as an excuse, it would interfere with his coronation.

There must have been jolly doings in this city of Kallundborg in former times, if you judge from the colossal drinking-cup now preserved in the Museum of Copenhagen, before the quaffing of which no man could be admitted as "brother" into the Guild of St. Knud.

REFSNÆS.

At some three miles distance from Kallundborg is situated the village of Refsnæs, the barest promontory of the island of Zealand—a scene of desolation now, but once the hunting-grounds of the Denmark sovereigns. It was here, while engaged in the pursuit of a stag, that Prince Valdemar, son of Valdemar II., met with a fate similar to that of our King William Rufus. Four gigantic masses of granite, now no longer to be found, once marked the spot. The event is thus described in the ancient ballad of 'Dronning Leonora:'—

> "Leonora the Queen in childbirth
> Her young life lost,—and died.
>   Alas! alas! alas!
> She came to Denmark from Portugal.
> She travels forth to God's joyful hall;
> She rejoices with saints, and the choir of angels,
> But her body lies in St. Benedict's earth.
> Court holds her lord in Kallundborg.
> He thought with time to kill his grief;
> Hardly had months gone nine
> The lord was willing to console his mind."

In fact, having grieved for nine months, he has had enough of it, and determines to amuse himself: "Saddle me," he exclaims, "Swedefux!"—and off he goes a-hunting. So hard he rides from dawn till night, that when he arrives at Refsnæs scarce a squire has been able to follow him. The beaters drive the deer and hare with shouts into the forest; a hart starts forth; Sir Eskiol draws his bow, the stag shall be his prey; the shaft pierces the prince's breast—he falls to the ground from his charger, and says to this world a long good night. Horror-struck, the attendants rush to his aid too late; he is dead. The affrighted waters of the Belt recede from the strand; the porpoises and fishes raise a loud lament—even the rocks grieve. When the King hears the fatal news, it shoots through his heart like a spear; he wrings his fingers till they crack, and then curses Refsnæs. "Hereafter shall no hare or hart be found— no tree shall henceforth live. On Refsnæs, where flourished oak and beech, henceforth shall grow the thorn and the brier—

"With sorrow they conveyed him to Ringsted,
Saint Benedict's church received the prince, 1231."

The curse of Valdemar was well fulfilled: no hare of the royal forest now exists; one solitary hawthorn, loaded with snow-white flowers, twisted and gnarled like those in Woodstock Park, alone attests the existence of the former hunting-fields. Well too might King Valdemar, and Denmark as one man, lament the death of the heir-apparent (already elected in his father's lifetime),[*] sole offspring of good Queen Dagmar, for three more vicious sovereigns than his half-brothers, sons of Berengaria, never ascended the Danish throne.

"Oh Denmark, had you known your grief,
You would have wept tears of very blood."

SLAGELSE.

Five miles to Slagelse, where we first dine, and then proceed in the cool of the evening by rail to Copenhagen. Slagelse is a tidy little town, once of considerable ecclesiastical eminence. The ancient proverb runs—"Roskild ringen, og Slagelse møgagen, fik aldrig ende" (the ringing at Roeskilde and manuring at Slagelse

---

[*] 1231. Valdemar, Leonora, and her child, were all buried at Ringsted.

never finish); alluding to the extent of her convent lands of Antvorskov, one of the richest monasteries in Zealand, founded by the holy Anders, a saint of much repute, who flourished in the thirteenth century. Holy Anders—only plain Anders then—accompanied a party of pilgrims to the Holy Land; he fell sick by the way, and became such a burden to his fellow-travellers —always wanting an arm, a rest—that, wearied to death, they took advantage of a sound sleep he indulged in somewhere near Joppa, to leave him to his fate, and rid themselves of so troublesome a companion. Great was his consternation when he awoke to find himself deserted; he gave himself up for lost, and prepared to die, when a voice whispered to him, "Be of good cheer;" and he felt himself suddenly raised in the arms of angels, carried rapidly through the air, and, after paying a flying visit to St. Antony of Padua on the way, and St. Olaf of Norway into the bargain, found himself gently laid down on the summit of a hill near Slagelse. "Good bye, Anders," said the angel. "If you don't know what to do with your hat when you say prayers, pray hang it, and your gloves as well, on the sunbeams."

On the summit of this høi was erected Anders Kors (cross). "In memory of St. Andrew, who slept at Joppa, and found himself here in 1205," ran the inscription, which was destroyed after the Reformation. Well, Anders—now holy Anders—grew in grace and reputation, and was in great favour at the court of King Erik Plovpennig. One fine day Anders prayed the King to grant to the poor church as much land to make a garden—merely to grow onions and leeks—as he could ride round on the back of a new-born colt. "By all means," answered the King, and went to his bath. Off

Anders set on his new-born steed, galloping like mad. "A miracle! a miracle!" roared the monks. "He'll ride round the whole island!" cried the courtiers; "stop him! stop him!" and rushed to inform the King, who quickly left his bath; but, before he was dried and dressed, Anders had ridden over such an extent of land as gave rise to the proverb I have above quoted.

After the suppression of the monasteries Antvorskov became a royal residence; and here Frederic II. died the 4th of April, 1587. He ordered the service to be held in his own room, as he was very sick; and when the doctor felt his pulse, the King remarked, "Let the pulse beat as it likes, we know the mercy of God will never fail." He then fainted; and when he recovered, he said, "It is a curious battle between death and life"—fainted again shortly after, and expired. Anders Bedel, the parson, in his funeral sermon, declared, "had he abstained from wine-bibbing he might have now been alive and in good health." The Danish proverb of "Han drikke som en koe"—he drinks like a cow—could not be applied to King Frederic. I plead guilty to not having understood it myself at first—a cow never drinks more than necessary. Frederic, like all early reformed sovereigns, was never quite at his ease when he thought of the church spoliation he had sanctioned. So he issued an edict forbidding the term "kloster" to be used by man or woman, when speaking of Antvorskov, under pain of the fine of a fat ox. The fines were exacted: the royal herds increased in numbers; but he could not beat it out of the peasants' brains—kloster they would call it, and kloster they did.

On the fine site of Antvorskov stands a modern

country-house built in the olden style — a pleasant walk through an avenue of shady trees, at ten minutes' distance from the Slot gate of the city. Slagelse boasts of an ancient church, in no ways remarkable from the rest of the ecclesiastical buildings of the country. On by the rail: we flit by Sorø, take up a cargo of small boys, and then again a stoppage.

SIGERSTED.

Ten minutes at Ringsted, enough at any time, and quite sufficient to point out to the right the village of Sigersted, once famous in olden story: for here dwelt King Sigurd, father of the fair Signe. Tall and straight as a lilievand * was the damsel, and beloved of Prince Hagbard, the Danish king's son; but Sigurd forbad the marriage. Lovers' wits are proverbial—secret nuptials take place; and Hagbard visits his bride, as Romeo did his Juliet, in secret. A spy denounces the lovers to the king, who orders his warriors to seize the prince; but they refuse, for Hagbard is born of a giant race. Then speaks out the spy: "Cut off first the hair of the princess and bind him in her tresses: his love for her is too great for him to burst such chains asunder." Hagbard is bound in her silken chains: the Princess Signe cries to him to break loose; but he refuses. "Never can I," he declares, "injure one hair of your head." The king orders him to be hanged; the lovers agree they will never survive each other, and Signe vows to set fire to her bower when Hagbard hangs in his chains. When he approached the gibbet, mistrusting the constancy of woman's love, he desired

---

* Stalk of a lily.

the soldiers to hang up first his scarlet cloak, to see how he would look hereafter. Scarce had the cloak swung in the air, when a volume of smoke arises from the bower of the faithful Signe, and Hagbard, satisfied with her constancy, is "launched into eternity." Then in rushes the "lille smaa dreng" before the king's board to announce the sad news how Signe and her maidens burn in the "høie loft," and all for love of Hagbard the Dane. "Extinguish the flames!" cries the king; "cut him down; I pardon them both."

> "But when they arrived at Signelit's bower,
> There she lay burnt in the flames;
> And when they came where the gallows stood,
> Young Hagbard hung in his chains."

Do not imagine the matter to have ended here. In a short space of time arrived from Ireland, where he was comfortably settled, Hakon, brother of the murdered prince. Silently, accompanied by his followers, he glides up the waters of the Suus Aa. To conceal their movements from the enemy, each warrior bears in his hand a branch of the beech-tree—Birnam wood coming to Dunsinane five hundred years before it was ever heard or thought of in Scotland. King Sigurd discovers the stratagem: a battle takes place, and he is slain in the contest. This stratagem of bearing boughs occurs very often in the ancient Sagas. When a battle was fought near Restaflarith, in Skaane, between the Danes and the Swedes, the former broke branches from the trees and fastened them to their horses. When the villagers saw it from afar, they exclaimed, "May Heaven destroy this walking wood, for it will make us pay bloody forfeits this day before the sun goes down."

SENGELØSE.

We steam on—on, but not fast—stop at station after station, till we arrive at Høie Thorstrup, passengers for Sengeløse; so I inspect the map; and here, not far removed, lies Snubbe's Cross, concerning which there hangs a story:—

It was in the thirteenth century that the Lady Snubbe, walking in the fields near Sengeløse, gave birth to a son and heir. Her husband, Sir Eskil Snubbe, a noble knight, caused a cross to be erected on the spot to commemorate the event, charging two of his farms alternately with the repairs necessary for its preservation. In the year 1817 a quarrel arose between the proprietors of the land, whose duty it was to do the needful, each declaring it to be the turn of his neighbour; so, as they could not settle the matter amicably, they pulled the cross down, and the name alone remains to prove the antiquity of the house of Snubbe with an *e*.

Off again, and in three quarters of an hour we are landed at Copenhagen.

ISLES—HORSENS.

A three hours' journey brought us to Korsør, where, on the quay side, smoked three steamers—one bound for Aarhuus, a second for the islands, and a third for Horsens. On the latter we embark with a head-wind and promise of two hours' extra passage. Towards five o'clock we pass the small island of Endelave, where myriads of flappers are trying their new-fledged wings on the water. Now as we enter the fiorde a small islet of emerald green appears faint in the horizon, flat, almost level with the waters: this is the island of Hiarnø,* death and burial-place of the poet king. A heap of stones, carved over with ships of rude workmanship, marks the place of his interment. His grave rests undisturbed by the antiquaries, though not by the cattle; for many years since a mad bull tore up the turf with his horns and brought to light an ancient sword. The labourer who inhabited the farm on which the grave was situated declared that from that hour nothing but ill-luck happened to him. And now in the background rises the sister isle of Alrø, the resting-place of his Queen Alruna. There is something poetic in the idea of these two early Scandinavians, each sleeping in their own small grassy isle, the waters of the fiorde flowing between them.

We coast by a wooded aitch, with an extensive farmhouse, the property of Baron Juel, Vaarsø by name; a smaller, still green and desert, called Vaarsø's Calf; then come shipping, the towers of Horsens, windmills hard at work on hilltop, none só busy as the Jutland windmill. We land upon the pier, and, after ten minutes' walk, take up our lodgings at Jørgensens.

---

* Hiarne had reigned for some years when Friedlev the heir, whom the Danes imagined to have been dead, returned to his native country, and Hiarne, after a battle in which he was worsted, fled to the island of Hiarnø, disguised as a peasant: he later repairs to the court, and gets employed as a salt-boiler in the Royal kitchen. He keeps his person so dirty, the king orders him to be washed, after which he is recognised. The king inquires of him "Did you come here to take my life?" "No," replies Hiarne; "but to decide the matter by single combat." Friedlev agrees, and Hiarne is slain and receives honourable burial in his own island.

CHAPTER XXIX.

Boller, the place of banishment of Christina Munk — Her regal state — The copper nail in a bed of gold — The eatable snail naturalized by a Frenchman — Coffin of Count Griffenfeld — Præstegaard of a Jutland clergyman — Agnete and the merman — The English Cinque Ports — Legend of the Elder Queen.

BOLLER.

June 15th.—OUT of respect to the memory of Christina Munk—not that she deserved it—we determined to visit Boller, the scene of her banishment after her divorce and expulsion from Frederiksborg. She remained here in confinement until the year 1646, when, at the intercession of her sons-in-law, she was released: they pleaded that her imprisonment reflected a disgrace upon her children. From that time matters went better; there was even a prospect of reconciliation between her and the king; and she was at her mother's in Funen, on her way to Copenhagen, when the news of his death reached her. She is said to have burst into a flood of tears, and, after a regular good cry, to have exclaimed, "Well, who ever would have thought I should have shed tears for Christian's sake?" Christina remained at Boller till her death, living in great state—a state which was particularly displeasing to her step-son the king, who sent commissioners down to Boller to see what she was after, and beg she would show the proofs of her right to the title of Countess Slesvig-Holstein. On their arrival they were received at the gate with flourishes of trumpets—a somewhat regal proceeding, which Christina, when she found out who they were, very much alarmed, declared to be a mistake. Proofs she could produce none beyond a letter in King Christian's own hand, directed to the well-born Mrs. Christina Munk, Countess of Slesvig-Holstein. When she was accused of writing "we," she gave no answer, but went off into a tirade of her persecutions, &c. &c. From this time we hear no more about her.

An old moated mansion is Boller, surrounded with garden, farm, and wood, running down to the water's edge; it is now the property of Count Friis. In the gardens stands a pollard lime-tree, under whose branches, supported on trellis-work, many hundred men might dine. Splendid oaks too, of whose possession an English park might be proud. Christina must have known these trees, and perhaps under their shade may have wept—not her fault, but its discovery—and thought what a fool she had been to sacrifice honour, position, and the fortunes of her children,* for the attention of a chamberlain of her husband's court. In earlier days Boller was the scene of a romance more tragic still. Queen Margaret, like all women, was a matchmaker; she hated a too small but powerful nobility, and it was her policy to swamp them by marrying the younger sons to rich heiresses of the commercial classes, and *vice versâ*. On her giving the high-born Kirsten Thott in marriage to her favourite Jeppe Muus, son of a rich burgher, the indignant bride presented her husband with a gold ring, in which was encrusted a copper nail, with this inscription:

---

* The youngest of whom Christian refused to recognise. Ellen Marsviin sent her off to Cologne, where she was brought up as a convent boarder, and later took the veil.

"Arte dig knaber nagle, die ligger i guld" (flourish, copper nail, thou liest in gold). Queen Margaret counted not on the vengeance of the bride's betrothed, Holger Munk, the lord of Boller, who, to the rage of the queen, picked a quarrel with the bridegroom, killed him, and married his widow the next day.

There is something very attractive in these Danish country-seats, reminding you much of England as it is still in many parts, and was formerly, before the villanous taste of sundry landscape-gardeners destroyed our fine old gardens, and laid low our trim avenues. Our grounds are well kept, radiant with American shrubs and flowers; but in nine places out of ten where can you walk and meditate?—straight you cannot go; either you tumble into an iron fence and march into the centre of a flower-bed, or get stranded among the rock-work, a foot upon zig, a foot upon zag: no reveries, no brown-study in an English garden, and very little shade into the bargain. In France you have your clipped charmille—your terrace, wide and imposing—your plate-bandes, laid out perhaps too formally, but very charming altogether, and adapted to the climate of a joyous sunny land. What I enjoy in these Danish residences is the combination of all these advantages together. Your garden gay with old-fashioned flowers, glorious roses; then, further removed, the lime avenue—"se perdant dans les bois"—those lovely woods running always to the water's edge. The only thing I disapprove of is the stagnant moat, telling of fever; it must be unwholesome, and should be let off from time to time.

Not far removed from the château of Boller stands the parish church of Uth. If you love old stone monuments of armed knight and high-born lady, visit it, and you will be gratified: Gyldernstierne and Rosenkrantz—old Jutland names; the latter perhaps the most distinguished of Denmark.

In the afternoon we drove over to Steensballegaard, the seat of Baron Juel, on the opposite side of the fiorde to Boller, remarkable for the beauty of its site. The entrance through the gaard, or farmyard—the moated grange itself, surrounded on one side by a square of farm-buildings—shocks an English eye; but when gentlemen farm on the scale of Jutlanders—feed and lodge some hundred retainers—it is necessary to keep these matters near at hand. An avenue of limes, some half a mile in length, led us to a hill-top, from whence we mounted to an adjoining høi, commanding the country round and the fiorde below. Hiarnø and Alrø, Vaarsø and her Calf—glorious woods and pasture-lands—a real Danish landscape. The country is refreshed after a long drought by frequent showers. The Helix pomatia— eatable snail—here abounds: excellent for consumptive patients. You find them in England in the " Pilgrim's walks "—Sir Kenelm Digby too introduced them in the neighbourhood of Croydon; his wife, the Lady Venetia, affected them much for the benefit of her complexion; so tradition says: and here at Boller, as well as at Lethraborg, the only two places where they exist in Denmark, they were introduced by a Frenchman.

VÆHR.

We returned home by Væhr, a small village, the last resting-place of Griffenfeld, who, after twenty-seven years' imprisonment in the fortress of Munkholm, near Tronyem, died at the house of his only daughter,

Baroness Krag, A.D. 1697, in his sixty-third year. We stopped our carriage at the præstegaard to demand the church keys; the pastor himself accompanied us. Griffenfeld's remains lie in an oak coffin, above ground, placed in an open chapel or dormitorium. A simple inscription on a gilded plate informs the reader that within repose the mortal remains of Christian V.'s Grand Chancellor; this plate, however, moves with a secret spring, and below appears a second, on which are inscribed his honours and titles, in all the pomp of heraldry. "The illustrious, noble, and well-born, &c. (son of a small wine-vender — rather too much that), Knight of the Elephant, Denmark's Lord Chancellor," followed up by the history of his disgrace, date of his imprisonment and death—an inscription the family dared not exhibit at the period of his death. His wife is buried in a vault below.*

We returned to our carriage through the præstegaard, the pastor having invited us to visit his domain. It may amuse you perhaps to have a description of the parsonage of a Jutland clergyman. You first drive through an archway into the gaard or square court—a yard surrounded with farm-buildings: opposite stands the house occupied by the family; a few lime-trees are planted in the centre; a house-dog barks violently, as though he'd break his chain; cocks, and hens, and chicks stalk about; carts and horses; but no manure—all clean, though somewhat untidy. The houses consist mostly of one story: you enter rooms scrupulously neat and

---

* Baron Krag, his son-in-law, has a long epitaphium; twice ambassador to Paris; three times married; twelve children by Griffenfeld's daughter; a very grand wig and lace jabot, picked out most tastefully in white marble.

clean; windows opening on the other side into a flower-garden; lots of roses, lilacs, and common flowers. Here the garden led into a hanging beech wood, with walks and seats; a sö or lake below—small, but large enough for the enjoyment of a boat, and fish in plenty. Then there is sure to be an orchard and vegetable garden, and a lime-avenue leading somewhere. The Danish clergy are poorly paid; but, farming on a considerable scale, their poverty is not of a repulsive kind, like that of towns: they have plenty at hand—eggs, butter, milk, poultry, pigs in profusion, cut their own turf from the never-absent mose for winter fuel. I inquired of our new acquaintance how many cows he kept. "Very few," he replied; "I have but a small farm—only twelve." Complaint is made that when their farms are too large they are apt to think more of their cows than of their parishioners. From those with whom I have become acquainted, I should say they were a well-educated, mild, gentlemanlike set of men: their wives good and useful helpmates, doing their duty in their state of life, and, like their husbands, simple-minded, and entirely free from all pretension—the very great charm of the Danish nation in general—at the same time void of all mauvaise honte or awkwardness. These præstegaards may be little soigné to our refined ideas; but I don't feel quite sure that the farm-house plenty which surrounds them does not fully compensate for the absence of the neat green entrance-gate, and the laurel-girt drive round the well-mowed grass-plot, before the house-door of an English parsonage.

SKANDERBORG.

June 17th.—Breakfasted this morning at Skanderborg. Lucky we did not sleep there last night. One hundred Danish students from the University of Copenhagen, on a walking tour through Jutland—very joyous—serenading the authorities wherever they go—were camped in the hotel, like a swarm of locusts. They had not, however, devoured everything, but we fared perhaps better for their presence. We are now in the land of plenty—no more "portions" served by rule, but large buffets spread out with a dozen cold dishes, meat and aspics, eggs and salad—eat as much as you like at two marks a head. We did not remain long at Skanderborg—just time enough to walk down to the castle islet—regret its destruction—to wonder whether it was within that sole remaining turret the havfrue (mermaid) danced on the floor while she foretold the fate of good Queen Dagmar; who, Christian-like, instead of "frying her on the fire," as the she-woman-fish anticipated, clothed her "in scarlet red" and had her conducted back in safety to the waters of the Kattegat.

I should really like to know what fish has given rise to the fable of the mermaid and man so prevalent in these northern seas—havfrue and havman, as they are called—for in Denmark no legend is complete without them. When in early days a young girl committed suicide by drowning, the act was set down to the blandishments of some merman, who enticed her to the depths below; as in the beautiful ballad of 'Agnete,' where the havman "stoppede" her ears and "stoppede" her mouth, and carried her to the coral caves below. Agnete lives with her spouse for nine years, and bears him seven children; when one day she hears under the water "the church-bells of England ring," and is seized with a very proper desire to attend mass. Her fishy lover grants her permission, stops her ears and mouth, and leaves her on the strand. Agnete follows into the church her mother, who asks her, "Where have you been these last years nine?" She replies, "Under the deep water with my lord the havman." Once on land, Agnete shows no desire to return. The merman follows her to the church—"his face is fair, his eye is blue, and his long hair shines like living gold"—but as he enters the door, "all the saints and angels avert their heads." "Come back, come back," he cries; "Agnete, your children cry after you.

> "Oh, think upon the great; oh, think upon the small;
> Oh, think upon the little one who lies in the cradle."

But Agnete, heartless creature, refuses, and replies—

> "I won't think upon the great or think upon the small,
> Hah! Hah! Hah!
> Nor think upon the little one who cries in the cradle,
> Hah! Hah! Hah!"

Long and dreary was the way—sometimes catching a glimpse of the Mos-Sø on the hill-top—till we arrived at the ancient but tumbledown church of Dover. We are all among the Cinque Ports to-day. Further on to the left lies Rye. Sandwig, in ancient times written "wich," lies by the sea-coast. Strange our five most ancient harbours of importance in England should all bear names of Scandinavian origin. Hastings derives her title from the pirate chief: and Winchelsea—Vinkel Sø; though who this Vinkel might be who dared to name a part of our ocean Sø, as though a boggy tarn in his own marshy Jutland, I am unprepared to say.

A pouring rain—one of nature's own shower-baths—catches us just as we arrive at the end of Knud-Sø—a lovely lake—not blue to-day, but agitated into wavelets by the stormy breeze—all sand here. Slowly the "wagen" trails its way through the ruts; on foot we fare worse; impossible to walk. But we mount the hill-side, and after a heavy tug arrive at the kro of Tulstrup. Here the panting horses rest to bait. The shower is over—sun bursts out—we can gaze at the lake below from the village cemetery on the adjoining høi. Humble and towerless is Tulstrup church; its bell hangs suspended to a wooden belfry in the churchyard, itself of most unpretending form and principle; but the small degraded edifice, built of granite, is surely of noble foundation—a thank-offering probably, though no legend attests the supposition. It is of early date; a round arch doorway, adorned with early carvings—as works of art on a par with King Gorm's Stone at Jellinge. On one side a yawning wolf (løve lure, the old sacristan calls it) on his hind legs, as large as life, with huge protruding tongue; on the opposite a damsel, resembling those very primitive wooden dolls you sometimes see displayed in a huckster's shop—large head, immoveable arms, long feet, and petticoat parted round the waist. In her hand she holds a distaff, as I imagine it to be, and looks ready to faint away from fear of the ravenous wolf—nothing but a church-door between them. At the other entrance we have the Angel of Christianity trampling upon the Dragon of Paganism. Above, the same lady seated, with an infant in her arms.

The angel holds a purse of gold in his hand; my ideas are that the lady has given a purse of gold to build the church, in consequence of a vow she has made. Deaf old sacristan knows nothing, not even to what saint the church is dedicated. We go in; at one end lies an enormous oak chest, cross-barred over with iron bands into a tartan pattern. We try to raise the lid; it requires all the united efforts of aged sacristan and stronger self to do so; and now we find two small square compartments—same form, same pattern—fitted with massive lock and key, expressly to contain the church plate, and preserve it safe from robber hand; but where is it? Two blue glass vessels serve now for the sacrament; on the altar-table the very candles are wooden savealls; a small fat-lamp inserted in the top is used at Sabbath Vespers. Churchwardening flourishes here, even in these high latitudes. The ancient granite font is painted verdant green, like a suburban garden gate. The open seats bear date 1587.

In the churchyard I stumbled on what I have never before met with—a grave covered over with the roughly severed trunk of a tree, unbarked, rudely-fashioned; a sarcophagus like that once placed over the grave of Queen Hedvig at Søborg.

And now they summon us from the høi-top, from which we have made out another lake, Lille-Sø by name. The horses are baited; on with our journey. We just distinguish the winding of Juul Lake and a little promontory jutting out into its waters, terminated by a sepulchral mound—the Scandinavian who chose such a site must have been a poet—when, as we climb the hill before arriving at Linaa, concerning which place I have a story to relate, down comes again a torrent plump upon our heads. We take refuge under railway wrappers, and may have passed through a paradise for what we know. When we again peep forth from our shelter, the postboy points to a branch of elder-flowers the maid-servant bears in her hand, shakes his head, and then points to the clouds fleeting through the air. Mademoiselle Thérèse, in her ignorance, had plucked during our halt at Tulstrup a branch of these flowers, preservatives, if steeped in water, against tan and freckles, without first demanding permission of Hyldemoir, "the elder-queen," who avenges any molestation of her tree, and no peasant would dare to pluck its flowers without first addressing her in the following words:—" O, Hildi, our mother; O, Hildi, our mother! let me take some of thy elder." These words thrice repeated, she grants permission willingly enough, but, according to the postboy's theory, it was the neglect of this observance which caused this pelting hail, this inhospitable reception to the Highlands of Jutland.

Dark is the superstition of the peasant as regards the elder-queen, and woe to the child who sleeps in a cradle of elder-wood. No sooner does the mother quit the room than Hyldemoir appears; vampire-like, she sucks its life-blood from its breasts, she pulls it by the legs, and torments the helpless infant in every possible manner. Still the elder-tree has been revered from the earliest times, and the peasant as well as the artizan loves to plant it near his dwelling; it brings good luck to the baker and to the gardener; leave it alone, and Hyldemoir will do you no injury.

The elements have ceased their war; and now we enter a glorious valley, hills on each side coated with beech and pine—beech in their golden foliage still;

the heather brown, the reindeer lichen white and abundant; later the leaves will become brown and the heather purple, so each season has its charms if mankind will only see it. We are now on the royal chaussée; electric telegraph on each side of us. The horses are fagged as we are. We meet troops of peasants, cows, and horses—evidently a fair going on—reach the end of the plain—pouring rain again—turn down a hill, catch sight of a lake, a town, a confused idea of river and other matters—all very charming when you are dry, but disgusting when you are half drowned: and so we made our entry into the most youthful of Denmark's cities, her youngest daughter, the town of Silkeborg.

CHAPTER XXX.

Silkeborg — Cup of Bishop Peter — The Jutland lakes — The treasure-seeker — Himmelbjerg, Queen of the Jutland mountains — The fiery beacon — Lovers of Laven Castle — The paper manufactory.

SILKEBORG.

We found the "Dania" in a terrible state of bustle, no chance of rooms before evening; after a long delay we got our dinners served, and it was a wonder we did, such a crowd as there was below—farmers by the gross buying, selling, and chaffering. Towards sunset the fair took itself off, and we were left in peace and quietness. Hans Andersen had described to us what we were to see, and lent us the translation of his charming little book, 'To Be or not to Be,' which told us the tales and legends of the neighbourhood, for, to the English traveller, Silkeborg is still a terra incognita; the very maps of our country, as well as the Handbook, ignore its existence. When on our arrival at Copenhagen last autumn we spoke of our tour in Jutland, the first question invariably was, "How did you like Silkeborg? Not seen Silkeborg? Is it possible?" until we felt quite cross, and began to look upon it as a sort of Jutland "Mrs. Harris," expressly invented for our botheration. Then we began to inquire what and where Silkeborg really was, and soon learned how some ten years since it was nought but a beautiful and dreary waste, the resort of gipsies, uninhabited and uncultivated; and how in the space of a few years it had risen to the rank of a flourishing town of fourteen hundred inhabitants, increasing daily in wealth and prosperity. Fourteen years have now elapsed since Mr. Drewsen, struck by the advantageous site, on the lake side, with the abundant waters of the Guden Aa, determined to turn to account this useless stream, and establish there a paper manufactory; he did so, and succeeded: his paper gained the great prize both at the English and French Exhibitions, no manufacturer having yet equalled the glazing of the material, which is formed by a machine of his own invention. The manufactory stands at the entrance of the town, near the bridge which spans the Guden Aa; beyond stands the modern residence of Mr. Drewsen, in the midst of a fair and fruitful garden, now a wilderness of roses, the old-fashioned yellow cabbage—so luxuriant in the Lion Court of the Alhambra, but most capricious to bloom in England—the Damask, the York and Lancaster, and the Cinnamon, varieties long since expelled from modern English gardens. If you fancy, because Silkeborg is the youngest town of the Danish dominions, she has no history of her own, no legend, you are much mistaken; on the very ground where we now stand once proudly frowned the towers of her castle, a stronghold of the Bishops of Aarhuus. Put by the paper and its manufactory, and fancy yourself carried back to the twelfth century, when Bishop Peter Bagnsen * held the diocese of Aarhuus. For reasons best known to himself, he determined to build a château

---

* Died 1204. His mother Ingeborg was niece to Sir Asker Ryg, and sister to the murdered cousin whom Bishop Absalon canonized. See vol. i. p. 106.

fort on the very banks of the Lang-Sø; so he journeys forth to fix the site, accompanied by a prior and a stalwart knight, one of his relations; and in an open boat they sail down the Guden Aa to the borders of the Lang-Sø. "Build it here," exclaims the prior, pointing to a promontory hard by. "Nonsense!" said the knight; "trust to my judgment, I am a military man;" and they wrangle and dispute until the bishop's patience is quite worn out, when a sudden gust of wind catches his silken skull-cap, and away it flies into the deep waters. " Let it go," exclaims Bishop Peter : " where the cap stays its course, there will we build a fortress, and call its name Silkeborg."

We have three days' sight-seeing before us, taking matters quietly in homœopathic doses, so we started this morning at ten o'clock. Our road ran by the Lang-Sø, where all the world seemed busy making bricks, on to the Amalia Kilde, by the forest side, a spring quite chalybeate enough to be nasty, good water spoilt by a taste of rusty iron. This spring is a favourite picnic and tea-drinking spot of the Silkeborgians: seats, and large wooden tables capable of dining twenty-four, are placed on the lake's bank, under the shade; a rustic open-air kitchen, where you may fry your own fish, and then eat them afterwards. How the old women in this country pass their livelong day, sitting out of doors, without dying before morning, was to me a mystery, until I witnessed one day the ascent of an aged matron into a stuhlwagen. She wore ten knitted woollen petticoats at the smallest calculation; you might have plumped her down flat in the middle of a bog without her perceiving the dampness of her situation. From the age of fifty until she is gathered to her fathers, a woman in Denmark betakes herself to knitting warm petticoats, at the ratio of one per annum, which she wears over that of the preceding year, until she becomes a moving mass of woollen fabric, defying rheumatism, lumbago, damp, and all such sublunary evils to which age is heir; but the old women know best. There is an old Danish proverb—"Man klæder sig paa Fransk, og fryser paa Dansk"—Dress like a Frenchman, and you'll freeze as a Dane.

The woods* have become close and stuffy in these unpruned regions; the cranberry is in full bloom, and the small trailing æren-priis, as they here term the veronica, of brilliant blue; a dwarf genista too, with golden flowers. After resting at Drewsenhøi, commanding the village of Lysang-bro, on the opposite side of the lake, we again glance at that named after King Frederic VII., whence we had a glorious view over hills clothed with beech and pine, and the moor below was studded with heaps of turf ranged in pyramids, first one, then two by two, looking like some funeral train wending through the valley. Suddenly we turn to the left, when a panorama bursts upon our view, a net-work of deep blue lakes as far as the eye can gaze; there may be five, there may be ten, they are so tangled one within another. We proceeded onward a little longer, and then returned home through a wood carpeted with the trefoil leaf of the wood-sorrel. Huge anthills rise pyramidical under the pine-trees—the black ant, from which formic acid and vinegar are extracted in Norway. We find dinner waiting; soup, veal-cutlets admirably dressed, salads, and compôtes

---

* These woods were visited by Christian IV. "Oct. 21st, 1616, 'Drog jeg' from Skanderborg to Silkeborg. 22nd was I in the forest, and ordered timber to be cut down."—*Christian IV.'s Journal.*

of five or six varieties, large dish of wild strawberries, and plenty of rich cream. The apartment too has been swept and garnished, and a little salon arranged for us; sofas and chairs dragged in, pictures hung on the walls, bowpots too of pinks and roses. The landlady hopes we are comfortable; she has done her best; of course we are pleased. I don't know what Jutland may be some ten years hence, when intersected by railroads and civilization; at present, if you meet with aught but civility and attention, it is your own fault. In the evening we again drove out, and a charming drive it was; but blue lakes, green woods, and brown heather, though beautiful in themselves, sound tiresome on paper, and you have already had a dose of them.

June 19th.—Little Lina, the Blenheim spaniel, was wagging her tail, imploring of Jacques, the man-servant, to put her up into the carriage before everybody, dreadfully afraid she might be forgotten among those big hoop petticoats, indispensable necessaries for ladies travelling in Jutland. We were all ready to start, and seated, when a black cloud appears overshadowing the whole heaven, but the weather cannot be worse than it was the day of our arrival. We may come in for a rainbow among the hills; no use waiting, so we crossed the bridge over the Guden Aa: the river is covered with water-lilies, and teems with trout, pike, and crayfish. The eels, which they served us en aspic this morning for breakfast, came from the lake hard by, where a small striped skipper-house, now turned into a beer-house, with tea-garden, skittles, and poppinjay, was once the residence of the keeper who superintended the taking and sale of the eels, in earlier days a royal monopoly.

Some years since an enormous pike was found dead on the Guden Aa's bank, together with an eagle, whose claws were firmly imbedded in his flesh. The bird had pounced upon his prey, and the fish, unable to extricate himself from the talons of his enemy, plunged beneath the waters, dragging his antagonist along with him; so they both perished, and are now preserved stuffed, as they were found, in a private collection at Silkeborg.

A two hours' drive brings us to an old striped gaard. An aged peasant opens wide the gate; four skillings is his fee. We pass through, leave the carriage on a plateau by the forest side strewed with paper and burnt ashes, relics of the students' picnic, and then in two minutes' time we stand upon the Himmelbjerg, five hundred and fifty feet above the level of the sea—a mere molehill to Alpine travellers, but here equal to as many thousands in a highland range.

June 20th.—These Jutland lakes are strung like birds' eggs on a thread, connected by one continuous stream, the Guden Aa, up whose placid waters in days gone by many a viking has sailed his victorious craft, laden with the spoils of England, Gaul, and Italy; and in these more peaceful days steamboats, bearing the red-cross flag, will ply from Randers upwards, when Silkeborg has become, as all men prophesy she will, the Birmingham of Jutland, bearing this time not plundered riches, but the produce of honesty, industry, and enterprise.

The otter will then be chased from his lair; he now abounds, and along the banks you may mark his track. Salmon, too—so plentiful, that by law no servant of Randers town can be fed with its flesh more than once a week—will soon disappear. The banks of the Guden

Aa are flat till it passes near Silkeborg, and there we string on to its waters the Lang Sø, about which I have nothing to tell you save the story of the treasure-seeker—Peter Guldgraver—a Holsteiner by birth. To him was revealed in a dream the existence of a mighty treasure, buried long since by the ancient lords of the castle. Find it he would: in the year 1780 he sold his Holstein farm, and came a stranger to the wide Jutland waste; he dug and dug deeper and deeper, till money wasted and hope grew sick; still he dug on. Some say he died, buried by a fall of earth just when the pickaxe had struck upon the hidden treasure, and that his whitened skeleton still lies clutching at the gold almost within his bony grasp, like that of Diomede found beneath the ashes of Pompeii. He fell a victim to the malice of some Jutland witch.

String on quickly to our flowing stream the Ørn Sø, the Bras Sø, and later the Borre Sø—well viewed in its mild woodland beauties from the Amalia-høi; and now we stand on Aasen Point; the vaster Juul lake lies at our feet. But observe only the hills opposite: look at those two gigantic mounds, sepulture of some warrior king; look at the smaller ones raised for humbler men. What an eruption of hillocks! brown and bare, too, are these barrows, once, no doubt, clothed with beech and silver birch. Fire has passed over them, ignited by some gipsy camp or careless benighted traveller: so we string on to our thread the Juul Sø, spotted over with islands, and we stand again upon Himmelbjerg—Himmelbjerg, like the Anglian Thyre, pride of the Danes and queen over all Jutland mountains.

She stands alone before the lakeside, queenlike, holding her court; her ladies range themselves behind her.

To the left stands the grande maîtresse, a fat stumpy old hill, tricked out in purple and yellow squares and patches of roseate clover, red, purple, and yellow—very bad taste if you will—but the grande maîtresse never knew how to dress herself; she gets her gown from that dowdiest of all court milliners, old Mrs. Nature. Behind Himmelbjerg stand her ladies, attired in green, fresh and springlike, plumed in feathery beech—somewhat sunburnt, it must be owned, from constant exposure to the weather. One is distinguished from the rest, for she bears from early times a fiery beacon on her crest, lighted in the days of Skipper Clemens, and even in the present century, to summon the land to arms to repel the invader or suppress the opror.* Last of all defile before her a range of youthful hillocks: lowly they bow before their queen, in their clothing of purple and brown, relieved by garlands of golden broom, glistening with crystallized sand, somewhat heavy ; but travellers can't expect to find much "chic" in Jutland.

Mark well that point to the right, on the opposite side of the Juul lake, a small promontory clothed with wood: there, says tradition, once stood the towers of Laven Castle. Here, in Pagan times, resided a petty king, whose only daughter was wooed by a neighbouring Smaa Konge like himself, but the father forbad the mar-

---

* Beacons are common enough in the Danish dominions, as we later found. In former days it was the custom to "send the *Budstikke*," a small piece of wood with the name of the king cut at the two ends, passed from man to man, to summon the people to war; a branch of willow, burnt at either end, was also used. He who missed the "gathering" was hanged to the same branch of willow at the entrance of his own field, and his house burnt to the ground. When at Frederiksborg the king showed me a small piece of stone inscribed with Runic characters—the only specimen, I believe, still in existence—which was formerly used in the duchy of Slesvig for the same purpose.

riage. The lover introduced himself into Laven Castle in disguise; some say as a blind harper. Be that as it may, the tire-woman one morning at early dawn found her mistress's bed untenanted, like in the old song—

"Lady Jane she'd gone off with that silly blind harper,
That silly blind harper who plainly could see.
Twang-twankadillo, Twang-twankadillo, dillo, dillo, dee."

And now the coursers are saddled, and hot pursuit gains on the flying pair: closely the maiden clings to her lover's neck. They pass where Sveibæk ferry-house now stands—you see the spot before you—then reach the forest, and near the old ranger's house among the oaks he loses his hat—"Hattenæs" the place is still called—and then, closely pressed by his pursuers, he tries to ford the river. Horse and riders both plunge into the stream; the courser stumbles, sinks, then rises again, and now sinks deeper and deeper and gradually disappears, for no human aid can avail them — horse, king, and damsel suffocated, drowned in the morass, which closes above their heads, before the eyes of the agonized father. The place where the king lover lost his life is still called by the peasants of the country "Kongensdyp." Tradition tells no more; but maybe the body of that fair princess has been rescued from its muddy grave, and later reposed beneath the green høi on that little promontory before remarked, jutting out into the waters of the Juul lake.

But if Himmelbjerg holds her court here on high, an English princess, not less powerful—Morgana, sister of good King Arthur, fairified by tradition—reigns below on that black moor, striking wonder and admiration into the minds of the simple Jutlanders. We did not meet her—she was absent during the time of our visit.

Endless are the traditions of this wild half-unknown country. On the moor near Silkeborg once stood a large square stone, inscribed with Runic characters, illegible to the most wise, even to the witches of the country. The peasants saw it and revered, regarding it with a superstitious dread; for beneath lay hid a treasure of solid gold, the size and weight of a full-grown Jutlander (18 stone, or thereabouts). One day a stranger herdsman laid his tether on it; the stone sank deep into the morass and disappeared, but not for ever, for the wise women say that in some future time, when Denmark's king shall be a prisoner in a foreign land, the stone will reappear, and the treasure be found,— a king's ransom.

We now string on the Knud Sø—last week all wavelets, to-day calm and unruffled—and next come Rye Mølle Sø and the Rye mills (pronounce it Reu), where once a cloister stood, oft honoured by the presence of King Christopher, who loved to hunt the wild boar in this neighbourhood. Old folks will still tell you tales of ravening wolves, and show you the pits for wild boars: races both long since extinct. Now come the Ves Sø and the Guden Sø, and then in the distance, not visible to the eye, links on the Mos Sø, our old acquaintance, full of fish; later comes Skanderborg. Our chain is now complete—twelve lake eggs on one thread of waters: a very pretty collection, is it not?

After one last glance we bid adieu to Himmelbjerg, and, stopping one moment at the old eastern well to draw a draught of water, drive home through the heath and forest. Only look how the dormice scamper among the ferns, wide awake, for to-day is the longest day, and that day dedicated to St. Vitus. Old style it may be; but the mice know nothing about that, and stick to their old customs.

Ducks and wild geese abound on the lakes; plovers and black game on the moors. You can sail, if you like, in a little boat on the Guden Aa from Silkeborg downwards, threading in your course the waters I have here enumerated, sleeping at the roadside inn of Rye. You can fish, you can shoot—only do not get bogged, like the Smaa Konge: you can draw, you can botanize, living cheaply and well at the "Dania;" and, if you have time to spare, while away many a pleasant day in the midst of the varying scenery of Himmelbjerg and the lake-bound city of Silkeborg.

We did not leave Silkeborg without visiting the "Fabrik," in which I was agreeably surprised. No rampageous machinery tearing itself to pieces, but quiet sedate cylinders, rolling noiselessly along in company with running water. We were first introduced to the rags, specimens of which hung suspended, like clothiers' samples to a card, twenty-five varieties, mostly of very coarse material; and here for the first time I learned how the finest writing-paper used for billets-doux is made from coarse home-spun worn-out labourers' shirts and dishclouts; then came the old sails—sails that have borne a gallant craft o'er wave and ocean, in process of time become transformed into that thin satin high-glazed tissue, oftenest pink or yellow, used by smart shopkeepers for lining handkerchief-boxes, and sometimes, though I pity those who use it, into "old-fashioned foreign post." Coarse toile d'emballage, as the French term it, such as encases bales of cotton, and that used by gardeners for basket-covering, again finds favour in the packing line in the form of coarse brown paper.

I climbed a ladder to inspect the rags previous to their purification. Heavens, what filth! and to think they must be sorted into twenty-five heaps and don't breed a pestilence! When sorted they are tumbled into a huge boiler, shovelled in with quick lime, and there simmer for twenty-four hours (thirty-six would not be too much), next carried up stairs, all dye and dirt removed, and then boiled for twelve more. Having now gained a clean bill of health, they are combed to death and destruction, become masses of whitened pulp, like fresh-scraped charpie for a Parisian ambulance; next, when reduced to a finer substance, like curds and sour milk, it is carefully strained in running water. Now, as water-gruel, it passes over a green canvas; at the third cylinder spreads out like wafer on a coarse blanket; later it begins to dry, and then for the first time runs alone, and, bravely leaping over the chasm between the two cylinders, falls dry and solid into the arms of the chopping apparatus, which clips it into three and prunes its edges; then it is rolled up a mile in length and handed over to the opposite side of the establishment for glazing, for which process a patent has been taken out by the proprietor in all the countries of Europe. In other manufactories the paper is glazed in sheets already cut; here in one long rouleau it passes between hot cylinders—goes in one side rough, and comes out on the other glazed with varnish: the process to an unintellectual eye appearing as simple as it is successful.

CHAPTER XXXI.

The fish and the ring—Fortunes of the house of Stubbe—The traitor page—Marsk Stig, the outlaw—Château of Friisenborg—Artificial egg-hatching.

———

LINAA.

June 21*st.*—THE horses are ordered at six o'clock—it is nearly seven before they arrive—postilion overslept himself. We retrace our steps as far as the village of Linaa, concerning which I before promised you a story.

Many centuries ago there lived, in the neighbourhood of the kro where we now stand, three sisters, Linaa, Dall, and Bjara by name, as remarkable for their piety as for their riches. Their father, a fierce viking, on his departure upon some marauding expedition, confided to their care his treasure, and then disappeared from the face of the earth—killed in battle, slain, or drowned; so his daughters wisely dug up his gold, instead of leaving it to grace in modern days the cabinets of the Musée Scandinave, and divided it among them; each determined to apply a part of her share to a good purpose very much in vogue at that period—the building of a church. Three sacred edifices soon rose proudly on the banks of the adjoining lake, on the spots where the villages of Linaa, Dallerup, and Bjarup now stand. For matins, mid-day, and vesper song, these pious damsels passed the water in a boat—quite edifying it would have been to the surrounding population, but unfortunately there was no one to see them; Jutland was then a bleak, bare desert, quite uninhabited. One Sabbath morn the sisters as usual rowed across the waters of the lake; Bjara held the oars, Linaa steered, while Dall was busily employed looking out the morning lessons in her Book of Hours. The bark now touches land; the sisters leap ashore—when suddenly Bjara misses from her finger her golden ring, the gift of her viking father. "My ring, my ring!" cries Bjara; "somebody must have taken it; lost—stolen!"—and she begins to hunt in every corner of the boat, but without success; so, waxing wroth, she invokes maledictions on the head of the man, woman, or living thing, who may have deprived her of her ornament. Loud and fearful were her curses; in vain her sisters tried to pacify her. "Bjara, dear Bjara! how can you be so wicked?" exclaimed Dall, while Linaa wept bitterly. Their entreaties were of no avail; but now, as they gain the church porch, the waters of the lake begin to swell, overflow, and gradually disperse themselves over the plain, leaving the bottom dry, and the fishes, eels, carp, salmon, perch, and flounders, all stranded upon the heather. "It's a fish who has swallowed my ring," triumphantly exclaims Bjara; and quick and sharp as a policeman she passes in review the different members of the finny tribe. The eels wriggle; flounders perform somersaults in the air—no guilt there; pike open wide their jaws,—"Put your finger down if you like," say they; "you'll catch something, not the ring"—when, reposing on a bed of reeds, puffing, blowing, she espies a bloated carp: "Here's the culprit," she exclaims—out with her bodkin, rips him up without mercy, and draws forth from his stomach her lost treasure. Anon the waters again become troubled, and recede quickly, fish and all, to the basin of the lake. Somehow or other, though, the lake never recovered Bjara's malediction; gradually it thickened, dried up, and the Bjarup Sø in course of time became a Bjarup Mose. See how the curse recoiled upon Bjara's church. The foundation soon gave way, the effect, some say, of the inundation; it is now a heap of ruins, while Dallerup and Linaa both stand, picturesque objects, though perhaps a little churchwardenized. We are at Mollerup: let us observe the storks —one, two, three, four nests, each with young ones ready to fly—not quite courage yet; and here arrives the male —what has he brought them home for breakfast in his mouth? a marsh frog! More nests still in Laasby: happy village! rather too productive perhaps, for the storks bring "triplets" to the Danish peasants, as common an occurrence as twins in England. In our own tongue we have no term like "trillinge;" we borrow triplets from the dice-box—a very bad throw in either case; but the storks mean to be kind, though the present be unwelcome. Mind how you make game of the young ones; they never forget it—are very tenacious about their long lanky legs. As there is nothing to look at until we come to Skovby, I may as well tell what befell the Stubbe family—"gammel adelige familie uddodt," —all because they laughed at the young storks' legs.

You have all heard of Cadet Roussel, whose fortunes hung on his possessing three of everything—

"Cadet Roussel a trois habits,
Deux jaunes, et l'autre en papier gris,"—

the last not a solid article perhaps, but it rhymes

very nicely. Well, the fortunes of the noble house of Stubbe depended upon the mystic number seven:— 7 churches, 7 mills, 7 islands, 7 lakes, 7 forests, 77 ploughs, 777 windows in their manor; cows, pigs, horses, all in proportion; and 7 children, or 77 if they could get them,—so much the better, but 7 they must have. This last, as he proved to be, of the Stubbes, was a bad small boy, always making game of the young storks as they sat in their mother's nest on the house-top. "Stork, long-legged stork," he sang: I'm sure I forget what besides, but something very rude, at which they were highly affronted. "All very fine now, Mr. Stubbe; wait a little, and our turn will come; who'll laugh then?" muttered the old mother.

The young squire grew up and was sent to Aalborg College, where he received a first-rate education: learnt Italian and dancing,—and very useful he must have found the former accomplishment, living on his estates in Jutland, among the moors and forests; he spoke it however with a first-rate (Aalborg) accent. Young Stubbe grows apace, and somehow does not tame down. He is thirty now, and should think of settling: forty finds him an old bachelor, and fifty still. "Marry before it is too late and I close my eyes," exclaims his venerable mother; so marry he did—a neighbour's daughter. "Plenty of time, mother," he laughingly exclaimed; "you know we Stubbes always throw doublets; I shall have my seven children before five years are over." There is great joy at Stubbesholm, an heir expected daily. Young Stubbe rubs his hands— "Triplets, you'll see, mother, like the old lady on her epitaphium in the church-aisle—our grandam." "Hah, hah!" laughed the old stork from the top of the chimney, where she was listening; "we shall see when the time comes." The time did come, and a bad time too—dead twins—nearly costing the young mother's life; and months and years rolled on—more dead children, and more still, and Stubbe borne down with age and sorrow. Then says the old stork, "Vengeance is not ours; we must pardon his offences for his young wife's sake." Next time a living baby comes, fresh and blue-eyed; and then come twins, and then a fourth, and twins again. Stubbe rubs his hands: six children living; one more and he is saved; and so he would have been had he reckoned with the storks alone; but grim Death steps in—a fit of apoplexy after the christening dinner of the last-born child: he is carried to the church vaults, father of six children. The fortunes of the Stubbes now ended: like others of ancient lineage, they passed away—one lake "Stubbe Sø"* marked on the map alone recalls their memory.

At Skovby pause one moment. Turn to the right and gaze towards Storring; there you will discern two mounds of earth, not far removed one from the other — Dronninghøi and Steilehøi they are called. Here, on the first-named, stood Queen Agnes of Brandenburg, widowed queen of Erik Glipping, who was slain by the Grand Marshal Stig† and other confederate

---

* Stubbe Sø is in the Mols district.

† Marsk (Marshal) Stig Andersen Hvide was of the same family as Absalon and Duke Porse; like the latter, he made a grand marriage. Concerning the intimacy of King Erik and this lady there was great scandal, and it was to revenge the insult offered to his honour that the marshal plotted, and later executed, the murder of his sovereign. Marsk Stig was renowned all over the North for his splendour. In an old Swedish lay it runs, "Stig, he proceeds to the marble halls: there he invites the king to his home so joyfully; he invites the king and all his men, the queen with her damsels fair. When they came to

nobles, near the village of Finderup, as I shall relate when we arrive there. Here she stood to superintend in person the execution of his traitor page, Rane Jonsen, who betrayed his lord and master into the assassins' hands. Rane suffered death upon the wheel, and Agnes feasted her eyes with the sight of his dying agony.

Marsk Stig with his brother nobles took refuge in the little island of Hjelm, where after the manner of the day he turned pirate; as the outlawed Earl of Huntingdon he took 'to the greenwood-tree, and soon became the terror of the neighbourhood. The ruins of his castle still exist.

FRIISENBORG.

We leave the road and make for Friisenborg, château of Count Friis. We stop for one minute at the village church of Hammel, to look at an early carving of St. Hubert over an ancient round-arch door, and admire there an admirably preserved grave-stone of exquisite execution, fresh as from the sculptor's hand, of Valdemar Parsberg and his wife Ide Lykke —noble and high-born, date 1589. The Parsbergs have passed away; they were once possessors of Friisenborg, but resisted the establishment of absolute monarchy by Christian V., and together with all the old Jutland nobility from that period disappeared from the state of affairs: many emigrated to Sweden.

We enter Friisenborg through a Gothic gateway

Childe Stig's gate, there plays a hind, there dances a hart, so joyfully; and when they came to Stig's court the fences were of steel and iron wrought, the floor was made of marble stone, and the walls were inlaid with white ivory."

emblazoned with the family arms, drive to the court entrance, where the moat is large and surrounded by horse-chesnuts of splendid growth, send up our cards, and demand permission to visit the gardens. The old château is quaint, flanked with antiquated towers, whitewashed too, all except its stone foundations; the whitewash contrasts queerly with the marble bust of its long-wigged founder Count Mogens Friis, black as time can make it, inserted in a niche above the doorway, with an inscription saying how the Grefskav was created in his favour by Christian V. in the year 1671. In five minutes' time we are joined by Count Friis and his countess, who themselves do us the honours of the place, and press us greatly to stop: we finish by remaining over dinner, leaving for Aarhuus towards the cool of the evening.

Of the château I say little: its interior is grand and at the same time habitable—the Riddersaal, a magnificent apartment, hung with family portraits, works of art, many of historical interest: among them are portraits of Eleanor and Corfitz Ulfeld, and Christina an elder sister of the Reventlow Queen—Countess Friis by marriage, pretty, and not such a fool as her sister. Count Friis Friisenborg,* Juel—Wind—Friis—is the richest nobleman in all Denmark. His father is still alive, an aged man, but inhabits Boller, having by royal consent ceded the County to his son, the present occupier of the place. In another year the château will almost cease to exist; it is to undergo an entire restoration at the hands of an able architect, in the style of the

---

* Friis of Friisenborg is a distinct family from Friis of Borreby, of whom more later.

country: how wise the Danes are to stick to it! when completed it will be one of the finest residences of its style in Europe. And Frederiksborg may bless its stars that the future Friisenborg is not situated in the island of Zealand. In the ornamental poultry yard there were several hens sitting on their eggs. The nest is that to be met with in all the peasants' houses—a truss of straw tightly bound towards the end, and opened funnel-shaped towards the top; the straw being neatly turned in at the opening and fastened down. They are placed between a wooden bar and the wall-side, and very clean and tidy they looked. The custom of "egg-hatching"—there is a finer term—in ovens appears to have been practised in Denmark in Christian IV.'s time. He writes word to the hen-woman—"When the chickens come out of the eggs which are in the ovens, let the girl have some swan and some turkey eggs." *

We are now in the land of "beeves," large numbers of which are here fattened for exportation for the London market. Molesworth, in speaking of Jutland, says,— "This is the best country the King of Denmark has; but neglected on account of its distance from Copenhagen. Quantities of beeves and oxen are exported to Holland annually, to fatten in the rich pastures of that country."

Towards sunset we took leave of our kind hosts, and after a three hours' drive are again installed in our old quarters of last year, in the hot, dusty, bad-smelling city of Aarhuus.

---

* Dated, Frederiksborg, 26th June, 1630.

CHAPTER XXXII.

Siege of Kalø — The lord of Mols — Danish Whittington — The Lady Hilda Trolle — Round church of Thorsager — Château of Rosenholm — Origin of the Rosenkrantz name — Holger the savant — Erik's rebuke of Cromwell — Jutland clergy — Claushohn — Meeting of King Frederic and Anne Reventlow.

KALØ—THORSAGER.

June 24th.—SOMETHING invariably occurs to prevent our starting early: horses were ordered at six, but a heavy downfall of rain—true outpouring of the heavens—caused us to defer our departure until seven. The sun then made his appearance, and, the dust laid, nature seemed quite refreshed and glistening. We cut the high road, as we always do when possible, make out a menu of the places we desire to visit, submit it to the postmaster, who writes out a ticket, all charges included, no extra pourboires or pikes, money paid down. A stated time—rather a long one—given within which the postilion is compelled to perform the journey, or none at all, when you wish to loiter on the road, as to-day for instance. Posting in Denmark, two-horse carriage and all expenses included, amounts to nine pence per English mile.

Our road runs along the bank of the fiorde, a charming drive; as we approach the further end the ancient castle of Kalø—where in early days was founded a cloister by some English monks—stands picturesquely planted. You may reach it on foot when the water is low.

Afterwards it was the prison of Gustavus Vasa, from whence he escaped to Lubek when on parole. Later Kalø was given to Ulrik Frederic Gyldenløve by Christian V. The generosity of the kings towards their natural children gave rise to a saying—"Bastards have better luck than children born in wedlock;" in the case of the Gyldenløves, it may be added, they deserved " better luck."

These are the most extensive ruins in Denmark—not saying much to be sure; but an old tower still stands, and they look picturesque on their green island.*

Not far from Kalø lies the Mols district, the Jutland Bœotia—not that its inhabitants merit the reputation of dullness more than their neighbours, but they have got the name of it, and endless are the "Joe Millers" retailed at their expense.

One day the lord of Mols came into Aarhuus, and there ate some salted herrings, so good he had never tasted the like before; so he purchased a hundred, and on his return home put them into his pond, leaving them a year's grace to increase and multiply. When the year had gone by he determined to fish: he fished from sunrise to sunset, but caught not one herring; so he caused the pond to be dragged, and all he took in his nets was one large fat eel.

"Here is the culprit," cried the lord; "here is the

---

* When Kalø was besieged by the Count of Holstein, Gerhard the tyrant, provisions were exhausted, and there remained in the castle but one sow. But, to make believe they possessed more, the besieged three times a day pinched the sow to make her scream; and as the enemy purposely sent a beggar-woman to the castle to report the state of the garrison, they every time gave her a larger piece of bread. Hence Count Gerhard believed them to have abundance, and raised the siege in the seventh winter.

devourer of my herrings!" So he summoned the whole village round, and they consulted on the death the fat eel should die. "Burn him alive," said one. "Collar him," said another, "and I'll eat him afterwards." "Hang him," advised a third. "No," interrupted an old man, "he'll slip through the rope. I myself was once nearly lost at sea, and I know from experience there is no death so cruel as drowning."

So the device of the old man met with general applause, and he was invited to accompany his lord in a boat out at sea to drown the eel, who, when he was cast into the water, wriggled, twirled, and twisted for joy.

"See!" exclaimed the old man to the lord of Mols, "see how the eel writhes—what a hard death he is dying!"

A little higher up the coast lies the Castle of Katsholm, concerning the foundation of which there hangs a tale much like that of our own Dick Whittington. A bad unjust man died, and left his property between his three sons; but the youngest, who was an honest lad, when he had received his share, said to himself, "What has come with sin must go away with care:" so he determined to put the money to the water ordeal, and cast it into the lake, knowing that what was unjustly got would sink and the rest float. He did so, and one farthing only floated; with this farthing he purchased a cat, not far from kittening time, and went by ship to a foreign land where rats and mice abounded and cats were unknown. There his kittens bore him little cats in their turn; he sold them, made a large fortune, returned to Jutland, and there built a castle, which he called Katsholm.

ROUND CHURCH, THORSAGER.

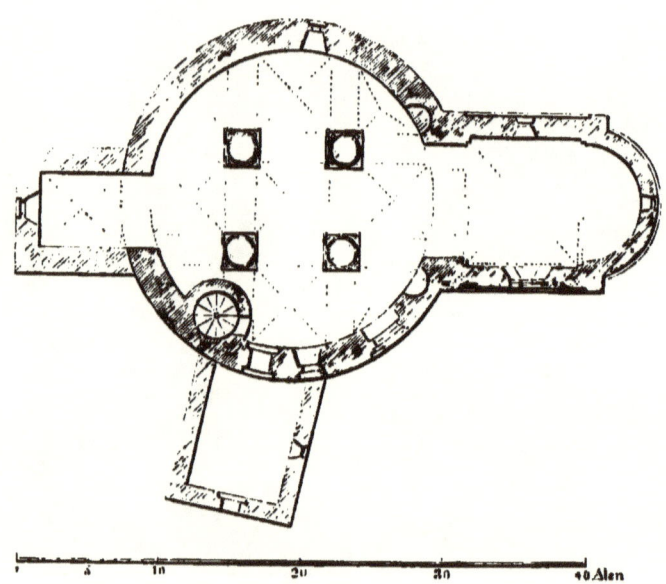

SECTIONS AND GROUND-PLANS OF CHURCH, THORSAGER.

But Katsholm was not always inhabited by honest people, for in the last century Lady Hilde Trolle, Baroness of Høgholm, dwelt there—a bad harsh woman, who had sold her body to the evil one for certain sublunary advantages. When the appointed time arrived she was in bed with her daughter; a terrible noise was heard on the staircase, and she well knew that her last hour was come. She bade her daughter rise and see who was there, in hopes the demon might make a mistake and carry her off instead, but the girl resolutely refused to do as she was bidden. Then the door flew open, and the lady was dragged out on the staircase. Terrible shrieks were heard, and all died away. The next morning her head was found on the stairs torn from her body, for the agreement had been only made for her body, and the demon kept to the letter of his bond; so it was buried in the old coffin of a former possessor of the castle, whom the Lady Hilde had turned out of his last abode to make use of his bones for her necromancies.

And now we go on to Thorsager to visit its far-famed round church—the most perfect of the eight still existing in Denmark.* It stands well on an elevation, a picturesque object as you approach, towering like a castle above the village. Its construction is assigned to Bishop Peter, our old friend of Aarhuus and Silkeborg, though, had he trusted to chance and his silken cap in this case, and the wind as high as it is to-day, there is no knowing where the peasants might have had to run for their devotions. Some say that there existed in early

---

* Two in Zealand—Storehedinge and Biernede; one in Funen—Horne, at Faaborg; one in Jutland—Thorsager; and four in Bornholm—Osterlars, Nykers, Ols, and Ny. Storehedinge is octagonal.

days a temple of Thor on this site—later Christianised, as was often the case; the round part cannot be of Bishop Peter's day, he may have added the rounded apse, the gabled tower, and the porch; but architecture in Jutland was behind that of other countries. This church is of an earlier date than the twelfth century; the original building is circular, the round-vaulted roof supported by massive columns; an interior circular tower leads to the belfry above; and from the strength of the supporting columns, it may be inferred a tower far more imposing than the small existing extinguishers had formerly risen from their bases. Hanging to the church walls were white and silver garlands, placed according to ancient usage to commemorate the death of some youthful maiden—a custom which existed in England formerly. Thirteen storks' nests on the village house-tops, all teeming with young, did we count from the churchyard of Thorsager.

It is curious to witness, when travelling, the gradual transition from the Pagan worship to that of the Christian faith. In Brittany you see the crucifix planted above the menhir, sanctifying the Pagan monument. "Let the idea soak in," thought the priests,—"the old man may still in his heart adhere to his early worship, but the child will bow to the cross later,"—and a fine jumble of Romanism and Paganism still exists there to the present day. Here Thor formed a stumbling-block to proselytising monks in the tenth century. Before the porch and doorway of Thorsager church lie two simple grave-stones of very early date, inscribed with Runic characters, hardly legible even to those who understand them : on one is a single cross; on the earlier stone a cross also, but a cross so strongly resembling the hammer of Thor, it might do as well for one as for the other. "How little difference!" must have argued the monk; "another point only and the hammer becomes a cross;" so the giant's chamber became abandoned, no more gold ornaments interred. The cross is engraved upon the stone slab—very heathen-looking cross—but there must be a beginning to all things; in the next generation Thor and his hammer are forgotten. Workmen were busy whitewashing the old brick edifice, lich-gate and all. What a wicked waste of quick-lime does take place in Denmark! It was refreshing, on arriving at Rosenholm, to feel ourselves again among respectable old red brick, relieved by Gothic mouldings, white stone copings, and armorial shields picked out in their proper colours.

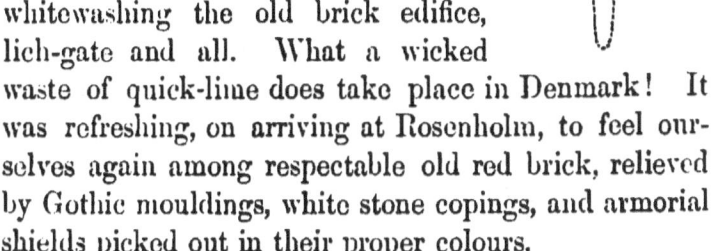

ROSENHOLM.

We were received at the entrance by the brother of Baron Rosenkrantz, and soon joined by the rest of the family—residing at that time in the castle—who conducted us round the apartments, pointing out to us the most remarkable of the numerous collection of family portraits, and those of historic interest, amounting to many hundreds in number.

The château of Rosenholm was founded in the sixteenth century by Jørgen Rosenkrantz—the earlier manor of the family, Hevringsholm, having been destroyed by Skipper Clemens and his band. Above the entrance he caused to be placed the following inscription, after the fashion of the day,—

"We have not built a durable house,
But we hope later to possess one."

The portraits date from the sixteenth century—beginning with the father and mother of the founder. Passing over the various sovereigns, of whom we have already had a sufficient dose elsewhere, among those of Jutland interest we have the portrait of fair Ellen Marsviin, mother of Christina Munk, who determined, as you will later hear, if she did marry an old man, it shouldn't be for nothing. Here hangs Holger Rosenkrantz, the savant, who founded at Rosenholm two schools, one for young girls, another for youths, whose education he superintended himself. Next is Erik, the youthful ambassador at the court of Cromwell, under Christian V., in buff jerkin and falling collar; on his first presentation his ill-mannered host scoffed at his youthful appearance: "A minister without a beard!" "If," replied Rosenkrantz, "my sovereign had known it was a beard you required, he could have sent you a goat; at any rate, my beard is of older date than your protectorate." The Protector collapsed, and so the matter ended.*

---

* Among the heroines of this family was Anna, wife of Holger Rosenkrantz, lord of Boller. She had been grande maîtresse to three successive Queens of Denmark, and was banished the country by king Christian II., who received in ill part the good advice she gave him. When Frederic I. ascended the throne she was recalled, and arrived at Ringsted, with others of the nobility. The soldiers of the exiled monarch still committed great excesses in the country; the lady Anna advised them to desist, as their king could never regain the affections of his subjects, which advice so irritated them, as well as certain citizens of Copenhagen, that they massacred her without mercy. The lady Anna appears to have been too fond of giving advice unasked. Two Miss Globs, at that time on a visit to her, nearly

Another Rosenkrantz, Palle, was sent to England as ambassador in the time of James I., to arrange the payment of 300,000 crowns, lent, at 6 per cent. interest, by King Christian to James, when King of Scotland. James was so pleased with Rosenkrantz that he gave him his portrait set round with diamonds.

Then we have Olaf, the apologist for the nobility and denier of the divine right of kings—pronounced a traitor, exiled, his property confiscated; next Rosenkrantz, minister of Christian VII., in grand gala dress as Knight of the Elephant; and endless others, all more or less distinguished in their way, many bearing round their necks massive gold chains to which are attached portraits of their sovereigns. Then the Jutland alliances of the family: Eleanor Ulfeld; the Reventlow Queen — far superior to that of Frederiksborg;— Krag, Krabbe, Høg, Friis, Sehested, de Reetz, Brahe, Gabel, Lange, Bille, Bielke, and other families, many of them since passed away—chronological portraits of 350 years, interesting even to a stranger but slightly acquainted with the history of the Rosenkrantz family.

We visited the gardens and the woods; never saw so many snakes, harmless though they are. Game too abounds in the forest—foxes, hares, and birds of all kinds; grand fox battues, you will be shocked to hear, every autumn. (Count Friis hunts his foxes with a small pack of beagles.) I wonder what my old fox-hunting friend would say to whom I once spoke of this custom: "Shoot a fox, Sir? zounds! I'd sooner shoot a Dane;" and he would have done so.

After much kind pressing we remained to dinner;

---

underwent the same fate; but their beauty excited the pity of the bystanders, who rescued them.

dined in the old Riddersaal, where above the carved chimney—fireplace fitted with chenets of the period—hang Jørgen Rosenkrantz and Dorthe Lange his wife, 1567, and other splendid full-length portraits.

The name of Rosenkrantz, well known to all readers of 'Hamlet,' is of great antiquity; all you hear of that blood is good, illustrious, and well spoken of in the annals of the country; and the Jutland peasants will point out, around the manor of Hevringsholm, which is said to have been in their possession from the sixth century, numerous barrows, where the earlier members of the family lie interred.*

It was a mystery how, in Jutland, where the great names are of primæval simplicity, mostly signifying the names of animals—daa, hog; brock (badger), &c.—anything so romantic as Rosenkrantz—crown of roses—could have inserted itself. It appears that Sir Otto Nielsen of Hevringsholm accompanied Christian I. to Rome on a pilgrimage, and the pope of the time presented the sovereign with a golden violet, Sir Otto with a crown of roses—strange present to a Northman; in consequence of which honour Sir Otto thenceforth adopted the patronymic of Rosenkrantz.

There exists a tradition that Rosenholm will fall in its own ruins some Christmas-eve; but as long as the

---

* There is no doubt that this custom of burying under høis continued long after the introduction of the Reformed faith. In former days there existed a Runic stone in the churchyard of Tømmerby, near Skive, unfortunately removed by Sir Iver Krabbe to Torstedlund, with the following inscription:—

"My name is Vidric Viis,
My father dwelt in Floieriis.
I built this church for thee,
But you must pray for me.
My father lies in Aalchøi,
Myself I lie in Vegelhøi."

little turret-shaped clock, of the sixteenth century, engraved with the arms of Jørgen and his wife Dorthe Lange, continues to wag its pendulum and strike the hours, no ill will befall Rosenholm, and, from the activity it evinces at present in the salon, little alarm need be excited for the future fate of the family whose destinies its good works hold within its power.

People talk much of the ill will existing between the landlord and the peasant in the country; but to-day I was struck, on admiring at dinner a massive silver ewer engraved with trailing vine-leaves, to find by the inscription it was an offering of affection and gratitude from the peasants of the adjoining village to Baron Rosenkrantz, on the celebration of his silver marriage: there was also a bread-basket of the same metal presented by the servants and retainers of the family. After dinner we drove down to visit the village church of Hornslet, a very St. Denis of the family, dating from the fifteenth century: here we have them all again— Erik, governor of the castle of Bergen, who received Bothwell on his arrival; Holger and his wife; Erik, no longer to be snubbed, but Erik, portly "Legatus ad Anglos," in company with three ladies, his wives, all dressed in white satin—as though they had inherited each other's gowns. Then there is a library in the church for the use of the population—the gift of Holger the savant; and lastly a chained book bound in copper, with a list of the monuments, inscriptions, and epitaphia, a legacy to the church from Erik's widow; and a deal else about the chronicles of the family.*

---

* In the collection of engravings by Schatten is the frontispiece to the funeral sermon, representing the epitaphium of Erik Rosenkrantz, in which an angel is pictured as descending from heaven and placing a crown of roses upon his brow.

In the Rosenholm archives was preserved the private collection of royal autographs extant from the time of Christian III. downwards; the letters of Erik during his embassy to England, as well as the correspondence with Ulfeld, Christina Munk, Tycho Brahe, &c. They were unfortunately removed, after the death of the minister Rosenkrantz, to Norway, and consumed in the conflagration of Frederikshall, 1826. Jørgen Rosenkrantz, founder of Rosenholm, was in the household of Queen Dorothea, and employed on all occasions by Frederic II. He was sent envoy to the Emperor, Duke of Saxony, and other potentates. In his journal, 7th October, 1564, we find: "Travelled from Leipsic to Vienna, to have audience of the Emperor Maximilian, who received me in his own chamber; and there was no one else — we were alone. But his council and all his servants were in the next room, and could hear our converse; and he gave answers nobly and well."

We drive through the extensive forest where in 1849 the German army encamped itself: they luckily advanced no further north, but were speedily expelled from the country. The sun was sinking behind the hill —half-past nine—as we drove through the village: suddenly a bell began to toll. "What is that?" we inquired. The sunset bell always rings as the sun goes down— the ancient curfew of England, as it still exists in old cathedral towns. Do not imagine we leave to-night for Randers, our kind hosts will not hear of it; so here am I, sitting in an old tapestried chamber, writing my journal. My windows look on the moat. There are no ghosts, and my tapestries are pleasant to gaze upon—a hunting scene and a picnic; a boy page plays the cithern, while couples dance under the greenwood tree. No fear of ghosts among such light-hearted beings. The stove too—such an antique stove—with bas-relief and cipher of Frederic IV.; and there is the king too, with a lady on each side—his two queens perhaps—no, they are Justice and Plenty; the king on horseback; hand issuing from the clouds places a crown upon his head, "proving thereby the Divine Right of Danish kings." Queer to find this in the house of a Rosenkrantz! a family who suffered from its opposition to absolutism, but such was the Jesuitism of the day: as the Portuguese missionaries caused sacred subjects to be painted on china, for the conversion of the Chinese—very rare these pieces are, the Emperor ordered them all to be broken up—so the absolute Government of Frederic IV. caused the Divine Right to be propagated on the stoves.

Friday, 25th.—After breakfast we drove over to Bulskovgaard, a residence belonging to a brother of the possessor of Rosenholm, near the fiorde, overlooking the island of Kalø and its ruined castle; dined; and at five o'clock took leave of our hospitable friends. The old Danish proverb of "De Reisende have mange Herberge, og faa Venner"—"Travellers find many inns, but few friends"—is not here realized; on the contrary, the Jutlanders seem "At holde Kong Artus hof"—keep open house—a proverb the open table of that mythic sovereign, at which all knights found a cover ready, gave rise to. At Bulskovgaard M. de Rosenkrantz showed me a piece of porcelain clay found on his estate, of which he forwards large quantities every year for the fabrication of porcelain at Copenhagen. Our way ran through a wide expansive country, windy and bleak, which, were it not for the regiment of turf-heaps ranged like huge black "pastilles à brûler" along the morass, would have reminded me of parts of Dorsetshire: every house is protected by a wood; every village nestles in a dell. The Jutland clergy are not badly paid on an average: he of Hornslet, the village church we last evening visited, enjoys an income of 1000 thalers, about 120*l.* English, house, &c.; he of Mørke 3000, about 360*l.*: part is paid in money, part in tithes; and it may be consolatory to their English brethren to hear the clergy have as much difficulty in getting tithes paid in Jutland as elsewhere. In Aalborg and its neighbourhood their tithes depend upon the price of corn. Considering the cheapness of the land they live in, they are not badly off; added to which, their wives and families are more simple in their habits than those of an English clergyman; no young man of good family ever choosing the church as his profession. In each village there is a school and school-house, furnished partly by the Government, partly by the community, an apothecary and doctor: gymnastics too are the fashion, poles and gibbets erected for the boys in every "handsbye" we pass. We are quite pleased this evening to come across a pair of ruined village stocks, quite out of fashion here as in our own country.

CLAUSHOLM.

We are now on our way (if we are not first blown to shreds) to Clausholm, the birthplace as well as deathplace of the Reventlow Queen.

In early days this manor belonged to the Brok family, great people once in these parts. In the year 1404 one of this family, Jens Brok, was slain by another Jutland noble, by name Jens Løvenbalk. The Broks demand vengeance against the murderer from the great Queen Margaret, who orders a reconciliation next year to take place in her presence at Helsingborg.

She condemns the murderer to give his victim a splendid funeral, which is to be attended by the members of both families, to ·found an eternal mass for his soul in St. Clement's church of Aarhuus, and also to send at his own expense six pilgrims to six different holy places, Jerusalem and St. Iago in Spain among the number; as well as nine more to the most remarkable shrines in the North: that done, the culprit was to be considered as whitewashed.

Clausholm afterwards came into possession of the Grand Chancellor Reventlow, father of the queen, who here died in 1708.

It was three years after the death of her father the king first met the fair Anna at a royal masquerade at Koldinghuus.* With Frederic it was love at first sight; he at once declared his passion. Anna replied, she must "ask mamma," and ask mamma she did, and received a box on the ears for her comfort; for the aged countess was a woman of high and honourable principles. Six months later Frederic determined to visit Anna at her mother's house of Clausholm, where he was received with great politeness by the widow of the Grand Chancellor. The dinner concluded, he had the vulgarity to leave a roll of 1000 ducats in his napkin,

---

* Frederic caused this meeting to be commemorated by a charming painted ceiling at Frederiksborg, representing the masquerade at Koldinghuus.

which the high-spirited lady observing ordered in the king's presence to be distributed to the poor of the hamlet. The king, disgusted at his want of success, returned to Skanderborg, where the sister of fair Anna, as well as her brother, informed him that she really cared for him.

The servants were gained, the waiting-maid of course. When the king drove up by night to Clausholm the fair Anna came out from a side-door to meet him, and was carried off by the king to Skanderborg, where he contracted with her "a conscience marriage," created her Princess of Slesvig, and for ten years lived with her, the husband of two wives, until the death of his first queen, when he espoused her a few days afterwards.

Christian VI., after the death of his father, wrote her a short letter with his own hand, stating how, after so many years' disgraceful living with his father, her subsequent marriage and coronation, she deserved the severest punishment. He accuses her of stealing jewels from Rosenborg, but allows her to retain Clausholm, granting her a pension of 28,000 thalers, a capital of 100,000, and a box of diamonds bequeathed her by his father.

Her mother, after a lapse of seven years, consented again to see her. Then she retired, banished by her stepson, and died twelve years later from an attack of small-pox, 7th January, 1743.

As we drive up, her arms still appear painted on the massive wooden doors of the castle gateway.

She was a great fool this Anna Sophia, and piqued herself on the writing of bad verses, which she caused to be engraved on the gold tankards in her possession. On one vase of gold, found among her treasures, three feet high, date 1717, with her name and cipher under a royal crown, is engraved—

"Ma main m'a sçu gagner cet or par son adresse :
Que ne doit espérer mon cœur par sa tendresse ?"

On another—

"It pleased the king to be tricked and lose this gold, the contents of which he will taste. But the loss is not great when the king loses gold to a person who is faithful for ever."

In Rosenborg is preserved a gilt vase, ordered by Frederic to commemorate his marriage with Anna Sophia. He had much better have said nothing about it.

It stands well embowered in woods, does Clausholm—terraces, allées, and slopes—without any exception the prettiest old place we have yet visited. Such a dream too of an old-fashioned garden—the pen of the poet Crabbe could alone describe it. No flower blessed with a botanical name would dare to blow within its hedges. A guard should be set to watch the entrance and ask, "Avez-vous fait vos preuves?" "Have you been painted by Van Huysum?" Roses and tulips, lilies and candytuft, sweet William and marjorum, gilliflowers and traveller's-joy: when plucked they would only form "posies," and could be placed in nothing but a "bowpot." It would be pleasant to dream of Clausholm—a souvenir of the past.

CHAPTER XXXIII.

Bruusgaard and the Bruces — Randers' commerce, her gloves and beer — Duel of the Counts — Manors of the Scheel family — A midnight wandering in Jutland.

———◆———

RANDERS.

WE then made for Randers, passing by the manor of Bruusgaard, pronounced Bruce, still a common name in Jutland. With all due respect to the memory of Scotland's mighty Bruce, Bruce in the Danish tongue signifies nothing more nor less than "muddle-headed." An hour and a half's drive brings us to the bridge of Randers, which crosses the clear water of the Guden Aa.

Saturday, 26th.—A most successful little town is Randers, one of the pleasantest in Jutland, not situated on the fiorde, as Murray declares, but at seven miles' distance. Guden Aa still teems with salmon and trout; excellent fish, preserved against nets, but open to flies at large. They don't rise. It might be picturesque, too, little Randers, were it not too genteel and seized with the fear of the "bumpkin fever." Such old timber houses, chessboard and striped! such carvings! Prout, how he would have loved them! but striped houses are here deemed vulgar, village-like; so they paint them stone colour, and hope that travellers may mistake them for plaster, if not stucco. On Guden Aa's banks bristles a little merchant fleet of shipping—

deals en masse from Norway and Sweden, for the Jutland peasants are inveterate builders; then, too, they export corn and fish, their far-famed dry salmon fetching a higher price in the market than any other. Pork, too, they salt in Jutland, and Randers manufactures linen—quite a little commerce of their own; on the other side is the barge laden ready for Silkeborg—an eight days' passage.

To-day is market-day; such a rich market! Look at the butter: the meat of best quality, 3½d. a Danish pound, two ounces more than the English; second quality, 3d. Look at the potatoes and other vegetables; above all, those splendid pots of yellow piccotees laden with flowers. Observe, too, those old Jutland peasants, —their picturesque costumes, Hessian boots, velvet breeches, and old-cut coat of our grandfathers' days, covered with huge silver buttons. And the women bringing their rolls of home-made linen to market: how solid, how well-to-do they look! a pleasure to see them! no finery, but good, wrought, stout, homespun dresses. The young men, sad to say, run after modern fashions, adopt the town-made trousers, and fight shy of good mud-preserving Hessians. Randers possesses one fine church, dedicated to St. Morten, founded, as a fresco on the walls denotes, "In memoriam," by good King John, who all devoutly hope "requiescat in pace." You walk over sepulchral stones, —knights, burghers, and ladies, plenty of them, none remarkable that you ever heard of. Not far from the church stands an hospital for one hundred and fifty aged men and women, clothed and fed, as well as pensions of twenty-five dollars yearly paid to out-door pensioners,— a charitable foundation raised on the very spot where, in the wars of the Counts, Niels Ebbesen slew in single combat the rebel Count of Holstein; for Randers, like other towns, has her history, and has played her part in her country's story. Her gloves were famous in the eighteenth century; French ladies much affected them and wore them at night: they were said to render a fair white hand whiter still; and the proverb ran—"As well known as Randers gloves." Randers, too, in early days boasted a manufactory of equal but less enviable notoriety—her beer. In the year 1586 no less than six murders committed within her walls were attributed by the judge to the effects of this intoxicating liquor. The German proverb ran—"He who comes from Randers not intoxicated or beaten is a lucky man."

But good, as we all know, sometimes comes out of evil. In the days of Skipper Clemens, when, after the battle of Svenstrup Heath, Rosenkrantz * and Banner, beaten by the peasant forces, retired on Randers, they were there besieged without success; for the "boers" found so much beer in the cellars outside the walls that they gave themselves over to intoxication, and Randers proved to the rabble forces of the Jutland Jacquerie a second Capua.

We visited the public gardens, the airy barracks for the young cavalry recruits, and their spacious stables; turned into the Town-hall to look at the modern picture of the duel between Niels Ebbesen and the Holstein count, and the charming portrait of Lena Brok, who

---

* One of his brothers, Otto, fell in the fight—you may see his tomb at Krogsbæk church, raised by his spouse, a Gyldenstierne, and over his coffin lies the sword he on that day so bravely wielded in the mêlée.

left her money to the town to portion off poor young maidens. We feel quite in England to-day, what with the Bruces and the Broks; and here again was a portrait of old John Caroe, pronounced Carew, ancient burgomaster of the city. Then on to-day's journey or near it we have the villages of Dyrby, Raaby, and Beilby, and again at the table-d'hôte they served us "gooseberry fool."

GAMMEL-ESTRUP.

The horses are announced; we start for Gammel-Estrup, the ancient Herregaard of the Counts of Scheel—"gaard" in Danish answers to our English word "court," of which some two or three are always added to the main building, offices, stables, &c. A very ugly road we drove over. Before arriving at our destination—far to the right lies Ammel Hede (heath), properly called Amlets Hede, which is mentioned in Saxo Grammaticus as one of the places so named after the Danish prince—we met with a fox wending his way leisurely along the roadside. Don't imagine he cared for us—not a whit: as the wagen passed he turned round, sat up just like a pointer dog, or fox in the fable of Maître Corbeau. He would have given me a paw had I requested him. The towers of Gammel-Estrup now appear in sight. We drive as usual through the gaard and gateway, cross two separate moats—bright sparkling running water here, connected with the Randers fiorde; swans in numbers, and cygnets too—quite right the heraldic bearings and supporters of the house of Scheel—and then descend in the inner court of the castle. Count Scheel was absent, but his brother-in-law, Captain Sparling of the

VOL. II. F

Hussars, had kindly given us a note to one of the family, who did the honours of the place. We walked through the garden: in green "caisses" stood gigantic orange-trees in full blossom and perfume, nearly coeval with the building, which dates from an early part of the sixteenth century, commenced before, but not finished in time for Skipper Clemens to burn it to the ground. Of red brick, flanked on the entrance side by two octagonal towers, crowned with open-work battlements, it reminded me of Hampton Court.

When once in these Jutland courts, and you have visited the Riddersaal, you have seen the best. Here it is a spacious oblong room, the conventional form; heavy ceiling richly decorated in compartments once painted; walls hung with ancient tapestry, representing some twelve châteaux, all, like this, ending in "Up," * possessed by the family in the last century, when the Count of Scheel of that ilk is said to have ridden from Grenaa to Viborg, a distance of sixty English miles, without once quitting his own estates; but said Count Scheel, a fast young officer, loved cards and dice as well, and he gambled away estate after estate. The saal is entirely hung round with oval portraits, many of them very charming, by Juel. We are now well "up" in these pictures, and recognise at once one old acquaintance. I was quite glad again to see the Arveprinds, son of Juliana, and his fair wife of most destructive eyes, "fendus à l'amande," with just a Chinese "squeedge" at the corners; they are hereditary too, and are reproduced in a second generation in the person of her handsome granddaughter, the Princess Augusta of Hesse.

---

* "Up" is a corruption of thorp."

Here hangs, mounted on his white horse, the portrait of Count Jørgen Scheel, 1740, minister to the Court of the Empress of All the Russias in the last century, one of the handsomest men of his day; at least the Empress Catherine appears to have been of this opinion, for with her he was in great favour, so much so as to excite the jealousy of the favourite, Orloff, by whose artifices he is said to have died poisoned at St. Petersburg. We then climbed the corkscrew tower to the rooms above. Long corridors hung with portraits: Christian IV. and other worthies, royal and of gentle blood, sadly in want of restoration. Such black wood, brass-bound chests stand ranged along the passages, full, may be, of the faded dresses of the originals of the pictures which cover the walls. Can't you imagine the velvet doublets and guipure-trimmed farthingales contained in such a tapestry-hung chamber? Grim knights and most prim ladies frown down upon you from their frames. Old beds of needlework (prodigies of patience and bad perspective, topped by stumpy panaches of discoloured feathers), handiwork of some former countess and her ladies; old mirrors, old toilets, powder and pomade boxes, tables covered with old Dutch tiles, &c. "Surely there must be a ghost-chamber here?" we inquired. There was once a ghost who haunted one of the largest rooms in the castle, fitted with two beds —no one will, however, sleep there, and it is now a lumber-room.

We must positively stay to tea. Seven miles Danish on to Mariager before nightfall. We hesitate, but it is all prepared, so we accept. A Jutlander would feel wretched if you quitted his house without breaking your fast. Tired of inquiring how many cows people keep, I ask this time, in my very best Danish, "How many horses?" Eighty-five is the reply, in the stable, for farm purposes as well. We are now in the horse country. There was a cattle-market at Randers this morning—mercifully we were spared a horse-market: last week there were more than a thousand brought in for sale; good strong animals they are too, perhaps a little heavy in the shoulder. Six thousand were lately sent to France, and orders came for three thousand more. The "Jagt," too, is excellent, deer, chevreuil, birds of all kinds in abundance, and fish into the bargain. We now take our leave, and jump out for one minute at Auning church to visit the monument of Count Jørgen Scheel. He reclines, after the manner of his day, in long curled wig and armour (Danes wore it later than other nations), bearing in his hand a baton, of some kind he had probably used in lifetime; beside him an angel sounds the last trump, while about his head a sister seraph unfolds a roll of marble, on which appear in bas-relief the features of the Russian Empress—queer idea, considering the scandal of the times! Having tipped the "Deacon," as they here call the grave-digger—an odd jumble of clerical titles—we are again en route. Jutland farmers make their own bricks, bake them at the house-side, and build them to the ready established timber as soon as worked and dry. We meet a chevreuil browsing on the heath, and then a manor-house, which the talkative postboy greatly admires, painted bright yellow. No signposts, and bye-roads by the dozen. We miss our way, and after a great deal of hallooing and inquiring arrive at the ferry's side, whose barge, for convenience sake, is kept midway out at sea, and has to be fetched by a cockle-shell. The postilion too, tells his horses to "stande"—not to staae—"stille," he constantly inquires the "vay," no longer "vei;" and begs to know if we start tomorrow in the "forenoun," or the "afternoun,"—very bad Danish, "quite incomprehensible the Jutlanders," so folks told me in Copenhagen, but very like the English language. Well, we get over the ferry, and walk on some mile and a half on the straight road, and are hallooed back again. Who ever would have imagined that woody path to the right? And now it is eleven o'clock and twilight, and all the world asleep. We drive over a bare waste; ought to pass through the villages of Tweed and Kirby, so pronounced at any rate.* We stop, knock up the people in the village, tap at one casement; no answer; on till the tenth; a voice replies; by this time the nine others are awake—all heads out at once, half asleep, directing, or more probably misdirecting, our steps—such a chatter—might as well have disturbed a hen-house. "Turn to the right:" some eight different paths diverge like the points of a star. Here's a puzzle; of course go wrong; are received at the entrance of a farm-yard by a furious watch-dog; turn again; we wander, benighted—no sign, no post through the land. See, there's the fiorde: we approach it—no such thing: a long line of mist rising along the valley from the Mose, but the road is good; two miles we rattle along at a merry pace; all wrong again—'tis a herregaard. "Oh!" exclaims the postboy, "if I had only turned my stocking inside out we should never have lost the way."

---

* Trede and Kærby.

A Jutland remedy. We are at last in the bon chemin; half-past one o'clock, no watchman to tell it though, nothing but sleepy ruminating cows and frightened tethered sheep under our very carriage-wheels. Those most uncomfortable creatures, the larks, are already up and about, swelling their voices in praise of early morn till ready to burst. Rising with the lark in Jutland must be never going to bed at all. The heavens—twilight long since over—become rosy-tinted, betokening the sun's early arrival. We now enter a forest—all beech and heather—the fiorde in sight. We drive along the heights above: how calm, how beautiful! A small capped snow-white tower — 'tis Mariager — nestling among the trees; below lies the little village. We rattle down the hill-side, knock up the Gjæstgiver and his myrmidons: by five o'clock (sun long ago up and about) we are in bed and asleep. N.B. Never go wandering after nightfall among unknown cross-roads in Jutland.

CHAPTER XXXIV.

The village of Mariager — Story of Sir Hem and Sir Sem — Poor Mary's well — A black stork — A Jutland plain — Sea of barrows — Wicked Baroness of Lindenborg.

———◆◇◆———

MARIAGER.

Sunday, 26th.—WHEN I rose from my bed this morning and gazed from the attic window on the scene below, it seemed, had we searched all Denmark over, we could not have selected a calmer, quieter spot to pass our Sunday than the small village of Mariager. Our inn is of the humblest description: whitewashed walls, but cleanest of beds; a better breakfast, tea and all, could not have been served us at the Clarendon, on prettier porcelain or finer linen. The landlord gathers us his finest roses to decorate our table, set out in the village ball-room, an indispensable necessary in these dance-loving lands.

How pretty, too, is the cloister church of Mariager rising from among the trees, distinguished from her village sisters by her high-arched lancet windows and stately gable; she reminds me of some fair lady, who, like La Vallière, has retired secluded from the world, to seek consolation and that peace which this world affordeth not, in solitude, meditation, and prayer. She is still grande dame, even in her adversity. The people, too, respect her, poverty-stricken though she be; they have planted and trailed a natural archway of limes, under which you approach her cemetery. The village runs down to the waterside, and possesses there a wee harbour all of its own, where two or three Norwegian vessels unload their planks upon the jetty. Not far removed is the small bathing establishment, and over the little custom-house floats the Danish flag.

Very quiet and composed is the village of Mariager on this Sabbath morn: a few peasants in their Sunday's best, patterns of rustic neatness, are now on their way to church. A stuhlwagen drives by laden with six Jutlanders, sober old-fashioned folks; beside the driver sits a musician, with distended cheeks, playing most vigorously on the flageolet. A wedding or something must be going on: we go and see, and meet a return christening, a small baby, well wrapped and nigh suffocated in a coloured blanket. As we enter the churchyard we meet the stiff-ruffed parson, who calls his "deacon" to accompany us. Deacon, an Old Mortality, knows all the tombstones by heart, and is anxious to display his knowledge. Well-worn knight and ecclesiastic, whose inscriptions will soon be trodden away, and become things of the past, like the families in whose houses they were erected—most of them slain at the battle of Aalborghuus [*]—lie here interred.

Very English do they sound to our astonished ears: the Hogs, Broks, Lockes, Lawson, Galt, and Benzon; the list closing with good Bishop Crump (crooked), last Roman Catholic prelate of Aalborg, who, the Reformation once declared, ousted from his diocese (stift), retired to Mariager or its whereabouts, and lies buried among his relatives, not far removed from

---

[*] 1534.

Sir Otto Crump and his noble and high-born lady Dame Anna Locke. While deciphering his epitaphium on the carved stone, thinking how calm and quiet must have been his end, removed far from this world's strife in placid Mariager, Old Mortality opens wide a gate, and there before my eyes lay extended the worthy Bishop, all dust and bones past corruption. By his side lay the bodies of two cloistered nuns—I trust no facetious innuendo of the early Reformers—and in the same sepulchral chamber lie bundled together old crucifixes, figures of saints, and objects of papistic times, placed aside until again wanted.

This convent church, whitewashed and slated, rising from her leafy frame, would have inspired the muse of some poet of the last century—Gray, Goldsmith, or the like. But here am I gossiping about Mariager, and quite forgetting her early history. "Early history!" you reply; "no doubt about that; some establishment of fat monks or idle nuns, all in honour of the Virgin—trust them to choose a good situation! plenty of fish, plenty of game in the forest hard by: they knew well what they were about, forsooth!"

But Mary the Virgin had nought to do with this foundation. Mary, a virgin, and a luckless one too, endowed with two hearts (" La femme à deux cœurs," of which I have heard say, is no novelty),—hers was a sad history. It was long, long ago there lived on the banks of the deep blue fiorde we now gaze upon a youthful damsel, before-mentioned Mary, the fairest, the richest in all North Jutland: she had suitors, as you may imagine, in plenty—all Jutland at her feet—but distinguished among the train two alone found favour in her eyes, Sir Hem and Sir Sem—Sir Hem, the blue-eyed, the golden-haired, a Northman "pur sang;" Sir Sem, of mixed Oriental blood, black-eyed and olive tinted; his mother, a fair Eastern maiden, had followed some stout Varangian,—her dowry a string of Cufic coins twined among her tresses,—from the marble halls of imperial Byzantium.

Fair-haired Sir Hem, black-eyed Sir Sem—what could poor Mary do? "I cannot marry both," she piteously exclaimed; and she felt her heart always warmed towards the present one; and that, you know, as she confidentially owned to a female friend, would never do after marriage. Hers was the old story of

" How happy could I be with either,
Were the other dear charmer away!"

"I can no longer stand this shilly-shally!" exclaims Sir Hem.

"No more can I," replied Sir Sem.

"We must fight it out, and he who *falls*—"

"Hold, brother! he who *dies;* there must be but one survivor. We will fight naked to our waists."

"Agreed."

The rivals now fall to—clash, clash, go the swords (long swords, heavy as the iron bar of a gaol gate)—clash, clash, clash again; the golden tresses of Sir Hem are now dyed scarlet red; the clear olive skin of the brave Sir Sem blanched pale with loss of blood. Clash, clash, they go—now fainter, cla-ash, cla-a-ash, till they sound no longer, and each knight sinks dying, side by side, in a pool of clotted gore.

"Brother," murmured Sir Hem, "your hand! we fought for love, not hate." A slight, feeble pressure responds, a whispering faint " Good-night!"

"Stop them, stop them!" exclaimed the frantic Mary, when the news of the combat reached her. "Stop, oh, stop! I'll marry you both,"—and she rushes to the spot. Too late—she casts herself on both the bodies at once, and gives way to her agony of grief. Survive them she will not—she who had caused their death; so she makes her will, bequeaths all her possessions to the Church to found a cloister, and builds two churches over the remains of her lover victims, Sir Hem and Sir Sem—those two white village churches, Hem and Sem, you pass on your road, as we did, when we wandered about the wide plains in our midnight journey to Mariager.

"Now," exclaims Mary, "I have done with life!" and she casts herself headlong into the deep well adjoining the ancient monastery, of which one ivied and extinguisher-capped tower remains.

"But our beloved foundress," asks a brother of the prior who directs the building of the rising convent, where shall we bury her?"

"Hush, hush!" responds the prior, "not in consecrated ground, the holy Mother Church forbids us; but bide a time, leave her where she is, the story will blow over; we can't canonize a suicide, but we will work miracles at her cell." And gradually a rumour goes forth, how a love-sick maiden, deserted by her lover, at the last stage of consumption had recovered her youth, freshness, and peace of mind by quaffing the water from poor Mary's well. The spring became famous, though I doubt it did much good—it only made men more heartless—"Stuff and nonsense!" they replied to the prayers of the helpless victims. "Go" (not as men say now, to the ——, but) "to Maria Kilde, and you'll soon be all right again."

Our landlord proposed a visit to Hor-höi, situated behind the Munksholm wood, the burial-place of King Hor, a sovereign unmentioned even in the most lying of Danish chronicles.

We did not go, having passed it the morning of our arrival; from its summit you can count on a clear day upwards of fifty church-towers, proving the flatness of the adjacent country.

HADSUND.

June 27th.—The sun is high in the heavens; the horses are ordered at four; we still linger, unwilling to quit so fair a scene, but an eight hours' journey lies before us to Aalborg, and we have had a dose of night travelling and losing ourselves. We have the choice either to go by Hobrø and the royal chaussée on to Aalborg, or by the more intricate road to Hadsund, and then, crossing the ferry, by Lindenborg on to our destination. Uncured of our hatred of the electric telegraph, we choose the latter, and drive along the water's edge: the green beech cap the overhanging banks; on the opposite side appear fine country residences, paradises in the summer season, backed by the never-wanting forest. And now what is that? We stop the carriage: a stork, a black stork, fishing in the waters—black as a raven—the first we have seen; his dwelling-house, no doubt, in the forest hard by, for black storks build their nests in trees, avoiding the society of human kind.* He now flies away back with the produce of his chase to his mate and young ones, and we continue our journey. As we pass near a country house the scarlet postilion points to behind the road, "Stonehenge;" and there as sure as fate stands a lofty dolmen—Stonehenges, as the peasants call them in these parts. He talks to his horses, too: one he terms "ole ors," the companion "mare,"—hoppe is the correct word—just like a British ostler.

We were charged for four glasses of "toddie" in our moderate Mariager bill—brandy and water taken on our first arrival half perished with dew (dug), pronounced like our own by the postilion, after our nocturnal wanderings among the moses. Such a night as he'd passed—"Sicken a one he'd never kenned." All of which makes me half imagine myself somewhere in the provinces of old England.

We reach Hadsund ferry; boats of course on opposite side, and no man visible. Tu whu, tu whu! sounds the postilion, like some stranger at the castle-warden's gate. No answer from the ferry-house, a building, had it only an extra story added to it, as big as a mansion in Belgrave-square. At last two lazy men appear: we sit like Patience and admire the opposite château of Dalsgaard, embedded among the trees, and pluck nosegays of white orchises. The boat arrives at last, and we get over to the other side; half an hour's time after quitting the ferry-house we bid adieu to all beauty, and enter on one of those wide-extending myste-

---

* It is a curious fact that, although these birds breed every year, no one can tell what becomes of the young ones; the number of nests never increases.

rious plains typical of North Jutland. Picture to yourself a raging sea, all wave and battle, ferment and locomotion, suddenly stilled by the magic wand of a magician, to stay as it now is, never to move again, but become, after a time, like stagnant water, covered with duckweed, green, later black from the decomposition of vegetable matter. Such is the country we this evening drove through, wearisome to a degree, still not uninteresting: patches of corn, patches of heath, black soil, white sand, a curious irregular colouring not often witnessed in nature. Even the endless tumuli give a certain variety to the scene, standing detached, as they always do, against the horizon: some black, others green; one has been just flayed, for its turf's sake, or may be for its heather, manufactured by the women into brooms and carried to Aalborg market. Many and rich are the ornaments of silver and gold which lie interred within these ancient graves; each year brings them forth, and fresh objects grace the cabinets of the Museum of Copenhagen. A gentleman at Aalborg informed me that last year, on the property of his brother at Buderupholm, three Danish miles south of Aalborg, there lay in the midst of the field a large stone always in the way of the ploughshare, so the proprietor gave orders to the labourers to dig a hole by its side and bury it. On moving the mass of granite they discovered beneath three gold armlets of exquisite workmanship, for each of which they received from the committee at Copenhagen the full value in solid cash, 350 dollars, nearly 40*l.* of our English money.

On the same estate the peasants, while engaged in cutting turf (what a blessing these moses prove to the humbler classes!*)—the peasants discovered the body of a female pegged down in the bog, a spurious Queen Gunhild.

As we drove along I fell into a reverie, and tried to picture to myself the map of Jutland and the Danish isles, such as it might have been before the birth of Christ, when these long valleys, now half under cultivation, half mose, were still extensive lakes, sloppings of the great deluge, not yet dried up in time to pass away from the evaporation of the sun's rays and the labour of mankind.

That the waters are retiring in these parts there can be no doubt; the very names as well as the stranded appearance of the sites on which the villages are built attest the fact—Traudersholm (island), Engholm, and twenty others.

The worthy mayor of Aalborg told me himself that, where he used to fish some eighteen years since in the little lake of Gravlev, the land has been long since under cultivation, and from no draining process. The islands, too, of the Liimfiorde are gradually becoming connected with the land—Oxholm, and many others: while at the farm of Revs the proprietor continued, until fifty years ago, to hold the privilege of ferrying over travellers in his boat to Gudenholm, where carriages have passed over dry land for many centuries. It is more easy to realise this transition in a summer twilight, when there is a sombre mysterious gloom as far as the straining eye can gaze over this sea of hillocks.

After a weary three hours' drive we arrive at Lin-

* One thousand large turves here sell for 2s. 6d. English—they find no bog-oak though, as in Ireland.

denborg, an ancient château (Grevskab) of Count Schimmelmann, picturesque, quaintly begabled, and hardly visible from the trees which grow round, separating it from the grass-green moat, stagnant and noisy as an old French grenouillière.

"What a pity the evening is so far advanced!" we exclaimed; but it was no pity, for in the soft tones of twilight the old building looked more mysterious, in the midst, too, of such a wild country, embowered in trees—alone—isolated. Somehow or other at the moment its history had escaped my memory, otherwise for gilded gold I would never have traversed the road we trod drowsily along after nightfall, for there are dark tales of Lindenborg well known to the peasants of the surrounding country.

Ræsholm, as it was called until created into a county, has passed through many hands—strange it is how these manors changed proprietors in Jutland; none, I believe, save Rosenholm, descended from father to son for the lapse of three hundred and fifty years—later it became the possession by purchase of Claus Daa, a noble Jutlander, married to King Christian IV.'s granddaughter, Sophia, Baroness of Lindenov. Claus Daa came to an untimely death in the castle, no one knew how, "beside the red door," was buried and forgotten. Years rolled on, and the fair but very frail Sophia became attacked by that scourge of the female sex, a hideous cancer. Fearful were the torments she endured, not only of body, but of mind. As a last resource, she caused her suffering frame to be transported in a litter by four horses over the jolting roads and ruts to Aalborg, even in these days, as we ourselves can attest, a weary journey. To stifle her screams, she was accompanied by a band of musicians; at each paroxysm they burst forth into melody, adding to the torments of the sufferer. She reaches Aalborg, and submits to the surgeon's knife—an operation of no avail. Grim Death is fast approaching: she sends for the Bishop, and on her death-bed makes a full and true confession of the murder of her husband. She wished for more liberty for the indulgence of her guilty passions. She died; but oft on a wintry night the passing traveller still hears the tramp of the litter-bearers and horses, with the agonising shrieks of the suffering lady, surpassing in shrillness the trumpets and clarions, hired, like the gongs of an Indian suttee, to conceal them from the horror-stricken villagers. It is one o'clock—the very recollection of this story gives me the "creeps"—it is pleasant to see in the morning twilight the spire of St. Budolph, and to be lodged safe and sound away from all ghosts and goblins at the hotel Phœnix in the city of Aalborg.

CHAPTER XXXV.

Aalborg or Eel Castle — Its armes parlantes — Death of King John — Jens Bang and the miser's daughter — The Agger Canal — Skipper Clemens, leader of the Vendel boers — Hog family — Their high and ancient descent — Coat of Jørgen Bille — Great bog of Jutland — Børglum and Bishop Crump — The lady of Asdal and the flitch of bacon.

AALBORG.

June 28th.—WE are at Aalborg, Eel Castle—simple people those early Scandinavians, with their Flounder Castles and their eels; no Tonquebec here—no Château Gaillard in this country—all plain speaking; and here we are on the Liimfiorde, within two days' journey from Skagen, which people prophesied we should never reach. My first impression of Aalborg as we entered the town was favourable: old houses, antique and respectable-looking; narrow streets; and here and there a running Aa (I can't say river, and won't insult the natives by calling it stream), three of which pass through the city—Øster Aa, Vester Aa, and Blegdams Aa by name—each separate stream contributing as its share an eel to the heraldic bearings of the town—three red eels on a field or. The banks of the Liimfiorde are here flat; but an expanse of water is always pleasing to the eye; it runs from here four Danish miles down to Hals.*

---

* Where, in A.D. 965, Harald Graafeld, King of Norway, son of Queen Gunhild, was assassinated by Guld Harald, later murdered himself by Hakon Jarl.

Aalborg is not a town of sights, guide-book-speaking—no bounden duties; a most blessed circumstance: still there is quite enough to interest and while away a day, pottering about without any fixed plan or stereotyped project. The pavement is not famous, but there are symptoms of progress; three long streets have been lately repaved; gas was introduced here as soon, if not before, Copenhagen; and a liberal supply of water is forced by hydraulic pumps to the upper stories of every house in the place, from Bleg Kilde. There is no doubt that this valley originally formed part of the fiorde; the city must have then been almost an island, the truth of which theory is carried out by the oyster-beds found embedded in the rocks near Bleg Kilde—beds of unopened oysters, growing, as oysters do in nature, double, the round shell undermost—not separate, like the kitchen heaps of the Northern Museum, of which plenty have been discovered on the heights above the Liimfiorde.

Leaving the hotel, we stroll down the street leading to St. Budolph's church: the doors are open; odd women occupied in cleaning it out, each armed with a goose's wing—ancient Scandinavian duster, used, I have no doubt, in the time of King Gorm. St. Budolph's is like all churches in these parts—carving, paint, and gold.

We must visit that adjoining house [*] in the corner of the ancient Kloster court, gabled and ancient. Here, in the year 1513, Feb. 20th, expired King Haus (John), father of Christian II., Knight of the most honourable

---

[*] One of the few which in this part of the town escaped the raging conflagration of 1660 or thereabouts, since which date no fire has attacked Aalborg; hence her antiquated appearance.

Order of the Garter, and a good friend to England. He allowed our merchants an "alderman" in each Danish seaport town, to protect their commercial privileges. Fifty-eight years of age was King Hans or John: he rode one morning on horseback, strong and in health, from Ringkjöbing, escaping from a flood at Ribe: while passing a river he fell from his horse, broke his leg, caught cold, and died in the very room we are now about to visit, to admire the stone chimney-piece, sole remnant of his time. It is supported by two Jutland warriors—most formidable individuals they must have been—sword in hand, somewhat like pictures of one's childhood's giants, in painted helm and corslet and gilded moustaches, quite beautiful. A pious motto is inscribed above—"Protectio Domini, fundamentum stabile."

King John was not of a happy disposition; always seeing matters in a dark point of view. The year of his death he was sitting at a table with his friends in the palace of Copenhagen, when the almanac for the following year, just arrived from Germany, was brought into his presence; in this almanac it was declared that in " this year would die a great potentate," which the king immediately settled to be himself, and told his son and the courtiers his opinion; then, as Duke Christian did not contradict him, he turned wroth, and sharply remarked, "It might just as well be you, for death spares neither youth nor age." The presentiment however did not quit him; for when, after a rough passage across the Belt from Korsør, in which his vessel was in danger of being lost, he stood on the bridge of Nyborg, he apostrophised the water, saying, " Farewell Belt! you have treated me so ill that I shall never pass over you again." When the flood took place at

Ribe and he was compelled to quit the castle, he took refuge in the house of the oldest burgomaster of the city, and there remained some days. One morning he stood before the door, watching the ebb and flow of the tide, and the ice floating in the western haven. Turning to his courtiers, he said, "Let honour be given—over all lords and over all kings to whom we pay honour and worship, over all potentates in the world—to Him who, without gun or shaft, or any warlike weapon, alone can hold us by His will in this city; to Him alone must we yield ourselves prisoners—in love, honour, and victory—eternally!" From the time of his accident he declared he should never recover; and calling to him his son Christian, gave him much good counsel for his country's weal (to which the heir-apparent paid but little attention); and having received the Sacrament, " from which he derived great consolation," he expressed no fear of death, but died calmly. His saying was, " I wish that my inferiors should not fear me, and that my superiors should not despise me." He was the first sovereign who assumed the title of "majesty" in place of "your high-born grace." King John was betrothed to Princess Mary, daughter of Edward IV. of England, in 1476, but she died in Greenwich before the marriage took place.

In the town-house, if you care to mount the staircase, you will find many royal portraits, mostly rubbish, from Christian I. downwards: much to the credit of the corporation, they appear to have treated their pictures as we do our London houses, caused them to be repainted (three coats) every seven years; but you will see untouched among them our English Queen Louisa. She wears the very parure later seen on Queen Juliana.

Her portraits are more rarely met with in town-halls and public places than in 'the farmers' houses, where her memory is still cherished.

And now we come to the pride of Aalborg—the Svane-Apothek. In Denmark the apotheker answers to the French "pharmacien;" they hold there a much higher position than they do in England. As the lives of so many are intrusted to their care, they are not selected without a most searching examination. In former days travellers appear to have been lodged at the apothek. We find in Daniel Major's Travels, 1693, "At the apothecary's I was treated with hare steak, excellent salmon trout, and good aqua vitæ, and all at a cheap price." Again, in Holger Jacobeus' Journal, 1671, "In Odense lodged at the apothecary's, and drank lemon brandy." The signs of all apotheks in Denmark are swans or lions, except one I have seen named after King Solomon; this, of Aalborg, was built in the year 1623, and is the finest specimen of the Renaissance to be met with out of Zealand—such a queer old tourelle too it has, tacked on to the doorway. At the above-mentioned date there lived in the city of Aalborg a wealthy wine-merchant, Jens Bang by name, one of the olden school, liberal to a fault, honourable in his dealings with all men. Young too he was, and loved the daughter of old miser Knud Jensen, the eel-salter —the fairest maid in the north of Jutland. A rich son-in-law was much to old Knud's taste; but it made his heart bleed to see his money fly so freely; and when Jens Bang commenced to build the house we now gaze upon, Knud swore with a bitter oath that, if he did not at once desist from so extravagant an undertaking, he would end his days in the poorhouse. Jens laughed, and replied, "Well, if such is to be the case, it shall be in one of my own building." So he founded the "fattighuus" for aged men and women outside of the town, which bears his name. We are now standing on the new market, take the apothek en biais, and see, separated by the running stream called Øster Aa, on the opposite side, the ancient residence of Knud the miser—an old striped house, with high-pitched roof and long open gallery in front, reminding you of Chester's city: in this house died the wicked Baroness of Lindenborg; it is now a conditori; below the gallery is a cobbler's stall. Cannot you picture to yourself the fair Mette, Knud's "datter," fresh and piquante in her youth and beauty, in trim bourgeoise dress of the seventeenth century, leaning over the gallery, watching the progress of her future mansion; the miser father, with long white beard and velvet cap on head, appearing in the background, stick in hand, chiding the damsel for loitering, and sending her back to her domestic duties, not, however, before she has caught sight of Jens Bang, nodded, smiled, and waved her handkerchief in token of recognition, thereby enraging the miser doubly?—a scene like an old Dutch picture—a Mieris, or a Gerard Dow, exquisitely finished. But you turn up your nose at such subjects not high art.

Time rolled on; the miser died; Jens Bang espoused his pretty daughter, and the prophecy of the old man was long since forgotten. Jens prospered; he speculated, and purchased Sæby Gaard, a fine estate; all went well until the occupation of Jutland by General Wrangel and the Swedes. Wrangel inhabited the corner house lower down. You may visit his rooms—two splendid empanelled chambers of richly-wrought oak-once adorned with pious saws, long since painted over, but still discernible. Before quitting Aalborg, Wrangel imposed so heavy a ransom on the town, the burghers could not raise the sum; Jens Bang, open and generous as ever, came forward, purse in hand, willing to advance the money on the simple word of his fellow-citizens. He did so; was never repaid; became a ruined man, and died, as the miser had prophesied, an inmate of the poorhouse he himself had founded. Such is the story of Jens Bang, which adds an interest to the old house we all admire at Aalborg.

Look at this quaint entrance a few doors lower down —above, the figure of a lady stands in a niche; it is Christina Munk. The house belonged to her mother, Ellen Marsviin, whose effigy, as well as that of Ludvig Munk, her father, if it be them, guards the doorway; date, 1616. Around the head of Christina hung a swarm of bees—mason-bees—who from the memory of man have built their nests in the wall behind her head—pleasant vicinity. If you care for an antique font, circular, with the date 1166 plainly visible in the sculptured granite, there is one of gigantic proportions in the yard of Wrangel's dwelling-house—monstraceous carving too upon it; cherubim with faces as broad as Wiltshire cheeses; and pigs, or some other animals, with tails expanding at the points into full-blown lilies.

By the harbour—a new little harbour lately finished —stands the old palace, not the same probably in which King Hans was born, but its successor, a tumble-down affair, once moated, now filled up; the inner court more like a country gaard than a palace, all stripes and "cage-work;" and in this so-called palace did Guldberg and Juliana propose to incar-

CHAP. XXXV. THE AGGER CANAL.

cerate Queen Caroline Matilda previous to her removal to Zell: the English Government would not allow it. Jutland has always been the refuge place of ladies under a cloud: Christina Munk, Reventlow Queen, the Russian princesses, then Caroline Matilda, and, in later days, another illustrious lady too nearly allied to the present royal family to be mentioned.

There is much shipping in the harbour, for Aalborg's commerce is great in grain, in eels no longer, nor yet in herrings, once her staple commodity. The sudden opening of the Agger Canal in 1824 into the Northern Ocean, after a lapse of centuries, overthrew this branch of trade. The herrings—like the English, at the conclusion of the late war—desirous of seeing foreign parts, swam out into the open seas, and took so kindly to real salt water they never again returned to the brackish Liimfiorde and the nets of the Aalborg fishermen. Whether this canal be an advantage to the commerce of Jutland is hard to say. On the charts is marked down eight feet of water, at present there is scarcely four; and only a few days since some vessels returned which had been waiting since December last, unable to pass into the open ocean.

In the construction of the new harbour the workmen came on a ship of early date, to judge by the timbers; there they lie, black as coal before you, supposed to belong to Skipper Clemens' time, when Aalborghuus was surrounded by water.

Skipper Clemens was a naval officer of rank, as his name denotes, leader of the Jacquerie who remained faithful to the fortunes of second Christian; Clemens led on the Vendel peasants against the nobles who tyrannised over them as well as over their imprisoned sovereign. Fearful was the revenge of the boer race: murder, rapine in its worst forms. Clemens, at the head of many thousands, defeated Banner and Rosenkrantz at the battle of Svenstrup Heath, and installed himself in Aalborg. Scarce a manor in Jutland remained undevastated, most burnt to the ground. Clemens was dislodged later by Rantzau, and defeated in the battle of Aalborghuus, taken prisoner in a moor four English miles from the city, in the parish of Storvorde, conveyed to Kolding, and there broken on the wheel and beheaded.

At this very time a farmer in the parish of Storvorde holds his lands free of all taxes, a perpetual grant from the Danish sovereign, in consequence of Clemens having been captured alive within his house.*

We have nothing more to visit but the Frue Kirke, a building of the early part of the twelfth century, whose round-arch doorway is a most remarkable specimen of the architecture of the period. The carvings are quaint and primitive, scarcely more advanced as works of art than those on the sculptured stones of King Gorm at Jellinge; the dragon appears, as usual in all ornaments of this date. The deacon proposed we should visit the tombs, or rather the coffins, of the "Normen," as he called them, who, by records still existing, are proved to have been here interred.

---

* Several letters still exist, in the collection I have before alluded to, between King Christian and Skipper Clemens; in one of which the monarch thanks him and his companions for their faithful services, and desires them to go to Scotland to procure aid. Then again, 31 Dec. 1525, Clemens in a letter begs of the king to send them more assistance.—Signed, "Fynd, Rempe, and Skipper Clemens, your poor, true, and humble servants, as well as Skipper Jackmyn." Faithful servants they were to their harassed lord; they did however an immense deal of mischief, as we all know, in Jutland.

THE HOG FAMILY.

Sigurd Slemmedegn, or bad deacon, a king of Norway, was wrecked in 1139 off Aalborg, where he passed the winter. He got slain the following year in some battle against Harald Gilleson, and is said to have died a terrible death. His friends brought over his body and interred it in St. Mary's church—so the priest of the same church, Kield Kalff, attests. Then there is an Olaf somebody—another, I doubt not, remarkable individual in his day—who lies by his side. The vault was so crowded up with Skeels—pronounced *Scales*, like Shakespeare's Lord Scales—and Beens, great people in their time, if you may judge by their quarterings—that the massive oak coffins of the Normen were scarcely visible.

The chapel under which the Normen lie is styled the Høg Chapel, and here may be seen one of the finest monuments of the Renaissance period existing in Denmark or elsewhere, erected to the memory of Sir Erik Høg, one of Christian IV.'s crack men, of Biørnholm, and Dame Sophia Lange, his wife, date 1647. "The noble knight and his high-born lady" are represented standing in niches, in the surrounding ornaments of which are introduced their sixteen quarterings, the best blood of Jutland. Sir Erik around his neck bears suspended the favourite order of King Christian IV., the "armed hand." Many of this family are here interred. There is good Gregers Høg, Protestant Bishop of Aalborg, who left a sum of money, still paid in pensions to poor of his blood (female) in Copenhagen. And now let me inform you that this name, Høg though it be, has nothing at all swinish about the matter. Høg, in the Northern language, signifies "*a falcon.*" I first made this discovery one day while perusing an ancient ballad. A damsel gallops in on her palfrey, "hog on hand." Surprised at her strength of wrist, I looked it out in the dictionary. To go the whole hog, and be an out-and-outer, you must write your ø with a spoke, a letter which does not exist in our English language. Lady Høg, with a spoke in her ø—I am sure it looks very distinguished. Observe how a name which in England we certainly do not consider euphonius, though highly respectable, here stands foremost among the highest of the land. At Slagelse hangs the epitaphium of a pretty girl, in costume like Lady Jane Grey, a fair Jomfru Karen Høg, who died in the palace of Slagelse in 1610, lady of honour to good Queen Sophia of Mecklenburg. But in Jutland, cela pullule, as the French say.

We have Field-Marshal Niels Høg in King John's days; Jørgen Høg, possessor of Kieldgaard and Krabbesholm; Stygge Høg, of Eskjær; Sir Jacob Høg, of Vang—we shall see him to-morrow between his two wives; Mogens Høg, of Todbøl Aastrup, one of the finest manors of Jutland, presented to Sir Niels Høg, by King Christian II., for services rendered to that unlucky sovereign. At Vennebierg appears a monument of Sir James Høg, of Trudsholm. Go where you will, read what you will, you have Høg—Høg—Høg, possessor of all possible manors, buried under rich monuments in all possible places.

In the year 1683 Iver Juul Høg, seduced by the fascinations of baronial pearls, deserts the cause of the old Jutland untitled nobility, and appears, fresh ennobled, in the hostile ranks as Baron Høg of Høgholm; he or his son, Knight of the most noble Order of the Elephant, dies in the year 1700, and this name, illustrious for centuries in North Jutland, became as a thing of the past, their tombs uncared for, their existence almost forgotten.

June 29th.—We were to cross the ferry by six, and meet the carriage-horses at Sundby, a small rising village on the opposite side of the fiorde. From the heights you have an admirable view of Aalborg, her two church-towers and her shipping—all of most prepossessing appearance. The postmaster, to do us honour, had routed out an old broken-down berline, which we declined, so three-quarters of an hour were lost in the change; and when the stuhlwagen does appear, it is small and narrow. There is no alternative; the large one has been under repair since December.

SULSTED.

We pass by Sulsted, in whose village church sleeps Sir Jacob Høg, of Vang (Vang the adjoining manor among the trees), in armour, between his two wives. Sulsted, whose priest, Møller by name, together with his brother, the pastor of Vadum, during the Holstein øpror of '48 and '49 engaged themselves as volunteers in their country's cause, and both rose to the rank of captain. So greatly did they distinguish themselves, the general commanding said, on their retirement to priestly life, that in case of need he should again call upon them for their services. As we pass by Aistrup our rotten carriage gives way; off flies the wheel and out we go—self like a cat, upon my legs—scarlet postboy rolls over like a ninepin and bites the dust: again an hour's delay. We visit the church and remark its old carved roodloft, the gift of Peter Munk and Karen Skeel. There stands the tomb of Jørgen Bille—a wicked old soul he must have been, for the very red coat in his coffin to be so restless. There it lies, a coat of some hundred and fifty years since, broad lappels and bordered. Each time the neighbouring manor changes hands the coat is said to leave its coffin, stalk on its tails to the manor-house, and there hover about restlessly, turning up on every side—on the dinner-table, hanging over the arm-chair, flapping its lappels in your face as you pass the corridor, positively refusing to be quiet until replaced by the new proprietor himself in its former resting-place.

TISE—VILD MOSE.

We are now mended and arranged, just in time to stop at a kro to bait; so we walk on. Turn to the west, says the postilion, and then to the south-east. Jutlanders calculate everything by the points of the compass: we accomplish the west, but then stick on a bank till the carriage arrives, our knowledge aiding us to proceed no further. A dreary drive over a cross road brings us to Tise; where we ascend to the church cemetery to obtain a view of the Vild Mose—the most extensive bog in Jutland, if not in Europe—another slopping of the deluge, dried up, and, like many other sloppings, leaving a dirty black mark on the fair face of nature. As far as eye can gaze, and further still, extends a vast expanse of mose, seldom traversed save by the sportsman after blackgame, and he must leap from hillock to hillock, for the bog is formed of small sugar-loaf mounds; and should his foot miss its destination woe betide him—over he rolls in the mud and mire, and sinks, perhaps, never to rise again.

In the churchyard we again saw many of those old timber tombs—trunk of a tree rudely severed—chiefly to be met with in ancient churchyards situated on an eminence.

We are out of the land of cemeteries now; plain green mounds, like an English village. The church is in full whitewash, as they all appear to be at this season. At the threshold lay one of those black liigsteen, as they here call them; engraved with a huge sword, like those of Canute's time—that of some warrior dead, perhaps not in the odour of sanctity, but allowed, as a privilege of birth, to sleep at the church entrance in peace.

The workman employed in the repairs pointed out to us Børglum Kloster, and related the story of its founder, the Holy Knud: he had it all at his fingers' ends. The Danes, as a nation, are singularly well-informed on the history of their own country. We then passed through the village of Tise, cowering at the hill's-foot—houses built very low, ducking from the wind, very snug, and windows small.

BØRGLUM KLOSTER.

The moor is all alive with tethered sheep, tethered geese, and tethered everything except the plovers, of which we never yet saw, certainly never yet ate, so many as to-day. Before arriving at Børglum Kloster we first distinguished in the distance what appeared to be rugged walls, standing alone, ruins of some gigantic castle; on nearer approach we find them to be bakkes, or klints as they here call them, of driven sand, not dunes, but upright walls, shutting out the sea from the inland country. Børglum Kloster resembles all suppressed convents. It may have been a lively place in the days of Knud,* its founder, not then Holy, but somewhat oppressive, severe. Here he intrenched himself against the "ǿpror" of the Vendel peasants, with whom he was everlastingly at loggerheads — Vendel men, who later poked him to death through the window of St. Alban's church at Odense. Børglum was once a bishopric. Her last prelate was Bishop Crump; these Crumps appear to have had no luck, and always come in at the death of Romanism in Jutland. He lies in the rummelig (roomy) abbey church, as it is called, all alone. Børglum is now a private residence and farm, little changed — a courtyard planted with limes, the ancient font a trough. If you care to count windmills and churches from these heights, you may so till your fingers ache; but we go on to Lykken, to bathe once more in the briny ocean, and get some dinner.

LYKKEN.

A small fishing village among the sand; splendid bathing in a mischievous sea, but to-day as calm as a polished mirror. We order dinner; the ladies don their bathing costume, and, enveloped in their cloaks, walk down to the sea-shore. A delicious bath we had; sea like crystal — a few fishing vessels and nets and the klint behind, like one of those pretty sea-pieces by

---

* Or at the fêtes of May, when the image of the Holy Virgin was decked with the gold and jewelled crown, a present from the great Queen Margaret, borne on her brow for near two hundred years, till Christian III., hard up to pay his soldiers, melted it down.

Zeemann in the Gallery of Copenhagen. No meat to be had in this retired place, but excellent fried fish; and a dish of sour cream, as they call it, a national plat, served up with bread-crumbs and powdered sugar, very palatable. N.B. Denmark is the only country I know of where bread-crumbs are sold ready grated by the ounce or pound, a very dirty practice.

A change has come over the Danish flora since we came northwards. In Zealand all was white; here all is yellow—yellow water-lilies, yellow iris, yellow marsh cineraria, field chrysanthemum, galium, as well as potentillas and marsh buttercup.*

HJØRRING.

We leave to the right the church of Vennebierg—the first object discerned by British seamen on their arrival from England off the Jutland coast: and approach the ancient ecclesiastical town of Hjørring, restored to the arms of Mother Church now, away from all Pagan "ups," in the parish of their sanctities "Hans and Olaf." Hjørring was once the stift (diocese) of a popish bishop, whose country residence of Biskopstorp, hard by, makes one half fancy oneself in the North Riding, far removed from windy Jutland. The little town— where, in good King Frode's days, hung one of the three golden rings, and with its church embowered in wood, and its cemetery in form of a cross—like all old cathedral towns, piques itself on its ancient grandeur, as well as on its present respectability; no commerce here, scarcely any shops, but a small population living on their "rentes:" to us, arrived from the desert sands

---

* Froe peber—seed-pepper—Ranunculus ficaria.

and moors, it appears splendid. We walk in the shady public gardens, provided with merry-go-rounds and gymnastic poles, listen to the music of a German band we should have fled from distraught at Dover or Brighton, and think it exquisite. The family of the pastor offered us their services for an evening walk, so we climbed with them to a høi commanding a view of everything for thirty miles round; the sea at twelve miles' distance, which looks so placid this afternoon—too gentle to crush the sea-egg shipwrecked on its sands, or to buffet the stranded sardine—with a west wind in winter season becomes terrible. The natives hear it roaring, deafening all sound, all speech, when at Christmas-time they gather around their festive board, or lie wakeful in their beds, and address a prayer to Providence for the safety of those afloat upon its waters.

Some two miles Danish from Hjørring lies the manor of Asdal, one of the most ancient in Jutland. It is a farm-house, remarkable now alone for its side of bacon —a side of greater historical notoriety than even that of Dunmow, for this very flitch you see hanging up, a shrivelled rusty bone, dates from almost five hundred years.

It was in the early part of the fourteenth century that Karl Pølse, lord of Asdal, was accustomed to turn out his swine in the autumn to feed in the neighbouring forest together with those of the lord of Odden. The proverb at that time ran, "Odden the old, and Asdal the bold;" and a certain rivalry existed between the neighbours.

The winter drew nigh, and the swine, fattened by beech-mast diet, were now herded, and driven home to their respective farms. A dispute, however, arose concerning the possession of a certain bulky sow, followed by a train of some dozen squeaking piglings. "It's mine," exclaims the lord of Odden. "No such thing," replies the lady of Asdal; "I know her by her curly tail." "Fiddlesticks!" continues the lord of Odden: "that all depends upon the dryness of the weather. Yesterday her tail was as straight as your ringlets." "I'll go to law," indignantly answered the lady, not at all pleased at the implied insult to her tresses. So to law they went. The Jutlanders were, and I believe are, like their Norman descendants, essentially a litigious race. The authorities heard both cases, plaintiff and defendant—felt puzzled—scratched their polls. The matter might have remained undecided to this day, had not an ecclesiastic present suggested how on an old carved stall in Hjørring cathedral he had seen represented the Judgment of Solomon, and forthwith explained the history to the assembled Court, who unanimously condemned the sow to be split in twain, and a moiety handed over to each contending party, with orders to salt and smoke their respective sides and hang them up in the manor-hall—the judge declaring in his charge, that whoever preserves his side for the longest period free from worms and rust shall be pronounced the rightful possessor of the twelve little porkers, which, until the cause be decided, shall be considered wards in Chancery, and be allowed to feed, increase, and multiply.

Time rolled on: great had been the preparation of the lady of Asdal, and here she had the advantage over the lord of Odden, who knew more of the art of war than that of drysalting. What spices, what saltpetre (if then invented), what curing, what smoking she made use of I cannot pretend to say, but the side of bacon was a feast only to gaze upon. Little porkers grew and multiplied; the forest swarmed with curly tails and straight; the side of Asdal is still fresh as ever; that of Odden has a rusty look, but still no harm to speak of. Another inspection is over, the suit is still pending, nothing new "in re demurrer," as the papers say; but after a lapse of years corruption declares itself at Odden, decomposition later, and then, worst of all, defeat.

Loud are the rejoicings at Asdal, louder even than the grunting and squeaking of the herd of swine, handed over fat (strange to relate) from Chancery to the possession of its triumphant mistress. "Victory," she sings: "ever while Asdal stands shall that side of bacon hang untouched in my hall, or may my curse"—but, suffice it to say, the now shrivelled, rusty side still remains—historical—authenticated—an object of superstition, on which the fate of Asdal hangs—for now five hundred years. It was, you will agree with me, "a monstrous fuss about a bit of bacon."

We return to our inn, one story high—like all its neighbours, it ducks away from wind and blast; find bowpots of honeysuckles (suæ patte) in our room; the table laid with silver knives; and they give us rød-grød, a national dish, a species of red jelly, composed of currants, cherries, raspberries, or what you will, served up with cream, to be met with in all village kros in Jutland, and excellent it is.*

---

* In kindness to the rising generation, rice-puddinged, be-sagoed, and be-fruited, we give the receipt for rød-grød:—Take a pint and a

In the manor of Asdal vast forests once stood, and of late years there have been dug up the horns and bones of the wild buffalo and the elk, races long extinct in Jutland.

June 30th.—At six we start. Strangers are rare in these parts, and looked upon as objects of curiosity. This morning, on my opening the door of the adjoining room by mistake, there knelt the grown-up daughter of the landlady, her eye applied to the keyhole, watching the English ladies at breakfast, with intense satisfaction.

During breakfast a nosegay of fresh roses arrives, accompanied by an envelope containing the visiting-cards of our friends of last night, addressed "To the English family, from admiring Danes." Well, you may smile; but when a man is turned forty, and inclined to corpulence, it is very pleasant to meet with admiring "anybodies," I can tell you.

We are off, our carriage laden with honeysuckles, along a splendid chaussée, quite glad to see our old friend the electric telegraph again. There's nothing like a little absence. We are just as pleased to see its wires as you will be to meet your acquaintance next May in London—the very same people you are now, June 30th, sick to death of.

The journey to-day is picturesque, along the moors and heights. Tufts of yellow iris come out from the

---

half of juice, either raspberry, currant, or cherry, or mixed, and when it boils add three ounces of ground rice. Let it simmer for twenty minutes, and before taking it off the fire throw in an ounce of sweet almonds pounded and an ounce and a half of isinglass. Pour into a mould set into cold water, and serve it, when turned out, with thick cream round the dish.

coal-black mose—a good contrast, black and yellow; and further on runs a line of feathery cotton-grass, pure, white, and spotless. To us, who have made a six-weeks' "cure aux épinards" among the new-born foliage of the beechen forest in early spring, this varied colouring possesses a double charm.

CHAPTER XXXVI.

Old manor of Høgholt and its dairy-farm — Two sisters of Jerup — Pontoppidan — Jutland's most northern manor — Lighthouse of Skagen — Storm of flying sand — Wrecks — Melons and sea-nettles — Sweet gale and bog moss — Frederikshavn — The Jutland Dido.

HØGHOLT.

June 30th.—WE leave Aastrup to the left, gift of Christian to Sir Niels Høg, his faithful follower; and then, whilst the horses refresh at Hormested kro, walk down to visit the ancient manor of Høgholt, at a quarter of a mile's distance. The names of our great people of to-day are certainly not euphonious, though Banner has a certain illustration to the world at large, for, besides the hero of Svenstrup Heath, there is Banner, governor of Kalø Castle at the period when Gustavus Vasa was there confined, awaiting the arrival of his ransom. Gustavus, as you know, escaped, and Banner was compelled by angry Christian to pay the sum out of his own pocket—more than half his fortune; still he remained faithful to his sovereign to the very last, and played a prominent part in the reign of Frederic I. as well as in that of Christian III. Then we have the Dues, Dyres, Daas, and Globs (horrid name!), Becks, Bagges, Basses, and many others equally ugly and mean-sounding. We arrive at the lake before the old manor-house of Høgholt, embosomed within a triple row of trees. You enter the court by a bridge crossing the moat from behind; the moat green, its banks clothed with flowering elders. As usual in these parts, a quaint round tower rises from the inner court. The entry! Powers! had you met the milk-cart laden with its pails overflowing, slopping away upon the pavement, rich creamy produce of the cow—why, the bi-diurnal sloppings of the Høgholt dairy would alone have set up a London dairyman for life.

Fish were rising in the lake, and nets hung out to dry in the cherry-orchard show that the fresh-water produce of the lake is not despised. I am often astonished in England to see how people neglect the fresh-water stews, which in ancient days teemed with pike, carp, perch, eels, and tench. You reply, In England we are spoiled for fish. In London, yes; but in the country, no;—it's not you, it's the fish which are spoiled.

The excellence of fresh-water fish depends as much on the previous care bestowed upon them as on the art of cooking. I remember once, in an old French château, to have seen a kitchen in the centre of which were placed two fountains, with basins en étage, in which the live fish were kept sorted in pure running water for some days previous to their being dressed, and fed with dough, bread-crumbs, and clean food.

We quit Høgholt, reminding me much of "Mariana's moated grange"—a charming subject for the pencil, but not a place to live in. "I'm aweary, I'm aweary," others than Mariana must have sung therein. Pass my life in such a place! I'd rather drown myself in one of the Brobdignagian milk-pails. The moor grows wilder and more undulating—semé, as the heralds say, with strong-scented cream-coloured orchises *—how fragrant too it crushes under your feet! no wonder the bees thrive around in the cottage hives: look at the Lycopodium clavatum—the witches' own plant. What a network of green! pull up a piece—pull on—four yards, five yards in length; it breaks, you've handled it too roughly; you might have gone on for ever, it extends over the whole heath. Observe those long, tender shoots which rise pale-coloured above the brown heather: gather one—shake it—a fine dust, its seed, falls out; that dust is used by chemists; they place it in the boxes among the pills to keep them separate. Morison employs it. If it have a bad odour, it is owing to the sulphur they mingle with it, for the powder itself is fragrant. Hold it above the candle—see how it blazes like a firework, a godsend in early times to witches and necromancers. The sea now appears in sight, and then the town of Frederikshavn. We pass by the public garden, all avenue and shady walk; descend to Zimmerman's hotel to dine, and then proceed.

Our postilion was to drive us to the village of Jerup, some two miles' distance, and there engage us two boer's carriages to convey us to Skagen, and bring us back to Frederikshavn the following day.

After two hours' drive over a waste moor, well backed by the rising dunes of the opposite coast, blue in the horizon, carpeted with the flowers of the thrift,† we arrive at Jerup, a nest of dairy-farms, in former days a waste,

---

* Brøndgræs—water-grass.
† Faare leger—"sheep's-flower"—they call it in Zealand; in Jutland "the warrior;" here, in Vendsyssel, "daglig brod,"—daily bread; and they have enough of it in all conscience.

where lived only a poor cotter, with his two daughters. One day a poor woman passed by, and begged a little help in Heaven's name. Said the eldest sister, "My hen has just laid an egg; take it, and be welcome." But the youngest gave her nothing but harsh words. Then the poor woman struck the air with her staff, and there came forth a farm, which she gave to the eldest daughter. Again she struck the air, and there appeared a castle, in which lived a "smaa konge;" this she assigned to the youngest; but the girl became proud and haughty; her husband soon got tired of her, and sent her back to her father's cottage. The elder sister and all about her thrived—her cattle increased; her lands were reclaimed; and she and her descendants grew rich, as the farms round Jerup testify even at this time. After a delay of half an hour a peasant agrees to furnish us with two carriages—a low sort of stuhl-wagen, not on springs, but by no means rough, drawn by two horses—and bring us back to-morrow, for the sum of seven dollars each; waggons to come "strax"— immediately. Now, if there be a detestable word in the Danish language it is "strax;" it always signifies any space of time, beyond the endurance of human patience and resignation. At the end of two hours they come, a splendid pair of young chesnuts; they would not disgrace Hyde Park; the blacks too are good serviceable beasts, though less showy. Horse-flesh improves as we go northwards. From the stables we drive close to the sea-side, one wheel in the water along the hard sand. A terrible coast this; the very shells are pounded into powder by the waves—all save the pelican's-foot,* and that is strong enough to resist

---

* Strombus pes pelicani.

SKAGEN.

the wear and tear of wind or ocean. Pontoppidan promised us sea-cats, sea-mice, and sea-wolves. This part of Jutland, as far as the village of Aalbæk, is more densely populated by the peasant tribe than any we have yet visited — gaards, farm-buildings, cattle in abundance; and then later we pass by a wreck—a ship sunk among the shoals; dip into a quick-sand, and are dragged out again; then drive by the manor of Lindholm, the most northern of all Jutland strong holds, in Queen Margaret's time, of the noble house of Bugge. Twilight comes on; the lighthouse of Skagen is faintly visible on the horizon. We drive now inland —brown moor, relieved by shining sand, and dunes glistening in the evening shades like snow. Pass by old Skagen church-tower, half buried beneath a waste —boats on the shore, nets hung to dry. We enter the village, or rather settlement, toil our way through the 'sand; each cottage stands by itself on a square plot of land, on espalier-frames; to a network of ropes hang fish drying by hundreds; corn too and potatoes flourish. At last we reach a small, long, one-storied house, embowered in trees—the kro—our resting-place. We knock. Hallo! No answer. What traveller ever arrives at Skagen after midnight? At length the master appears, and later women but half awake; in ten minutes our beds are prepared, and before long we are asleep.

SKAGEN.

July 1st.—We wade out through the sand, knee-deep, to our bath before breakfast—fish split and drying in their netting-frames, and something else, by no means grateful to the smell: they look like peas; so I ask a woman where they come from? "The sea." Peas grow in the sea! Then calling to mind the stranded vessel of last night, I discover how Skagen has been doing "a little wrecking," like her Cornish cousins: a vessel, on her way from Stettin, ran aground last week. Our bath was less private than we imagined; for though we sneaked out early, almost unseen, the news got wind of ladies swimming in the Kattegat; fishwomen and children (the men had been out at sea since dawn of day) crowded the dunes, too happy to stare and wonder.

Breakfast over, we drive to the newly-built lighthouse, mount to the summit, and, glass in hand, gain some idea of the village of Skagen. Gazing northward, the land runs tapering finely down, like a bullock's tongue—though the name is derived from some ancient Scandinavian word signifying "nose,"—at whose extreme point the sister waters of the Northern Ocean, stormy and violent, embrace and mingle with the more gentle Kattegat, who, as she nears the meeting-point, makes believe to a little tide of her own. Kattegat is not an open sea; her velvet paws betray her; she looks meek and placid, but in the course of this present week has wrecked two vessels, stranded on the shore before they gained the open sea.

Turning to the south, before you lies the village, planted in the sand in the form of an English X. You will wonder why the fishers chose this place of sand for their settlement, when heath and dry moor—terra firma—were at command on the western coast: patience, and you will hear.

In front, to the right, stands the old lighthouse, now for sale, but no purchaser appears; who would wish to drag old materials over a plain of sand? by its side some pretty, clean, striped houses, backed by a little grove of trees; then again, beyond the village, in the centre of a baby forest, stands the house of the chief magistrate; you can hardly see it, so shut in is it from the wrath of wind and sand.

Further still, on the western coast, stands, rising from a mountainous sea of silver-glistening sand, the half-buried church of "Gammel Skagen," long since disused,—built, says tradition, of the stones brought by English and Dutch seamen; not improbable, as in old popish days these church landmarks fared well in offerings from the grateful mariner.

It was in the year 1775, on a common prayer day,— of which in the Danish Church there were formerly many, thanksgivings for fires extinguished and pestilence stayed, and other mercies long since forgotten,—while the inhabitants of Skagen were engaged in divine service, there arose suddenly a storm, accompanied by a whirlwind of "flying sand," carrying desolation over the fields and the village of this devoted settlement, and entirely filling up the holy well of St. Lawrence, whose water proved infallible even in the 18th century. Before the affrighted inhabitants could leave the building, where they still remained cowering for shelter, the church was half-buried beneath its fury, the doors blocked up, and they compelled to escape by the windows of the belfry. Since that period the building has been no longer used. The colony emigrated to the opposite coast, where the village is now situated.

We inquired if any English vessels ever touched at Skagen? "Yes," the man at the lighthouse replied; "when they are wrecked, not otherwise:" a visit more honoured in the breach than in the observance.

Behind the tower stands the residence of the people employed at the lighthouse—the head man a retired officer.

The melons of Skagen enjoy a considerable reputation in the gastronomic world, and fish in considerable quantities are exported to Sweden. The man at the Phare takes a pride in his flowers: splendid oleanders, passion-flowers, and picotees were blooming in his parlour-window. Whilst on high we observed a curious effect of the clouds over the Kattegat; three ships appeared in the horizon, the mist separating them from the water, giving them the effect of naval balloons floating through the heavens. Skagen, too, boasts one sepulchral tumulus—resting-place of some storm-loving Scandinavian. We now embark again, and drive to the "Nose's" point; stand one foot in the North Sea, the other one in the Kattegat, and do—I forget what, but something our host, who accompanied us, told us was the correct thing. Huge masses of glutinous substance, of brick-dust red and cobalt blue, lie stranded on the shore, some three and four feet in circumference, beautiful to look upon; what a trouvaille for a vivarium! These animals are said to possess medicinal qualities; and at Sandifiord in Norway there exists a sea-bathing place, where those who are martyrs to rheumatic pains go and make a "cure aux actineæ," bathe in the burning sand, and have their bodies rubbed down with live jelly-fish.*

---

* Pontoppidan, worthy old prelate, does his very best to get up a few remarkable events in honour of this the most northern village of Jutland. In the year 1281 a fish very like, not a whale, but a lion, ravaged the coast, devouring fishermen and women, cracking their bones like filberts. Passing over a few awful battles with the North-

We returned to our kro by the west coast, across the downs, partly converted into heath. Sheep browse on the waste, and the mutton is excellent, if such as we had at breakfast—like our own Southdown, or the Pré Salé so much esteemed in France.

Skagen has her flora: all the heathy tribe — hollowlip (hulleloebe), lapwing's-fat, and Our Lady's eye-tears,* as the peasants call them. Something crushed fragrant under my feet; an old Jutlander cries out to me from his cart, " Gather some of that shrub." I do so, smell it, and highly aromatic it proved to be—the sweet gale,† used both here and in Germany for flavouring pale ale; in Danish called Porse, like the duke. We pay our moderate bill and start—N.B. The women varnished our bottines—gratifying, but inconvenient, as the sand caked to them like scouring-paper—and, after two hours' drive, we leave the sea and cross the moor land—a pleasant change, as the day is cool and the air fragrant—till we again arrive at Jerup, and stop to bait our horses in their native stalls.

The Vendel boer, as they are here all called north of the Liimfiorde, ushers us into his house, which reminds me much of Brittany, with its ship-cabin beds and carved chest of drawers, painted red and picked out in

---

men, we, in the 16th century, come upon a child born with two faces— most inconvenient in this sand-driving country. Then Skagen has its crack men. One, son of a fisherman, became Bishop of Stavanger; another Bishop of Zealand; a third was Professor of Mathematics at Copenhagen; and many others, all well known under the name of their native town Skagboe, latinized into Scavenius.

* Epipactis palustris, Pinguicula, and Drosera.
† Myrica gale.

divers gaudy colours. The "huus fru" enters quickly, bids us welcome, placing on the table not "butter in a lordly dish," as they do in Norway—she brings a jug of fresh milk, and bids us drink. But with the furniture and wooden settles ends the likeness to dirty Brittany: here all is of a Dutch cleanliness. The women in their queer frilled caps and good stout dresses, clean and neat, knit as fast as they talk, and as their tongues run glibly the stocking advances quickly. We sit down to write our journals, and then an aged peasant in gray homespun, very white hair, and spectacles on nose, enters and wishes us good day—"Four people writing at the same time; we don't often see such a sight in these parts." He then examines our calligraphy—"You write the best," he says to one; "you next; you next; and you the worst," to me— a most unjust remark, and a proof of bad taste on his part. Had the ladies been ever at school? he was the schoolmaster: 'if we liked we might come across the road and write in his school-house at the desks— a tempting offer we could not accept, as the horses were already harnessed. The farmer himself accompanies us this time, to the great disgust of his son, who was looking forward to a lark at Frederikshavn, I dare say. The boy looks sorrowful, but father (a splendid fellow, like Rollo; one wonders how any horse can bear his tall athletic frame) is inexorable. We start; half-way exchange our spirited chesnuts, too young to be hackneyed about, for a pair of wicked-eyed ponies, in fur collars and blinkers (de la fourrure après Pâques, quel pays!), and arrive towards eleven at Frederikshavn.

FREDERIKSHAVN.

July 2nd.—On our arrival last night we found the hotel nigh deserted; were received by an important-looking boy of twelve years of age or thereabouts, who seemed awfully affronted at our calling him "lille dreng." It was not until this morning we became aware of the cause. The whole family, landlord, landlady, housemaids, cooks, kitchenmaids, boots, and waiter, had passed the night at a ball in the neighbouring "skov."

Our Vendel boers come in to wish us "farvel," "tak for idag," shake hands with us all round, and express their pleasure at having driven us. We would not like to part with little Lina, would we? If so—— Lina, affrighted, retires under the protection of her mistress's ample petticoats at the very mention of such a fate. Well! she might be worse off. Plenty of good milk at the farmhouse, and no sparing.

Frederikshavn is a pretty little town, beautifully situated, consisting chiefly of one long street, running down to the water's edge—its harbour protected by one solid martello tower, built by Tordenskiold, at the end of its citadel: the peasants still call it Fladstrand * — its ancient name. It was offered for sale in the last century for the sum of 4000 dollars. A change since then—plenty of shipping, clean houses, and charming shady public gardens, the pavement its only weak or rather rough point. All that can be effected in Jutland to make their cities desirable as resi-

---

* In former days the post passed through Fladstrand on its way to Norway, it being the nearest harbour of communication.

dences to the lower as well as to the higher classes is done by the natives themselves in conjunction with the authorities. It is a pleasure to see how happy the lower classes are: how they enjoy the advantages of air, shade, and water, of which the inhabitants of our own large cities are debarred. The Danes should be a contented and happy people, as I believe them to be; for never in any land will you see so little, indeed, such an entire absence, of poverty—perhaps among the higher classes not the great rent-rolls we meet with in England, but such a general appearance of "aisance" among all—from the highest to the humblest cottager.

The roughness of the climate causes the houses to be mostly fresh coloured externally every spring, and the constant burning of stoves during the long winters renders frequent paint and whitewash in the rooms a matter of course. This accounts for the exquisite neatness of the dwellings. When you do meet with a cottage of bad appearance, it is sure to be a condemned tenement. Don't judge its inhabitants hastily, but enter its doors —"look up the chimney;" and when you see three or four sides of bacon smoking for winter's consumption, a store full of potatoes, a chest full of good stout Sunday clothes, rest assured poverty is not there, and that in a year another cottage will arise, all black and yellow timber stripes, fresh from its ruins. Perhaps at this very moment the peasant is employed cooking his sunburnt bricks, and has purchased his double window, all ready framed and glazed, at the neighbouring market-town.

We passed by our old splendid chaussée on the Hjörring road, as far as Knivholt, and then, turning to the right, climbed up over the moor—a steep ascent—to a hoi near the pollarded church of Flade, her tower blown over by the raging storms; so we scrambled up a brown-skinned barrow, half dug out, all alive with ripe bilberries; and stood for some time gazing at the panorama before us, extending to Skagen. We plainly distinguished the lighthouse; and the little town of Fredericia, with its ships and harbour, looked prettier than ever.

If Flade church be exposed on her heights, her præsteguard snuggles comfortably, protected by a lovely beech forest, at the bottom of a natural punch-bowl, laughing at storm and winter breezes.

We now descend, and, after a most picturesque but somewhat perilous descent among farms and woods, gain the high road, which runs along the waterside, across a monotonous country on to Sæby. We pass by an ancient manor, whose name escapes me, once cradle of the Pack family, though long since changed hands. The small white church of Sæby is plainly visible, jutting out on the sea-side.

SÆBY.

At the entrance of Sæby we are received, as we cross the bridge which traverses the little Sæby Aa, by a nest of young storks, both parents out, left to their own devices. They evince a desire to fly: stretch first one leg, then the other, shake their new-fledged wings, give a hop,—courage not up to the point yet; like a schoolboy at the swimming-school, about to try his first header. Their resolution fixed, they make a plunge in the air, and come (as the boy does, à plat ventre on the water) tumbling, rattling down on the roof-eaves below.

No harm done! We order dinner at the inn, and adjourn to bathe. What a luxury, after a three hours' dusty drive, a plunge in a sea sparkling like this! To gain it we again pass the bridge ; lots of small trout playing in the river: a pure briny sea, and fresh running river water.

We have a peep on our way at Sæbygaard, an old country residence of the Bishops of Børglum. Not far from where we now are stands the manor of Lingsholm, some centuries since the cause of disputes between a widow lady—a Jutland Dido—and her nearest relation. The suit had lasted long, and was still undecided, so the widow proposed a compromise. She consents to waive her claim to the disputed lands on condition she may be allowed to sow this one year's crop, and reap it when it came to full maturity. Her antagonist, delighted at this easy ending, gives his full consent; the deed is signed and sealed, and our fair one commences her sowing. What does she sow? Wheat? no! Barley? no! Rape? no! You'll never guess! She sows a forest of beech-masts. Her right to cut them when they come to full maturity. This forest was standing not many years since.

CHAPTER XXXVII.

Manor of Voergaard — Skipper Clemens and Bishop Crump again — Lady Ingeborg Skeel and the architect — The message of her husband — Her disturbed spirit — Her prison, the Rosodonten — Her Sunday pastime — Her monument — The road-side inns of Queen Margaret — Jutland mode of boiling eggs.

VOERGAARD.

THE postboy turns off the high road to Voergaard, one of the most interesting châteaux, both from its architecture and history, in the whole of Vendsyssel, a splendid specimen of the early Renaissance, built of red brick and sandstone. As you pass under the gateway, rich in stone carvings, of a somewhat diabolical character, above stand two shields, the armorial bearings of its founders, Frue Ingeborg Skeel and her husband Otto Banner, with the date 1538. In the earlier part of the fifteenth century Voergaard was the property of the Børglum bishops. In 1534 it underwent the fate of all noble residences in these parts, was destroyed and burnt to the ground by Skipper Clemens and his band, "who hunted," says the old chronicler, "Bishop Crump" (Bishop Crump, who looks as good as gold on his tombstone) and "his Frille" (impossible to translate such a word when speaking of an ecclesiastic) "Elizabeth Gyldenstierne from their good rest;" so that the Bishop "krob udi muus hul"—crept into a mouse-hole; an exaggeration of the chronicle, for it was only in a baker's oven that he took refuge. Voergaard is burnt and sacked, and later comes into the possession of our present heroine, the lady Ingeborg Skeel, a woman of high birth and strong mind, endued with consummate taste, but unfortunately without the means of gratifying it. Build a manor-house she would, by hook or by crook, and one that in richness and beauty should surpass all her neighbours. So she sends for an architect, orders in timber—of that there is no want on her own estates—bakes her own bricks, and has sandstone over from the island of Bornholm. The first cargo arrives, and that she pays for, but when the second and the third appear her purse is empty, but her wit is sharp. A storm arises in the night; she sends down her trusty minions, causes the cables of the vessels to be cut, an east wind drives them ashore, and she, lady of the manor, by the ancient law of "flotsam and jetsum," claims the cargo as her own.

The building now advances, the towers rise; rich and quaint are the stone carvings around the windows and portals. Never were such yet seen in Vendsyssel. At last it is completed, but the architect must be paid, and where is the money to come from? Here's a puzzler again! Don't be alarmed: trust the lady Ingeborg. Where there's a will, there's a way; so she orders the architect to bring his bill receipted and prepared to receive his money. The architect arrives with the massive keys of the castle, ready to hand them over to its noble mistress. "But, before we settle our accounts," says she, "we will first go together over the whole castle, and see that all is right. Leave your bill here, Knight of the Keys of Bronze," she playfully adds, passing the bunch, weighing nearly half a ton, round his neck. "Leave them where they are, I insist; you shall not take them off!" so they proceed together to examine the rooms one after the other, and then pass —the poor architect groaning under the weight of his burden—over the drawbridge which connects the moat with the castle. "Stop!" she cries; "look at that eastern tower; surely, the piles have sunk. Lean over!" The man obeys. A push from the lady—he falls headlong into the moat, borne down by the weight of the keys, to rise no more.

When Ingeborg feels sure he is drowned she calls wildly for assistance. The body is withdrawn from its watery grave, but the receipted bill remains in her possession.

> She was a fine old Jutland gentlewoman,
> One of the olden time.

The husband, Otto Banner, was just as bad as Ingeborg herself, and the cruelties and extortions practised by both on their peasant serfs were beyond belief. At last Otto dies, and on the anniversary of his death the lady Ingeborg drives to church in great state, and says to Claus, her coachman, "I should like to hear how my husband is." The coachman replies, "My lady, that is not so easily known; but I do not think he suffers from cold where he now dwells." The lady became furious, and threatened the coachman with death if he did not, before the third Sunday, bring her tidings of her lord. The affrighted Claus applies to the parson of Albæk, "who was as learned as any bishop;" but he declined the task. Happily Claus had a brother a clergyman in Norway; and as, says the legend, the parsons of Norway are more cunning in these matters than any other, Claus went to his brother, who takes him at midnight to a cross-road in a forest, where he conjures up his deceased master. Claus delivers the message of the lady Ingeborg. "Tell her," replies his master, "that I have gone where a chair is preparing for her, and she will be taken when it is finished, unless she gives back the meadows of Agersted. But to prove that you have spoken to me, I give you my bridal ring to show to her." Claus reaches forth his hat to receive the ring, and waits on the third Sunday at the churchgate for his mistress. He gives the message and the ring. "Well," said the lady, "you have saved your life; but I will never give back the meadows of Agersted." Shortly afterwards there is a great funeral feast at Voer church, for the lady Ingeborg is to be buried; but do not imagine she rested quiet in her grave—she returned every night and made such unearthly noises in the courtyard, that the parson of Alsted was forced to conjure her down in a bog hard by, called the Pulse. But she still appears on Christmas-eve, when she drives over the drawbridge into the inner courtyard in a coach drawn by six horses, with fire glaring from their nostrils and mouths, and she is often seen in the Pulse combing her long hair with a golden comb. On every New Year's night she is permitted to advance the length of a cock's step towards the manor-house, and when she has reached it Voergaard will inevitably sink. Neither grass nor moss ever grows at the place where she has been conjured down into the mose, and, by help of the scorched spots in the adjacent field, it may always be ascertained how many lengths of a cock's step she has proceeded towards Voergaard.

The château consists of one corps de bâtiment, flanked by two octagonal towers; the wings, if there were any, have been destroyed. When standing in the courtyard among the milk-pails—for we have here 300 cows, each morning some ton and a half of butter made before breakfast*—I could not help thinking how well one of our water-colour artists might have limned this out. It is a wonder they never travel in Jutland; they would find living cheap and a new subject for their pencils.

The intendante came out with her keys, and asked us if we should like to visit the rooms: one, hung with splendid embossed Flemish leather, alone attests the former magnificence of the building. The oak and walnut carved doors still remaining show that Frue Ingeborg knew what she was about. As for the loft, you might lodge a regiment therein, and the timber walls are constructed with a solidity only to be accomplished by those who do not pay their reckonings.

Ingeborg, too, had no idea of being defenceless. In the cellars at the basement of her octagonal towers were placed cannons, ready to sweep the neighbouring country at a moment's notice. As for her prisons, the "Rosodonten,"—with its iron hooks for hanging and torture, her own invention,—without window, door, or opening, in which human bones were lately discovered, is one of the most horrible that can be imagined. In the year 1841 several murders were committed in the Vendsyssel, and the people suspected lodged in the prison of the Rosodonten. One night was sufficient; terrified, they declared, by the menaces of Frue Ingeborg Skeel, they one after another confessed their crime, declaring they would rather be hanged or lose their

---

* Calculating the Danish ton at 118 lbs. English, nearly 180 per diem.

heads a dozen times over than pass another night in such villanous company.

On quitting the court we drove to the village church, along the very road by which one Sunday morn the lady Ingeborg rode in her gilt caroche; and spinning by the way, for she was never idle, she sees a little child among the corn, plucking the ears and eating the grain; so she stops the carriage. "Come here, little girl; what are you about?" "Eating corn, please, my lady." "Oh! so you can't keep your hands from picking and stealing, can't you? hold them up!" The child obeys. Snip! snip! off go her fingers, severed by the steel scissors worn at the girdle of the relentless lady of the manor. We visited the church, where still stands the splendid carved oak "pue" used by Ingeborg in her lifetime; and in the Skeel chapel, out-topping the edifice itself in height, admired the splendid Renaissance monument, erected in her lifetime to her husband and herself. They are represented kneeling face to face. It is 80 feet high, and is, I am sorry to say, going to decay from damp and neglect.

DRONNINGLUND.

We went to visit Dronninglund on our way, a fine extensive manor, under restoration, once a convent of Benedictine nuns, founded by Frue Gro in the 13th century, by name Hunslundkloster, until it became secularised and stamped with an ₣ (Frederic and Sophia). Queen Margaret loved it much, and founded there an altar for herself and friends and perpetual mass for their souls. Of Queen Margaret's friends the less said the better. So thought her nephew and successor Erik the Pomeranian, when he chopped off the head of her particular pet, Abraham Brodersøn. Blessed is the memory of great Queen Margaret to all travellers in Jutland, for to her thoughtful care we owe the existence of our roadside kros. Among her laws and ordinances is one enactment by which she orders the establishment of kros on the highway at a distance of each four Danish miles, " where every man shall find rest for his money and his ease, as the lodging (it proceeds to say) in private houses in the villages costs dearer than in the mercantile towns."

Dronninglund looks like a convent still. In France, Italy, Spain, or anywhere you please, do what you will to these ancient ecclesiastical buildings—call them slot, gaard, lund, lyst, lust—the scarlet lady still peeps out in every corner. A thick sea-fog has just come on—havguse, they here call it—so we could not see much of the gardens, and, as we drove on over the dark moor, it became thicker and thicker. The wind began to howl, and some of the party to grumble. There are some countries one expects to be blown about in, and Jutland is one of them.

HJALLERUP.

It was past eleven before we arrived at Hjallerup kro, where we remained the night. Impossible to continue our journey; we should not have reached Sundby before four in the morning, and found the ferrymen all asleep. Clean rooms and beds and an excellent breakfast next morning consoled us for our misfortunes: a very Scotch repast—fish, flesh, and fowl, and eggs—piles of eggs boiled to a bubble, not by the clocks, not by the hour-glass, but according to an old Jutland custom. When the servant-girl boils the eggs, she is careful, as soon as they are put into the saucepan, to repeat twice the Lord's Prayer slowly and with reverence, for then the eggs will be well boiled, neither too hard nor too soft, and are sure to have a good flavour. When she takes the eggs from under the hen she never leaves less than five, for the hens can count up to that number and no more.

4th July.—Three days' rest at Aalborg. Not quite so for me, as I must be up betimes to visit Nørlund, some five Danish miles distant: my series of historic manors will not be complete without. The want of energy in womankind is fearful: no one will accompany me. As for Christina Munk, they have done with her, visited the place she died, and don't want to commence over again at her birthplace. So, unencumbered by capes and shawls, and other discomforts which invariably accompany the presence of ladies, I slip into my stuhlwagen at three minutes before five, without any feeling of irritation at being kept waiting. All smooth and serene this morning; electric telegraph rather in bad books to-day; road dull and ugly until we arrive at Svenstrup Heath, black and redolent with patches of fragrant thyme. Capital place for a battle: room for a charge, though the retreating cavalry would run a good chance of getting bogged, whichever way they took.

We pass by Buderupgaard, prettily situated off the road, remarkable as being the only manor which escaped devastation at the hands of Skipper Clemens. The road now improves. Near Gravlev, a village beautifully situated on the heights above, is a lake, now half-dried up; in a few years it will all be under cultivation.

Take the map in your hand and the high ground of

Aalborg Amt as your centre, you will find it surrounded by a continuation of villages bearing the name of holm or island; then again towards the east lies the " Lille Vild Mose," a huge bog extending over miles, the effects of one of those awful inundations of the sea so common in the earlier centuries. Having done its worst, the sea has thrown up dunes so high as to be called " Muld bjergene." Well, in the centre of this bog lie four small lakes, or Sø, now brought into cultivation. The turf, as we all know, grows upwards, and is now fifteen feet above the level of the lake's banks. Every year, as the plough passes over these lands, urns containing bones are turned up, composed of the same black Jutland pottery now sold at the canal by the Amagertorv in Copenhagen, ornamented with the zigzag decoration, such as you find on all the earlier round-arch doorways of the earliest Christian period, as the Frue Kirke at Aalborg. In one of them was discovered a small bone cross—perhaps brought over from Christian lands, as the burning of bodies is supposed to have gone out of fashion after the introduction of Christianity in Denmark. Be this as it may, it proves that the immersion of these lands took place at a period not very far removed from us in the history of the world's creation. Amber, too, is found on the highest eminences of Stensbæk, in the Vendsyssel country.

We now turn off to the right, and enter a forest of beeches, banks clothed with the vintergrøm * (winter-green) in full blossom; pass by the manor-house

---

* Pyrola.

of Tordeslund—a pleasanter drive now than in the days of Valdemar Atterdag, for documents exist in which he gives orders for its destruction, describing it as a "nest of robbers." Queen Margaret, however, spared it at the request of a "friend." And now we come to Nørlund, the object of my pilgrimage.

CHAPTER XXXVIII.

Nørlund Manor — Ellen Marsviin and Ludvig Munk — Meeting of King Christian and the fair Christina — Names of the Jutland nobility — Almshouse of Aalborg — Scottish guard of Christian II. — Prince Niels and his tutor — Duke Knud's suit of scarlet — Mermaid monument at Tiele.

NØRLUND.

Towards the middle of the 16th century, a knight of wealth and some renown, Ludvig Munk by name, not in the flower of his youth, courted a fair damsel, Ellen Marsviin, daughter of a neighbouring noble. You recollect we have already seen her portrait at Rosenholm—plump and fair, with laughing eyes, just the beauty to captivate a man of fifty. The young Ellen had no wish to marry, and Ludvig might have been her father; so she laughs at his suit, teazes him, as girls sometimes will do, and only renders his passion more ardent.

Where we now stand, surrounded by woods, was in those days a marshy swamp. Imagine the noble knight on his good war-horse riding by the side of Ellen's ambling palfrey: he presses hard his suit; it becomes wearisome; the maid, at last impatient, withdraws hastily her glove and casts it into the centre. "Build me," she exclaims, "a palace in the middle of this mose—a palace which shall surpass all those now rising around us (they had all been lately destroyed by Skipper Clemens and his band), with a tower from the top of which I can gaze on St. Budolph's church at Aalborg, and I am yours. Until that, leave me in peace and quietness." Little did she know Ludvig Munk. Before many months had elapsed a stately mansion, built upon deep-driven piles, began to rise; the foundations, too, of the tower are laid. The workmen are relieved day and night, for Ludvig feels he has no time to lose.

Touched by his constancy, fair Ellen marries him at once, long before the palace is completed, and became later mother of Christina Munk, who was here born, and whom Christian IV. first met on a visit to Nørlund, and shortly after espoused at seventeen years of age. Some authors declare Ellen to have laid snares for the king, and to have taken her daughter regularly to the Frue Kirke, and placed her in front of the royal closet to attract his attention. The bait did not take at first; but after a time his curiosity was excited: struck by her beauty and the richness of her dress, he inquired who she was; was told she was a daughter of the widow Munk; and, if the portraits of Christina in her early youth do not flatter her, she must have been very pretty.*

Christian accuses Ellen of having a hand in her daughter's disgrace—of being aware of " her daughter's flighty life, which she carried on publicly, and which did

---

* In addition to her personal attractions Christina Munk was one of the greatest heiresses of the day, a circumstance of which King Christian seems to have been perfectly aware, for I find a letter in which he urges Ellen to assure her daughter's succession ; and at the time of their mutual disgrace "he orders Ellen to deliver over the properties of Boller and Rosenvald for her daughter's maintenance. Without saying of him " Han meete Reden, og cy Fuglen,"—he thinks of the nest and not of the bird—he had no objection to the goods and chattels of his morganatic spouse as a provision for his children.

not agree with the honour of a Danish lady, and did not give us a hint of it; if she had done so, then we are sure Mrs. Kirstine would have never come into that labyrinth in which she later became entangled;" and " how, when the lady Ellen saw it became too bad, and that the boys and old women pointed fingers after her daughter in the streets, she commenced crying, and she would not tell us the reason why she cried."

The family of the present proprietor, Kammerjunker de Mylius, kindly did me the honours of the mansion. Few have suffered more from neglect, devastation, and injudicious restoration in the former century than Nørlund. The towers now are all under restoration. The room occupied by King Christian on his visit is still shown—the riddersaal. Upon the chimney-piece, date 1591, appear the effigies and arms of Ludvig and Ellen— young Ellen no longer, but Ellen fat, fair, and forty— overblown. She made a great mistake in not having had her bust taken soon after her marriage, before she ran to fat. The arms of Ellen puzzled me much—a heavy-looking fish straddling over a bend in a most uncomfortable position; but, on referring to my dictionary, I find Marsviin signifies porpoise. There is no romance about the names of the early Jutland nobility. Ellen Porpoise! all sentiment is at an end. Names derived from the swine tribe too were much in vogue— Urne, boar; Galt, hog; Griis, pig. In the wars of the Counts, 1534, we have a noble knight, Sir Bagge Griis, who is killed by a tile thrown from the house-top on his head by Peter Bedske (bitter), of Klampgaard, the shoemaker. Then we have Oxe, Kalf, Daa, Dyre, Krabbe, Trolle;* Ulvstand, wolfstooth (quite refreshing);

* When Harved Ulf went to fetch home his bride Mechtild, sister

with many others already mentioned, all equally ugly and equally illustrious in the history of their country.

Nobody ever bore the name of Hound or Dog, though the animal was looked upon as noble; and this may be accounted for by the custom that a knight when degraded from his honours was compelled to hold in his arms a " mangy dog," while his spurs were chopped off from his heels, and his sword broken asunder.

Nørlund suffered fearfully, in the Swedish war of 1658, from the visit of its friends the auxiliary Polacks, who tore off the leaden roof, &c.; it will require much money and time to place it in order. The gardens are small, but a wilderness of roses. Jutland is a land of roses, though few of the more modern species have as yet penetrated; but the old cabbage, the maiden's blush, the cinnamon, and, lastly, the Provins, sweetest of all its tribe, abound in the greatest profusion. Ludvig and Ellen sleep not in the village church, but in Funen. I first entered a cottage. On asking for the key, "Go thou to schoolmaster," was the reply as plain as ears could hear. Splendid swords I saw lying rusting, rotting, useless, on the mouldering coffins of their former owners; a series dating from 1500 to the end of the latter century, many of most exquisite workmanship. There was another Runic stone lying at the porch entrance of this little church—always been there, the schoolmaster told me. The way ran by the village of Bold, whose forest, now no more, once gave rise to the proverb, " As

---

of Birger Jarl, some warriors, rushing out of the wood, endeavoured to carry her off by force, their leader having disguised himself as a devil, that he might more easily frighten the guards. Harved, with one blow, severed his head from his body. From that day he changed his arms from a wolf (Ulf) courant to a headless devil (Trolle), adopting the name of Trolle instead of that of Ulf.

old as the trees in the forest of Bold." * On the heath sat a whole tribe of fox-cubs, quite tame; a chevreuil, too, was browsing by the way-side.

AALBORG.

5th July.—A day of rest at Aalborg. We visit one of the three hospitals the town possesses for aged men and women, sixty in number—all fresh and bright in its annual coat of paint—large airy rooms, and plenty of old Jutland women, in their queer frilled caps, spinning and knitting away. They are fed and lodged, and receive a mark weekly by way of aid for their clothes, which, added to the small sum they make by the sale of their yarn and stockings, keeps them in good trim; one of the old women reminded me of a bonne femme Normande by Gerard Dow—quite a picture, with what the Yankees call "a wealth of silver hair." Then there were others, cross and querulous, as the matron expressed herself, "as the old woman of Buxtebude." † The mayor of the town pointed out to me a street still called Scottingade, adjoining the site of an earlier Aalborg Slot, where once stood the barracks of the Scotch guard of the second Christian, hired from his

---

* I passed by the village of Aan; on the heath you observe those lofty tumuli, the greatest a giant's sepulchre, grave of the well-known Gunther, killed by his rival Kagul, when, according to the old song—
  " With spear and dart does Gunther strive
   The giant Kagul from his house to drive;
   But Kagul he drives Gunther back,
   Until his collar-bone does crack.
   Now Gunther lies in the earth cold,
   And Svenstrup belongs to Aan so bold."

† "As cross and scolding as the old woman of Buxtebude," is a Jutland saying. The said old woman is an historic character, the heroine of an ancient ballad: she married a giant at the age of 110.

uncle James III. King of Scotland, husband of the Princess Margaret of Denmark.*

Our hotel was once a house of some importance, built in the last century by Brigadier-General Halling, an officer in the English East India service he called himself. As a boy he had run away to sea, made his fortune in the East, and returned to end his days with honour in his native land. It was later discovered he had been a daring pirate, the terror of our English homewardbound Indiamen, and that the "honourably gained fortune" was the plunder of the captured vessels; the viking spirit bursting out, only eight hundred years too late: otherwise he might have been a smaa konge, and buried in a giant's chamber, his arms and ornaments around him.

HOBRØ.

6th July.—We have changed our plans, and, instead of floating down the Liimfiorde, adjourn first to Viborg, where papers and letters await us.

---

* A large number of Scots, says the historian, came at that time to Copenhagen. They were highly esteemed as warsmen, equal to the Germans and the Swiss. This caused great jealousy; and one day, when the Scots were assembled at a drinking-house, the Germans gathered round the house and challenged the Scots to come out. The Scots, finding their adversaries too numerous, refused; so the Germans set fire to the house, and the Scots had to crawl up to the roof, whence they threw down stones; but as the fire advanced they were compelled to jump down, and were all killed. The Germans took possession of the town and ran through the streets slaying every Scot they met. When the king heard of this uproar he came out and endeavoured to restore order, but without effect, though he rode through the streets on horseback. When he arrived at the Amagertorv, a Scot threw himself under the king's horse, demanding protection; but the German had no respect for the king, and slew the Scot under his horse's feet; for which outrage he was however afterwards beheaded.

It is not to the credit of the Vendsyssel country, but an old proverb declares "At Aalborg Sund ends law and right." Let us hope matters are mended since those days. We roll down a hill, and arrive at Hobrø, where we dine; and the fair fiorde, with the town and its church, lie clustered before us. Nothing can be more beautiful than the site, which the foolish town has not known how to take advantage of; built in one long street scampering up the hill on the Randers road. The church is of modern Gothic brickwork, striped horizontally in dark and pale red—the effect admirable. In the churchyard stands a Runic stone, the characters as fresh as though incised yesterday. After half an hour's drive we leave the Randers road, and turn across a moor, through a windy country, all drily historical, but no remains to make it interesting.

BRATTINGSBORG.

Later we arrive at Kleitrup Lake, where alone a few embankments tell the existence of Brattingsborg castle; to take which the seventy-seven knights of the ballad set out from Hald by way of Viborg. A cow, tormented by the flies, fords the moat, so they follow her example and scale the walls. It was when riding in the neighbourhood of Kleitrup that Prince Inge, son of King Niels, fell from his horse and was killed. His affrighted tutor fled, disguised as a woman, and was captured in a bog—people always got captured in the bogs in Jutland—and was buried alive, without bell, book, or candle, pegged flat on his back, a høi heaped up over his body.

From here, too, eloped the Princess Ingeborg, wife of Prince Henrik Skatelar. She fled disguised in knight's attire, and was caught in the streets of Aalborg. Prince Henrik, suspecting unjustly his cousin Knud Lavard, aided in his murder.* He pardoned the princess because she was deserted by her lover; but later caught somebody else, and buried him, like the tutor, under a høi.

Well, history compels us to gaze on this little Sø, which has seen a great deal in its day, but of which no traces remain: it looks very calm and quiet, with the white village church, built down by its water side, glad to have done with all these exciting times, and be at rest.

TIELE.

How the wind did blow as we proceeded! umbrellas turned inside out; can hardly sit in the carriage. My geography, too, is at fault: a new road has been opened this summer, and we are all at sea till we stop at Tiele to look at the tomb of a ridiculous puppy of the last century, a certain Capitaine de Levetzau, who left orders in his will that his sarcophagus (which looks like a work of Wiedevelt), all curves and allegory, should be supported by six undraped female figures, "in humble expression of his gratitude to the fair sex for the favours he had received from them in his life-time." Orders were given for the execution of the monument,

---

* The cousins had already come to loggerheads, at the marriage of Prince Magnus in Ribe, about dress. Prince Henrik appeared clad in a suit of sheepskin, while Knud Lavard dazzled the eyes of all beholders by the splendour of his scarlet raiment cut after the Saxon fashion. Henrik, boiling over with jealousy, sneeringly remarked, "Such new-fangled stuff ill befitted a warrior, and would afford little defence against the sword-cut;" to which Knud replied, "Scarlet cloth was quite as serviceable as sheepskin, when the wearer had the courage to defend himself." Prince Henrik never forgave that suit of scarlet.

when the Lutheran clergyman vowed no such impropriety should enter the church, even if he appealed to the Sovereign (it was under Christian VI., of pious memory, and Queen Madalena). "But they shall be all scriptural subjects," reasons the artist, by no means anxious to relinquish so advantageous an order. The pastor was inexorable. The artist, at his wits' ends, proposed the ladies should have fishes' tails and become mermaids. This settled the matter—allegory was all the fashion of the 18th century—so there they are, with their fishy continuations looking somewhat crushed, supporting the black marble which contains the body of the captain.

While admiring the sepulchral stone of Jørgen Skram, founder of the château, and his wife, a message was brought to us from the Kammerherrinde de Lüttichau, the dame châtelaine, begging us to rest ourselves in the house. On entering we find old acquaintances of Copenhagen, and pass a pleasant evening. Cows are diminishing, sheep increasing in numbers, as we approach the moorlands. Cows are called "cows" by the Jutland peasant, the sheep are the "English Southdown," and the horses used of "Yorkshire" breed. The château of Tiele is of great antiquity, and the only one we have yet met with not surrounded by a moat; very picturesque it appears among the splendid lime-trees, with its striped wings and ancient gateway.

On quitting Tiele we pass through the village of Lovel. The frequent occurrence of England's holm, England's this, and England's that, at first puzzled me. The word Eng signifies meadow, and Eng-land is merely common parlance for meadow-land. In two hours and a half's time we were safely housed in the hotel at Viborg.

CHAPTER XXXIX.

Pagan city of Viborg — Erik the Lovely and the harper — The Danish Luther — First of the Longobardi — Sir Niels Bugge and the Castle of Hald — Murder of King Erik Glipping — Church of Anscarius — Railway engineer — King Knud's invasion of England — Manor of Krabbesholm — Parson Mads the slanderer — Caps of Fuur Island — Mors, birthplace of Hamlet — His story as told by Saxo.

VIBORG.

THE ancient city of Viborg held high her head in Pagan times, rival to Leira and Sigtuna, for here were solemnised the chief sacrifices to Odin; and here, in an open plain before the town, were elected the Danish sovereigns for the provinces of Jutland.

Numerous and important were the events in history which here took place; far too dry and tiresome to enumerate: one alone I will mention.

It was early in the 11th century that Erik the Lovely, driven to madness by the strains of a wandering harper, slew four of his ministers; and to atone for his crime made a pilgrimage to the Holy Land. Then up rose all the Jutlanders imploring him not to leave them, and offering one third of their goods to purchase his peace with heaven: they wept, they begged on their bended knees, but of no avail. He started and died on his way at Cyprus, before his pilgrimage was completed.*

---

* Erik Eigod was one of the natural sons of Svend Estridsen. From the time of Canute the Great till Valdemar I. no difference

You have had enough of historic events; but when towns, like mortals, have seen better days, they like to indulge in the memory of their former grandeur, and talk about the grand doings of their early youth. And now Paganism is at an end, and Odin out of fashion. Thor has had a handle added, not to his name, but to his hammer, which is converted into a cross. Freia no one cares for now, so Viborg appears bright in a new light—the very odour of sanctity. Six-and-twenty churches rise within her walls, convents and nunneries, white brothers and gray; and such relics, too! All the pilgrims on their road to Rome take Viborg by the way, and are lodged by the hospitable monks. Some, indeed, go no further, perfectly contented with the treasures displayed before their admiring eyes: and no wonder; have they not here preserved a lock of the hair of the Virgin Mary? a fragment, too, of the five barley loaves, and, more curious still, the eye of one of the seven sleepers? Little use going in pilgrimage to Rome when such sights can be seen in our own native Jutland. In our cathedral, too, repose the bodies of our kings: first on the list Svend Grathe—a murderer he was. Then, too, there is Erik Clipping; he lies there, and we exhibit his bones to the wondering stranger, and display the marks of the square iron clubs by which he was murdered, still visible on his battered skull. These sovereigns honour our round-arched crypt, where we say masses both night and morning. A brave place is Viborg in these old Papistic days. A real Danish saint, too, once lay interred in

---

was made between natural and legitimate children, six illegitimate princes reigning one after the other in Denmark.

Viborg Domkirke, canonized by the pope, St. Kield by name. St. Kield was born in Vinding, near Randers. He was a very holy man, who performed many miracles, and became Bishop of Viborg. Before his sanctity was known, he was once expelled by the friars of his convent. A few days afterwards he met one of the servants of the convent who had been sent out to fetch water, and asked leave to drink out of his pitcher. When the servant handed it to him, he changed the water into wine, ordering the servant to take it with his compliments to the brethren of the convent, and to ask them to drink to his good health. He was immediately called back, and received with great joy. When after his death the pope had entered him in the number of the saints, his corpse was laid in a costly shrine and suspended in golden chains under the vault in the chapel of the cathedral of Viborg. This richly gilt shrine, called the arch of St. Kield, was always held in much honour until the Reformation, when it was taken down and placed behind the altar of the church, where at last it was burnt in a conflagration. But now, in the commencement of the 16th century, rumours are rife of a Wittemberg monk and his new heretical doctrine; the visitors to Viborg are few and far between. Then uprises a gray brother, Hans Tausen by name, and, in defiance of all authority, preaches the doctrines of the Reformation, and proclaims himself the Luther of Denmark, and Viborg, prosperous Viborg, the first Protestant city of the empire.*

---

* Hans Tausen was born in Funen, and first entered the kloster of Antvorskov, and travelled to Wittemberg, where he resided two years. On his return his new doctrines gave offence; he was first reprimanded

Bishop Jørgen Friis, the last Romish prelate of the diocese, accompanied by his halberdiers, endeavours to seize the recreant monk, but in vain; he is defended by the people. The discomfited bishop retires to his castle of Hald, and later quite forgot himself, for one of the accusations brought against him in Christian III.'s time was that he had been heard to say "he wished himself a devil to have the plaguing of King Frederic's soul with hot and cold in purgatory." With the Reformation ended the glories of this ancient city; her monasteries suppressed, her churches fell soon into decay; of the twenty-six which formerly graced her city, three only now remain. But though Viborg be fallen, her site none can take from her, on a hill-side overlooking the lake which bears her name. The cathedral, once her glory, built in the 12th century by Bishop Niels, has much suffered; it was burnt nearly to the ground in the earlier part of the last century, was then restored in the taste of the day; her fine granite arcades closed up with plaster, and her massive stones replaced with brick; her towers topped with a jockey-cap—degraded as far as degradation could be carried. Still her proportions are grand, and the fine round-arch crypt well repays a visit. Here long after the Reformation were, masses no longer sung, but morning prayer said daily in Glipping's honour. Svend Grathe has long since disappeared, though they still dis-

---

and then sent out of the way into Jutland. Near Veirup, in Funen, were some years since still seen the remains of a smithy in which Tausen is said to have been born. His father Tage was a smith, and extracted iron from the moor; therefore he was looked upon as a sorcerer, and was killed by the peasants. The place is still said to be haunted by the wife of Tage, who is heard calling after her husband; no one will disturb the ground, and dross and scales of iron are still found there.

play his bones, and Glipping's too; his armour (of the time of Christian IV.) still decorates the walls of the royal chapel. There is, however, some talk of a general restoration, if money can be collected; but the bishop is poorly paid, scarce better than a parish pastor; 4000 dollars, and a house with a garden near the cathedral, forms his annual stipend.

We visited the public garden, where the stone on which Tausen first preached "the truth" still lies. It is called Tausensminde, and bears a small inscription thereon, "Upon this stone in 1528 Hans Tausen first preached in Viborg Luther's doctrine." He became Bishop of Ribe. You have seen his portrait at Frederiksborg; a sour-faced man, like all the early reformers; he might frighten you, would never win.

8th July.—Viborg has still some vitality in her left — is repaving her streets and smartening up in expectation of a railroad. She possesses too a little commerce of her own. I observe the weavers sit at their open windows, busily engaged at their looms: look in at that man, his house shaded by two clipped limes; how neat and tidy all appears about him! look at his two bas-reliefs in biscuit, — one of the present king; the other by Thorvaldsen, the Genius of the Year. Observe too his flowers—his oleanders, his carnations—how carefully cultivated! and, above all, his own healthy, well-fed appearance, and his thriving family. He sings as he throws his shuttle at his "uld" (wool), a pile of Jersey jackets beside him. His next-door neighbour works on his own account, and stockings, as fast as completed, are exposed for sale in his window—see, there's an odd one; he is occupied at the fellow this very moment. Before every house is placed a red barrel; very smart it looks too. Viborg has a wholesome terror of fire; and these little casks are kept ready filled in case of being wanted —name of the owner painted upon them to avoid confusion; rather an antediluvian idea, but better than no protection at all. We step into the South parish church to admire its ancient altarpiece. It came first from Antwerp, and once adorned the far-famed church of Esrom Cloister; then, after the fire, which lapped up the churches and houses of the city of Viborg as a cat does cream, it was sent to replace the one destroyed. It is a wonderful production.

We crossed the lake to Asmild Kloster, founded in the twelfth century by old Bishop Gunner, who died here in the ninety-ninth year of his age. A very small portrait of Hans Tausen hangs in the whitewashed nave, whose aisles have long since disappeared.

HALD.

9th July.—A drive of an hour, partly by heath, partly by forest, brings us to Hald. We alighted at a manor-house of no pretensions, built by Guldborg (enemy of Caroline Matilda, and last representative of the Høg family). A more lovely spot than Hald cannot well be imagined — her purple waters, and the opposite banks o'erhung with luxuriant beeches; the foundations of her ancient castle rising abruptly on the little island, now hardly disconnected from the mainland, for the waters of the lake are low. It was from the castle of Hald that, in early times, when a dreadful famine oppressed the land, and corn was scarce, Aage and Ebbe, sons of King Snic, first of the Longobardi, whose høi you may see in Østi

Snede parish, accompanied by a band of warriors, set forth from their ancestral abode to seek fresh fortunes and new conquests in a sunnier clime.

In the days of Valdemar Atterdag the fortress of Hald held out against the sovereign, who besieged it in vain for many months. You may still discern the rampart constructed by the enemy on the lake's side.* The king, discomfited, retreated to Odense, and there summoned its lord, Sir Niels Bugge, to arrange the matter by compromise. Sir Niels departs, confiding in the honour of his sovereign. He bids farewell to his château-fort and Hald Sø for ever; for on his return from the meeting, at a village not far from Middelfart, in the island of Funen, he was slain by a band of fishermen, who were supposed to have acted at the instigation of the king. Valdemar, however, affected much virtuous wrath at this foul murder; taxed the inhabitants of the place; and to this very day the peasants of Middelfart pay a tax to the Government, entitled "Bugges mande bod."

Queen Margaret, who, like Richelieu, hated castles and a powerful nobility, gave over Hald to the Bishops of Viborg, on condition they should destroy the fortress. The bishops accepted the present, but preserved it intact; it was near head-quarters, and found convenient, particularly in Hans Tausen's time, for here

---

* The siege had lasted for several months, and Bugge was already reduced to famine; one cow alone remained of all his stock. To deceive, however, the enemy as to his resources, he caused the animal to be clothed each morning in the skins of her long since slaughtered sisterhood, and driven along the ramparts in sight of the enemy—black cows, white cows, brindled, and streak-dun—one after another. "Why, with such a provision," exclaimed the king, "they'll hold out for ever." So he raised the siege.

gallant old Jørgen Friis, in 1536, intrenching himself, defended his castle to the last against his Viborgian flock, who besieged him; they got the best of it though, and imprisoned the gallant church militant in his own tower. Hald then fell to the Crown; afterwards Guldborg dwelt there, and built the present mansion— ugly, and now out of repair. We walked to the pretty hamlet of Bakke, all streamlets and water-wheels, and, striding through the long grass, scaled the mound where once stood the earlier castle, surrounded by a double trench; the site of the second castle rises well from the lake, and must have frowned imposing upon its waters. You may drive round by the other side, if you like; it will repay your trouble.

FINDERUP.

We took Finderup on our way home merely as a change—Finderup, where Glipping was, as you already know, basely murdered by Marsk Stig and other Danish nobles. It was one dark November night—the eve, they say, of St. Cecilia (1286)—fatigued after a hard day's chace, he slept soundly in a farmhouse before the fire; his traitor page Rane*—he whom we have seen executed elsewhere, under the eyes of justly revengeful Agnes herself—introduces the assassins to the chamber of his lord. Fifty-six blows from heavy square iron clubs rain down upon the body of the unlucky sovereign, and all is over. The assassins fly the vengeance of the Church and his successor, to meet later the punishment awarded to their crimes. We passed two days

---

* Rane was a Hvide, but of a bad stock; own sister's son to Archbishop Jens Grand, most turbulent of prelates.

since the manor of Sødal, where Rane's mansion, Stapelgaard, once stood—confiscated and razed to the ground by order of Queen Agnes.

Finderup is a poor village on a desert heath: blighted by the foul murder committed there against "the Lord's anointed," it has never thrived. In duty bound we entered the miserable church raised over the spot, where in early days masses were daily and nightly sung in memory of the event. What keys! the little boy can hardly bear their weight. It's a miserable place, containing a small, narrow, white tablet to Guldborg, with a few more. Some English names are among those interred within the chapel—Knapps, Løvels, and Kjærs, which latter answers to Kier or Kerr, so here pronounced. To-day too we are not far removed from the village of Ryde; and Vinkel, with its little Sø, is not very distant. In the cemetery, above a maiden's grave, a white rose bloomed.

In the evening we drive with the Amtman,* Baron le Breton, and his family, to the village church of Tapdrup, the earliest Christian edifice in all Jutland — round arch with a soupçon Byzantine—built by Anscarius himself, who here founded a colony of early Christians, English and German mixed; for a time afterwards the colonists spoke the "plat" or bad German of Holstein. In the lake below the early Christians were baptized.

A party of Sir Morton Peto's men are in the hotel. They arrived one by one this evening after a week's

---

* The office of Amtman answers to that of Préfet in France. In the days of absolutism it was given to the grooms of the chamber when they married; now the appointments are filled up by men who understand their duties and perform them.

hard work, surveying the land for the proposed railway—a pleasant, gentlemanlike set of men; they came tumbling in, like Macbeth's witches, each giving an account of his spiritings, from east, north, south, and west: one had passed his time among the sands; a second had sounded the never-ending moses, forty-five feet deep here, and there no bottom to be found: a third has passed his week pleasantly enough on the wild moor among the sweet thyme and heather under canvas—he is young, and knows not rheumatism; the elder ones laugh—he'll soon get tired of that work. One arrives from Portugal, another from Canada: they like the profession; they see the world; and are away, removed from its conventionalities.

SKIVE.

Monday, 11th July.—A three hours' journey across a moorland brings us to Skive, passing on our way the small village of Fiskbæk—fish rivulet—which here runs into the Liimfiorde: no scarcity of these streams in Jutland; the whole country is intersected with them. The village, small as it is, boasts a certain historic notoriety; and its little church, perched on an eminence, no doubt to avoid what once was water, with a grey slate turban to its towers, rising up into a point like a cock's feather all on end. It was from this pert little village that, in the year 1085, Knud the Holy assembled an immense fleet preparatory to his descent upon England, his revolted colony. He passed with his fleet through the Agger Canal, lately reopened; then oprored the Vendel men, and he had to quell by bribes their insurrection; meanwhile, his Jutland nobles, tired of delay, and idle outside the Liimfiorde, came to loggerheads — some retired in disgust, and the fleet dispersed.* On crossing this valley a toll is exacted; a relic of the ancient ferry, long since disused.

Skive, like its neighbour village, stands on a hill, with a sea of verdant prairies at its feet — prairies watered by a fresh-running beck, like all the streams of this country, alive with trout. There is nothing exciting in to-day's drive, but it is calm and very English. A vast extent of heath has been lately planted with young pine-trees. Jutland has become too déboisé; the crops, owing to the constant drought, look fearful; there is no doubt that this drought is increased by the wanton destruction of the forests — evaporation augments, and the streams and lakes suffer in consequence.

We walk through the woods to Krabbesholm. The château is dilapidated, but unspoiled by modern restorations. Floriated crosses and shields, once no doubt bearing the arms of its founders, still ornament the work. From Field-Marshal Sir Niels Høg — by the marriage of his daughter in the reign of King John — a Banner widow — it passed to the Krabbes, who named it Krabbesholm. Many old places might be restored, but to touch a brick of Krabbesholm would be downright sacrilege: I would

---

* William the Conqueror sent gold to Oluf Hunger, one of the fourteen brothers of King Knud the Holy; and Oluf promised to hinder the king from putting into execution his threatened descent upon England. He it was who excited the riot of the Vendel men; and when the king went to quell the disorder, was left in charge of the Liimfiorde fleet. He persuaded the Jutlanders they would lose their harvest, and made them run away; the warriors from the islands alone remained, and were dismissed. The Vendsyssel men refused to pay the tenths exacted to the clergy, so the king sent his officers to harass the peasants. The people now rose in open revolt. The king fled to Snoghøi, and thence passed over to Funen, where he was assassinated.

leave its court unswept, the peasant's cart upturned where it is, never put away the milk-pans, and as for that old Jutland peasant-woman, turn her at once, like Lot's wife, into a pillar of salt; the ducks and the geese, the ever-raging watch-dogs tearing like mad round their kennels; the moat, part green duckweed, the remnant a bed of raspberries, should all remain. Look at the horse-chesnuts and the limes — what glorious timber!—how well they tone down in the evening's light the colour of the buildings! A very prim old lady in gray gown and snow-white cap, fit châtelaine for such a mansion, invites us to the garden. It is all avenues; a fine green turf, like that of a bishop's in some cathedral town in England; fine groups of limes, fish-stews, and flower-beds—not too many: and only for one moment stay and gaze at the old house—how well it covers up its faded charms! leaving only its best features, that fine old octagonal tower and quaint Gothic gable, peeping out from beneath their framework—that old horse-chesnut.

FOVLUM.

12th.—Our steamer starts at six. Krabbesholm looks still asleep, and the bathing-cabins damp and uninviting; our deck, too, is none of the cleanest, and the brass compass appears as though it had been up all night, dull and besmeared.

Skive fiorde is narrow, and her banks brown, varied occasionally by patches of cultivation and a succession of white structures. If her ancient forests still existed, it would be beautiful, for the ground undulates. The morning is gray and slightly overcast—best colouring for the scene before us. The lake of Hald, with its rich luxuriant beech woods and its deep blue waters, shone glorious in the bright mid-day; but cliff and moor, when barren, tell best in early morn. We now, after a wide opening, again thread our way through a narrow passage. Here the cliffs are green, clothed with soft thymy turf, such as the sheep love to browse upon. We pass Dolby and then Lyby, where, in 1375, a council was held by the priest-ridden nobility of Jutland, at which they agreed unanimously to preserve intact the rights of the clergy as a sure preservative against murrain, fire, plague, and sudden death. Our first stoppage is at Sundsøve. A long narrow tongue of land runs out to sea; a carriage laden with something awaits our arrival; they hoist the red-cross flag, and we receive a Jutland farmer, ten sacks of wheat, and pass on. The sun's rays, as though on purpose, suddenly light up that village church to the right, dazzling in new-born whitewash—that is Fovlum church, concerning which there is a tale to tell—curious, as illustrative of the Jutland jurisprudence of the middle ages. It was in the days of King Frederic II. that a Lutheran parson, Doctor Mads by name, who, though he had reformed his religion, had quite forgotten to extend the same advantages to the licence of his tongue, accused from his pulpit Sir Jørgen Lykke, of Bonderup, of destroying a church, and building himself a mansion with the materials—nothing extraordinary, considering the days of church spoliation in which he lived; but, unfortunately for Dr. Mads, it was false, as the sequel proves. The knight, indignant at the accusation, summoned the scandalous parson for calumny before Bishop Juels of Viborg. The priest is pronounced guilty, and condemned to suffer the punishment awarded by the law.

Now in Jutland there existed in those days an excellent law against scandal-mongers—one which might well be introduced into the still embryo Code Victoria in England — " That the individual found guilty of a calumny should himself undergo the punishment awarded to the crime of which he accused his neighbour." The punishment allotted to him who destroyed a church was death. So poor imprudent Parson Mads was condemned, underwent his sentence, and lies buried, head severed from his shoulders, in the parish churchyard of Fovlum. This occurred in the year 1566.

ISLAND OF FUUR.

We are nearing the island of Fuur, and now pass between the straits; green are its banks like an emerald —a village, a church, and a few boats. The women of Fuur are remarkable for their marriage head-dress—a " bonnet mirabolant," all beads and small feathers, more like the South Sea Islanders than the matter-of-fact inhabitants of the Liimfiorde. You may see one preserved, together with the crown of the bride, in the Musée Scandinave of Copenhagen.

If there be nothing absolutely to astonish in our sail of to-day, you will at least be struck by the never-ending variety of islands here, promontories there, continents looking down on them from behind quite dignified. Turning and twisting in every direction, a church or a manor attracts your eye. You pass on: the facsimile appears in another direction; why, it's all the same—you've only been spinning round like a tee-totum. Depend upon it, there is a great deal of beauty in a low country, if people will only look at it.

ISLAND OF MORS.

We approach the island of Mors—its little capital Nykiöbing is already in sight—tall church, somewhat pretentious; harbour, shipping, and red-roofed houses, and the indispensable skov at one side. Boat stops for half an hour, so we disembark and walk about. The strand is heaped with flounders, and barges unloading turf, too, which leads you to imagine Mors to be a dry island. Its church is a good specimen of brickwork, with thirty-five little niches, once populated by saints, in its two side gables—whitewashed, and the granite even painted gray. It was once the church of Dueholm Kloster, with whose monks the inhabitants were ever at loggerheads. These northern churches have always one advantage over others of more common architecture in the fine vaulting of their roofs. We have just time to take a turn through the town—horrid pavement, but clean; each window a conservatory—camellias the high fashion; whenever a household utensil is cracked, whatever may have been its use, it receives back rank as a flower-pot. Mulberries too grow here, as standards, more than they do at Aalborg.

The Morsagers were not celebrated for their bravery, if you credit the old ballad on the Vendel boers' revolt against Christopher the Bavarian, in which Tornekranz* lost his head—a ballad which the Vendel men, even

---

* Tage Heinrich Tornekranz - a very sensible name to apply to an illegitimate offspring, "Crown of Thorns"—is supposed to have been a natural son of a Rosenkrantz, and was brought up at the family manor of Hevringsholm. The family later flourished at Ry, near Silkeborg. The last abbot of Vidskøl, vitæ scholæ, was of this family, which went out in the year 1652; the last member having lived to be upwards of a hundred years of age.

at this present day, lose no opportunity of singing and throwing into the faces of the descendants of their pusillanimous neighbours:—

> "First, then, they ran, the Morsagers,
> And next the traitors of Thy.
> After them stood the Vendel men;
> But they disdain'd to fly."

Names of Morsagers written up here, there, and everywhere, are Hort, Portman, Brinckmann.

We coast along in the open sea, till we turn straight between two promontories of land, one of which runs high and commanding, out to sea—the very site for a feudal castle. Two spacious old gabled houses— once a mill, now a depôt for coal—stand by the strand side. This is Feggeklit, sacred in the eyes of all Englishmen as the birthplace of our Shakespeare's Hamlet—Amleth, as he is called in Denmark. It

Feggeklit, Island of Mors.

was at Feggeklit, in the island of Mors, in the very early ages, dwelt two brothers, smaa konges—Haardevendel, father of Hamlet, and his brother Fengo. For many years they lived in amity, resting alternately, each for the space of three years, while the other went on a pirate expedition. When Fengo witnessed his brother return laden with spoils, and the joy of his wife Geruthe, Fengo's heart burned with jealousy; he determined to remain at home, and get possession not only of his brother's wealth, but also of his wife. Pretending that Geruthe is ill treated by her husband, Fengo slays his brother. After their marriage Amleth, fearing for his life, feigns madness. He rolls about in the mud, and replies in a ridiculous manner to the questions put to him. The king, suspicious, endeavours by means of a woman's art to draw the truth from him. Amleth, on his guard, that day indulges in unheard-of vagaries. He rides out in the forest with his face towards the horse's tail, pretends to mistake a wolf for a horse, and wishes Fengo had many such chargers. Now comes the story of Polonius. Fengo absents himself, and gives orders to a confidant to watch the movements of Amleth, and conceal himself in the room when he is alone with his mother. Amleth, who has his wits about him, before entering into conversation with his mother, runs, as was his habit, round the room, flapping his arms and crowing like a cock. Jumping on a heap of straw (in her Majesty's bed-room!), he feels something underneath, runs his sword through, and withdraws the dead body of the spy. He cuts it into pieces, boils it, and gives it to the pigs. Then turning to his mother, who was weeping over his madness, he addresses her the most violent reproaches: "If you will grieve, weep not over my madness, but over your own shame and dishonour." Fengo, after the disappearance of his counsellor, feels more anxious than ever to make an end of his stepson. He then sends him to England; and here Shakespeare has followed the true story. Amleth adds to the instructions for the death of his companions, that the King of England is to give him his daughter in marriage. Amleth is still very queer; he refuses to eat or drink at the English king's table. On inquiring, he replies he will not touch food because "the bread savours of blood, the beer of iron, and the lard of dead men's carrion:" he adds also (very ill-bred), that the king has eyes like a bondsman, and that the queen in three things behaved herself like a servant-maid. They only regard him as mad; but after a sharp observation the king discovers Amleth was right in his supposition as regards the food: for the corn came from a field where a battle had taken place; the pigs had eaten a dead man's carrion; and in the fountain of the brewer were discovered several rusty swords. The English king now becomes uneasy, and, taking his mother to task, forces her to own that a bondsman was his father. Later Amleth declares that (shocking bad manners) the queen is not of higher origin herself: for, first, she hides her head in her cloak; secondly, in walking she lifts up her kirtle under the girdle; and, thirdly, after eating she picks her teeth with a fish-bone—all decided proofs of low birth; "but perhaps," he added by way of a sop, "her mother was a prisoner of war, which fully accounts for her low habits." The king (a most undutiful son) praises his wisdom, and gives him his daughter in marriage. Amleth now demands recompense for the death of his companions, and receives a considerable sum of gold, which he melts down into two hollow sticks; and, after a year's absence, begs to return to Jutland on "important family affairs." On his arrival he is asked after his two companions: "Here they are," he replied, exhibiting his two sticks. His answer is received with shouts of derision, and they look on him as mad as ever.

On his arrival at the palace of King Fengo, situated on the lake hard by, he found the family in full carouse, a wake subsequent to the celebration of his own funeral. Disguised, he joins the party, drugs the liquor of the carousers, and, when they are all intoxicated, first setting fire to the house, rushes to the room where Fengo lay asleep, awakening him with these words: "Fengo! your good men are burning to ashes; and here is Amleth, who will revenge the death of his father!" He then slays him. One hundred and fifty years since Fengo's grave was opened and an iron sword taken from it; what became of it none can tell.

Such, according to Saxo Grammaticus and the earlier sagas, is the story of Amleth, Prince of Jutland; he will again turn up later. A flock of sheep appear out at sea. They have waded out to a little island from Feggeklit and are caught by the waves. See, how they stand up to their knees in the water, awaiting till the tide permits them to return.

CHAPTER XL.

County of Thy — Superstitions concerning tombs — Plague of sand — Wicked Queen of England — Draining the Sjørring lake — The pedlar and the geese — Anne Boleyn — The Liimfiorde — Story of Liden Kirsten — Sale of a wreck — Old Abellona and her amber beads — Loss of life off this coast.

———

THYLAND.

WE now turn a point, and the little town of Thisted, with its church and harbour, appears quite unexpectedly: we are soon landed and lodged in Hotel Liimfiorde.

Thisted is in no way remarkable. It seems a most creditable pleasant-looking town, lately built, with a forest adjoining, planted by the inhabitants themselves for their own recreation, connected with which is a nursery of young trees, which are given gratis to the peasants who desire to plant their farms; but the taste is not in them, and it is only by inculcating the ideas in the schools they can hope for improvement. With so much waste land in Jutland, it is a pity not to employ it to some good purpose, and the people might as well grow their own timber as draw their supplies from Norway or Sweden. We passed our evening at the house of Baron Rosenkrantz, the amtman, where we again met a friend of Rosenholm, who has lately purchased an estate in the neighbourhood of the Sjørring lake.

The county of Thy is most rich in antiquities of all sorts. They are formed of black basaltic granite, which takes a high polish and appears to be fashioned with greater sharpness than those of the other materials.

The peasants have a superstition against disturbing the ancient cemeteries, so that, unless a new road is about to be made, or the plough passes over some ancient battle-field, they yet remain undisturbed. M. de Rosenkrantz related to me a story of an Öland peasant, on whose farm stands a lofty tumulus, under which, according to tradition, lies concealed a mighty treasure. This treasure may be used for the benefit of the proprietor of the farm when he shall be really in want of bread. Some years since the possessor of the farm, incredulous, caused a search to be made, and opened the barrow. A few days afterwards his house, as well as his farm-buildings, were totally destroyed by fire. The boers looked upon this misfortune as a judgment upon the perpetrator of the crime, and from that day to this the tumulus remains undisturbed.

A curious incident occurred, a few years since, on the island of Oxholm. A man, in endeavouring to cross the morass, sank deep into the mud. On withdrawing, after some difficulty, his leg, he felt something hanging attached to it. At first he imagined it to be a snake; but soon discovered it to be a massive neck-ring of solid gold, for which, when forwarded to Copenhagen, where it may now be seen, he received the sum of 500 dollars as its full value.

SJØRRING.

12th July.—M. de Rosenkrantz and his amiable family have kindly arranged an excursion for us—some on horseback, others in the carriage—to visit the lake and the once celebrated castle. We started this afternoon at four o'clock, a large party—three carriage-loads and four equestrians—for the Lake of Sjørring, distant four English miles from Thisted. We paused for a few minutes at a tomb placed in the churchyard, that of some Irish bishop and his wife wrecked off the coast. It consists of four granite headstones inscribed with fantastic crosses, hearts, and other emblems; in the centre lies a flat gravestone; a triangular block of granite placed between each of the headstones, on one of which is represented the figure of a prelate, with mitre on head and crozier in hand; on the corresponding side the figure of a woman.

The granite of the village churches of Thy is most admirably worked: they are all now towerless—long since blown down—and nothing more than one fine round-arch doorway here remains. In former days, when a church was built, each peasant brought a stone, ready cut and carved according to a given measure, as his contribution towards the building. Here lie many of those early timber tombs, but of a more primitive character, denuded of their bark; one carved with inscriptions and quaint devices.

We now walked up to the height at the further end of the lake, where, surrounded by a lofty vallum and a moat having egress to the water, stood the celebrated wooden castle of King Knud the Holy.*

The Lake of Sjørring, in those early days, opened into the North Sea, of which it was then a fiorde: a sort of Jutland Brest, the harbour of the Northern fleet.

---

* From this castle on the island of Sjørring lake eloped the queen of King Niels, "Ulfheld;" concerning whose adventure you may read a ballad of some two hundred stanzas. She married later the Swedish King Sverker, and was mother of King Charles of Sweden—making the confusion of history only still greater.

It is blocked up at the northern end by a succession of sandbanks—bakkers; and where do you think all this sand came from? From England—so say the men of Thy—for in ancient days there lived a wicked Queen of England, who, offended at the conduct of some Danish king, whom she loved in vain, from pure revenge cut open the " canal "—she worked for seven years with seven thousand men—which now separates France from her dominions, let in the waters of the Atlantic,* which came foaming, raging, rolling, bringing sand and destruction, stopping up the harbour and ruining the most fertile fields along the coast of West and North Jutland; but her revenge bore its own punishment, for, when the sluices opened, she approached too near, and was borne away by the overwhelming force of the raging waters. " Never mind," say they ; " our turn will come in time ; for a prophecy exists that the ' revolted Danish colony ' of England will again be some day recovered by a Danish king."

There are many small islands scattered among the waters of the Sjørring lake, where sea-fowl abounds in endless variety.† Here, too, the sea eagle builds her nest; you could scarcely distinguish her eggs from those of a barn-door fowl. The lake swarms with wild fowl, and the surrounding country with partridges, snipes, woodcocks, and game of all kinds.

Many years since, a pedlar passing near this lake was attacked by two robbers. He beheld a flock of wild geese flying along above his head, and cried, " If there

---

* The whole west coast of Jutland was inundated A.D. 1717, on Christmas eve ; and 1720, on new-year eve.

† In addition to the common sorts, too numerous to mention, are the Larus ridibundus, Sterna cantiaca, Anglica, &c.

is no one else to be a witness of my death, I summon the birds of our Lord to give evidence." A few minutes after he expired. Years passed away; nobody had got on the track of the evil-doers. One Sunday, when people were assembled in a churchyard waiting for the parson, a flock of wild geese flew screaming over their heads, at which a Holstein horse-dealer said to his comrade, "Behold the witnesses of the pedlar!" These words drew attention upon the horse-dealer, and when they asked him what he meant he lost his spirits, and at last confessed that he and his comrade were the murderers of the pedlar. Such witness bear the birds of our Lord.

In a neighbouring cemetery lie interred the bodies of a Lieutenant (?) Harboard and eight English seamen, lost in the "Polyphemus," Captain Vaughan, wrecked off the coast some few years since; and farther removed among the sand is the ruined church of Torup, whose congregation have long since disappeared, driven away by the spasmodic attacks of flying sand, sent of course from England. There once existed a Runic stone, raised to the memory of "Tuko, the Englishman, who here was slain by the Viking Isvard."

On another small island—iland, they here call it—in the centre of this lake once stood the fortress which guarded its entrance. No wonder at the men of Thy feeling vicious against the English queen who by her machinations blocked up and ruined so fair a harbour.

We turn to the right to visit the canal, to be completed next spring. The draining of this lake is undertaken by Captain Jagd, a Danish officer from the Isle of Funen. These Jutland lakes are, as before said, strung together like birds' eggs on a thread. A canal is cut to the nearest lake, turning, at the same time, the course of the beck or rivulet, by which a fall of from fifteen to twenty feet is gained; the sluices once opened, the drainage is soon effected. Captain Jagd has established himself at a mill adjoining, superintending the hundred workmen under his orders. Twenty feet of sand had to be removed before they came to the natural clay. I could not help smiling as I looked around on the "fixings" of the cottage. An English patent stove, purchased from the wreck of the "Polyphemus;" an oil painting of some English ruined abbey, from the "North Sea" steamer lately stranded off the coast; splendid shutters, carved and even gilt, from some Russian brig, also gone down. Then there was crockery from vessels laden with oranges and iron. No wonder the "customs" of the North of Jutland are not productive. The sea herself "provides" for the wants of the inhabitants.

The ancient law of flotsum and jetsum has long since passed away. The Government takes possession of all unrecognised waifs and strays: if claimed, they are sold for the benefit of the owners—a wise provision in a country where the sea proves too great a temptation to human weakness. In ancient days, before the repeal of this old law, not only did our own Cornish habit of wrecking prevail, but murderers cast the bodies of their victims into the sea, to be washed up again on the strand; thus proving their right to the possession of the property discovered on the person of the corpse.

On our ride home we ascended a kjæmpe høi (giant's chamber), once the scene of some fearful battle. As far as the eye can extend, a sea of barrows rise like bubbles on a pot of boiling water. There is no doubt that this county of Thy has, of old, been the scene of many a bloody conflict, as well as long one of the richest and most thickly-populated parts of the kingdom. Of the numerous ancient manors—Duel, Væstermark, Alstrup, Skovsted, and Rotbøl—mentioned in King Valdemar II.'s Jordebog—a sort of Danish Domesday—he measured out the land under his own inspection, settled the boundaries himself, leaving nothing to his underlings—a practical man was Valdemar the Victorious—all have long since passed away; many are now covered by some twenty feet of sand. Most of the villages in these parts bear names having allusion to the chace, showing that the country was at some period covered with extensive forests, as letters preserved in the archives from the various sovereigns who hunted there still attest. The village near the høi on which we are now standing—a splendid giant's chamber—destroyed some thirty years since, is named Hundborg, Hound Castle; another adjoining, Wolfen something.

No antiquities have as yet been disinterred during the excavation of the canal; but this draining of the lake is looked forward to by antiquaries as that of a Jutland Tiber, and marvels are expected as the results of the undertaking. The ilex would grow on the sand-dunes. It stands the climate here in Denmark, and rather enjoys a sandy soil. You may wade knee-deep among forests of this tree on the most exposed coasts of La Vendée and in the islands off the coast of Brittany. No tree resists the wind more effectually, as we ourselves know in England. The tamarisk too might be employed with advantage for the binding of the sand-heaps.

VESTERVIG.

July 13*th.*—We start from Thisted in the afternoon. The Limfiorde is to-day agitated like a wide sea; the cliffs of the island of Mors opposite are imposing in their height. Our road runs along the banks—a fair extent of mysterious country—all tombs, tombs—an occasional peep at a lake, backed by sand-dunes; white churches rising here and there, as though to hallow by their presence the sepulchres of the Pagans.

Our harness breaks. Scarlet postilion doffs his hat, and prays, "Lend os a scizzors!" which request is granted, and the damage is soon arranged. Pronunciation and spelling in these parts do not, as in England, run together side by side. A manor near our course, marked on the map as Todbøl, is by the peasantry called Tudorbøl; and stranger still, in the village of Snedsted there dwells at this moment an aged woman who rejoices in the appellation of Anna Boleyn —Swollen Anna. But we arrive at the village of Vestervig, stop the carriage at the lich-gate of the cloister-church, and enter the moorland cemetery. The church —date 1100 A.D.—was a rich foundation in bygone days, its tower a sea-mark to the in-bound vessels. It is dedicated to St. Thøger, a sanctity unknown in more southern climes, domestic chaplain to St. Olaf, whose body, you may remember, after a lapse of years, was discovered quite fresh and pure, smelling of nothing but the odour of sanctity, on which account he later received saintly honour: in the exuberance of their piety the Northmen tucked in his chaplain Thøger along with him into the canonization. Vestervig church is of solid granite; granite columns and round arches support the aisles, all most tastefully whitewashed. On entering the churchyard, to the right you will observe a long

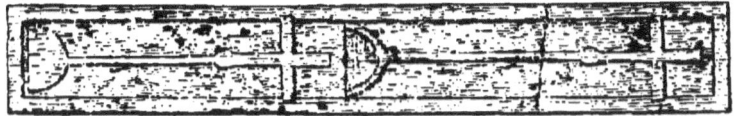

Liden Kirsten's Grave.

narrow sepulchral stone, hewn out of solid granite. Mark, it is broken towards the centre, and with a little imagination you may descry the print of a horse's shoe. The inscription, "Habet tumulus cum fratre sororem," is still pointed out by those who from long habit know where to find it. On the stone, some twelve feet long, are engraved two crosses; a headstone at each end. Two bodies sleep calmly within—their names known to every peasant in Denmark, old and young, rich and poor. All men have read and many wept over the sad story of Liden Kirsten and her lover Prince Boris.

I cannot do better than at once give you a résumé from the ballad,—a ballad sung in all the dialects of the North, in Norway, Sweden, Denmark, Iceland, and the Färoe Isles, in the Gaelic of the Orkneys; and again, in a different form, it appears in the Scotch under the title of 'Sweet Willie.' * We will now commence our story :—

"King Valdemar and Sofie,† they sat before the board,
    Under the roses two.
'They ' snackedt '—conversed together—full many a word."

---

* "She hadna well gane thro' the reed, nor yet well on the green,
    Till she fell down at Willie's feet, as cauld as any stane."
Again :—
"The tane was buried in Mary's Kirk, the tither in Mary's Quier.
    Out of the tane there grew a birk, and of the tither a brier."
† Sofie, queen of Valdemar the Great, was daughter of Duke Vla-

"Hear, oh, my king! lord and master mine. Will you give my brother Prince Boris little Kirsten to wife?" "That shall never be! Liden Kirsten, she is a noble maid, and Boris but a stable-boy. Never will I give my dear sister to a horse-thief!"*

Sofie now meditates revenge in her heart. Valdemar leaves, with his warriors, to fight against the heathen of Rugen, and Sofie, in conjunction with the "horse-thief," rules the land. Sofie says to her squires twain, "Bid Prince Boris come here to me;" and she orders him to betray little Kirsten. Boris refuses: "Never will I do so great a sin!" for he says it will cost him his life. Three months elapse. Again Sofie reproaches her brother, and finally wounds his vanity by ordering him to "cast the Runes," as he possessed of himself no power over Liden Kirsten.

The expression of "casting the Runes" requires some explanation. In early times there existed a superstition, that if an apple, inscribed with certain Runic characters, were cast so as to hit the breast of a maiden, she at once became powerless to resist the attractions

---

dimir of Halicz, and half-sister (somehow) to King Knud V.; a queen of very bad reputation, concerning whose ill deeds—murderings, burnings, poisonings of fair damsels both high and low—there are some twenty ballads extant. She lies buried in Ringsted church.

* Why Valdemar calls Boris "stable-boy" is a mystery not yet unravelled, and not likely to be; maybe, like many members of our own aristocracy, he dressed himself more like a jockey than a gentleman: and as for the term "horse-thief," we can only suppose him to have been on "the turf," and up to a thing or two—an occasional robbery—nothing more. Boris was son of Prince Henrik Skatelar (the lame), the history of whose wife, the Princess Ingeborg, I have before mentioned. He founded the convent of Tvis; and was much too near to the disputed succession for King Valdemar to look on him with a pleasant eye.

of her admirer. The vanity of Boris is now put on its mettle. He obeys the orders of the queen his sister, and the very day of Valdemar's return little Kirsten gives birth to a daughter at her house near Ribe.

Bent on revenge, Queen Sofie smiles under her "skind" (cloak) when the king inquires why his sister does not come out to meet him? She relates the story, but Valdemar is incredulous. He orders his squires to ride to Ribehuus, and conduct his sister to his presence. Little Kirsten lay in her dark room, surrounded by her damsels, when Sir Peter arrives, and on receiving her brother's summons she cries, "It will cost me my life!" but prepares to obey, and, taking leave of her daughter, whom she names Lucy Lille—she rides on her palfrey gray—ganger graa—to the palace, and is lifted off her horse pale as death.

"Shame on you, Sofie!" exclaims the king; "you have slandered my dear sister." As Kirsten enters the door she takes her brother by the hand. "Welcome!" she cries, "a good welcome home from the wars!" "Sing me a song!" demands the king. She sings one as well as she can. "And now, little Kirsten, you must 'threde' a dance with me!" They dance in and they dance out, little Kirsten under her brother's skind. Valdemar then turns to the queen: "Shame on you, Queen Sofie! you have slandered my sister." "Have I!" exclaims the queen, and, tearing open the dress of poor Kirsten, she presses her bosom: the milk flies out, and all is discovered:—

"Then the king became as red as blood.
    Little Kirsten as black as mould."

"Now," said the king, "all happiness is at an end! I had given my word that you should wed the King of

England's son, but now you shall die the hardest death I can devise!"

Kirsten sees it is all over with her. She begs for mercy, and then, resigned to her fate, makes her will. After other legacies, she bequeaths—

> "To Sofie my silver-bound knife;
> For she has sworn away my young life."

Then the king, in a passion, calls his small page. "Bring me in the whips! Bring me one! bring me two!—crescendo—eight! Bring me nine! for my sister shall surely die!" All the maidens and matrons grieve for her, except the wicked Sofie.

Valdemar now falls to. "Oh! stand up, Sofie, and entreat for me; for your brother has caused my misfortune." "No!" replies the queen: "my virtuous cheek would blush, were I to beg for such as you!" Valdemar lays about him with all his force, and the floor is stained with blood. Little Kirsten begs, "for Christ's sake, who died upon the cross," to creep under Queen Sofie's skarlagen rød, but is repulsed. "Don't touch it!" she cries, "or I can never wear it again." Whack! whack! go the whips. At last, with one cut out flies the heart of poor Kirsten. When Sir Peter sees this, he faints dead upon the bench.

Valdemar now has exhausted his rage. "Oh! Sofie!" he exclaims, "this is all your doing. Alas! my poor sister! Where shall we lay this red rose?" "Lay her?" replies the queen, "on Ribe bridge, to be sure; where I every day may gallop over her grave!" "That shall you not do!" answers the king; "we will bear her here to Vestervig Kloster, and I will give much gold with her to assoil my soul from this great sin."

He now sends for Boris, condemns him to lose his right hand and left foot, to be chained to the wall at the porch of Vestervig Kloster, and there "oculis defossis"—as the Sagas say—with his eyes dug out, to pray once a day at the grave of his little Kirsten.

Boris lived eleven years chained in this manner to the porch of Vestervig, and was afterwards interred in the same grave as little Kirsten under the "roses two."* In the year 1610 the grave was opened by order of the amtman. The coffin was found to be divided into two parts, each containing a skeleton, the one of a man, the other of a woman.

According to popular tradition Queen Sofie did have her way at last. She survived her king for many a year, and espoused a Landgrave of Thuringia, who soon divorced her. She did not however quit Denmark without having first ridden her "ganger graa" over the tombstone of her victim. The print of the horse-shoe, faintly visible to very sharp eyes, attests the fact, near the very place where the stone is rent in twain.

Tradition as well as the Sagas also declare that

---

* If this story be true, Valdemar was later punished for his conduct to Liden Kirsten in the fortunes of his own daughters, all three of whom were repudiated by their husbands without any just cause. The history of the youngest, Ingeborg, wife of Philip Augustus, is too well known to need recounting. A volume has been lately published in Danish, from the archives of the papal government, on this vexed question, which had much better have never been brought to light—evidence which in a modern divorce-court would have been received with "closed doors." Ingeborg was fifteen years of age, and is described as a "sunshine of northern beauty." She understood not a word of French; and during the trial could only utter the words, "Male, malo France!" pointing with her finger, "Rome! Rome!"—She lived in a convent at Soissons for nineteen years, and was then taken back again by her husband—and apply to Rome she did, as all men know.

Lucy was married to a King of England's son, though who he was I am unable to discover. Valdemar, on the whole, made a good thing of it; he disembarrassed himself of a dangerous rival, and gained possession of his vast estates. We sat down by the tomb of Liden Kirsten, read aloud the ballad in its own native Danish, and then adjourned to our kro, where we found our rooms already prepared for us.

Vestervig is the most considerable village in Thyland. "What is that house?" we inquire, pointing to one opposite. "The Raadhuus," they reply; then come three schools, an apothek, and the house of the mayor, to say nothing of that of the provost. But where is the population? Scattered about here, there, and everywhere, for miles around, among the sand-dunes.

THYBO RØN.

July 14th.—We have been to a sale to-day; not, as you may imagine, of "vieux Danois" porcelain, nor of the débris of some ancient château passing away from a long line of ancestors: nothing of the kind. We have been to the auction of the "North Sea" steamer, now embedded in the sands on the western coast, at a stone's throw from the fishing village of Thybo Røn. In company with Baron Rosenkrantz, the mayor of Vestervig, the English consul, and a whole boat-load of authorities, we embarked on board a sailing-boat at the village of Kirke, about eight miles distant from the place of our destination. A glorious breeze carried us dancing over the waves, the spray dashing in our faces, sufficient to brace up our nerves for a year to come. After a time the water becomes more shallow, the sandy bottom appears—we go bump—bump—bump, and later bu-u-ump; off again; a more decided bump, and then we are stranded to move no more. We are here relieved by a flat-bottomed boat, and re-embarked—punted along till within half an English mile from the shore, where we are met by three peasants in their country carts, who soon land us safe upon the beach. The masts and funnel of the shipwrecked vessel appear rising above the sand-dunes, as well as those of a Norwegian, her sister in misfortune. We adjourn to the kro, are received by mother Abellona, the mistress—a queer old lady, somewhat of a character—who hurries the ladies into a room to dry their saturated garments. I myself march out, my coat-tails tucked under my arms, for a walk on the common. Trust wind to dry you any day, versus fire, provided you have plenty of it, and there is no scarcity in Jutland.

I prolonged my walk to the sea-shore; passed first over one range of dunes, carefully planted with the sand-reed,* then ascended a second, and came down upon the strand.

A small tent was erected near the shore, and ranged in order for the sale lay the débris of the vessel—anchors, coils of rope, sails, sacks of coals, rusty-looking iron chain, kitchen utensils, &c. The articles of greater value were lodged in the village inn to be disposed of later.

The "North Sea" herself lay embedded in the sand, all on one side. The sea was rough, and the waves dashed

---

* Arundo arenaria.

over her: two more such nights and she will go to pieces.

It appears, when first wrecked, the engineer sent over by the insurance-company was advised to sell her outright. The insurance however was too heavy (13,000*l*.) for the company to abandon her without a trial. They counted on the west wind to bring the water necessary to again set her afloat. The west wind came, but with it breakers so violent she soon filled a second time. So, after an expense of nearly 2000*l*., the enterprise was given over.

There is one thing certain, that no vessel once stranded on this most perilous of all coasts ever can be got off. The east wind blows away the water, while the west brings with it breakers of such fearful violence nothing can withstand them. Many other vessels are here in the same plight, without speaking of the wrecks extending from hence to Skagen. Lower down lies the "Auguste," a French boat, and further still the Dutch "Harborg;" then comes a Swedish frigate, 74, and so on; a regiment of masts of phantom-ships lie embedded in the sand down the whole west coast of Jutland. In the year 1811 two English ships, the "St. George" and the "Defiance," first-class men-of-war, were wrecked on this coast. The masts until not many years ago were still above water. The "Defiance" may yet be distinguished at low tide, though not the skeletons of the Admiral's wife and three daughters in the state-cabin, as I was informed by a young lady a few days ago.

At this season last year ten vessels lay close together, wrecked, side by side, on the sands, and were standing, their masts rising above the waters. They have since gone to pieces, but each receding wave still discloses black timbers embedded in the sands. Having no intention of bidding, and being literally blown to shreds by the sea-side, I adjourned to the kro, where the sale was preparing—house of as unpromising an appearance as your worst enemy could ever wish you to be lodged in.

Abellona, an old Jutland name, is most anxious we should eat. She is a queer wrinkled old creature. Her head-dress a sort of turban composed of a shawl-pattern handkerchief, twisted round with a black coil of the same material; her jacket fastened by two large amber buttons (such as men wear on their coats) in quaint old silver settings. We ask her where she got them? Got them! they belonged to her grandmother, and hers before her. They are pretty—Pretty! pretty as Abellona is herself—and she laughs like an old witch.

Finding we admired the buttons, she pulls out from within the kerchief which surrounds her withered throat a necklace of amber beads as large as pigeon's eggs —clouded amber, such as the Easterns love—of the purest quality—collected for her by her sons when children—good for the eyes, she says; all the women wear them; and they are right so to do in this sand-flying country. She had two sons still alive, both pilots; and, as she told us how her two youngest had both met with a watery grave, shipwrecked in some winter-storm, her eyes filled with tears; then bursting into an agony of grief, she hastily quitted the room. Poor Abellona! she is not alone in her sorrow, for fearful is the loss of life on this raging coast.

The life of a fisher is a fearful one; not so much

to him, for he is at home upon the waters. He thinks little of the dangers of the deep. A sudden gust—a capsize—a struggle—and all is over. But to those who stay behind the anxiety is fearful: what sleepless nights in stormy weather—what expectation —what hope worn threadbare—too often wound up by the news of death and sorrow!

On the coast of Brittany — a coast nigh as perilous as that we are now standing on — are oft seen, after a stormy night, the wives and families of those who battle with the wave, standing with anxious gaze on the rock's extreme point to gain one look at the returning vessels; and again, when, after some months' absence, the fishing-barks arrive in harbour, among the joyous meetings of the sailors and their wives, among the hearty greetings of their fellow-villagers, you are sure to mark some woman —surrounded by her children, too young as yet to understand the cause—weeping bitterly, supported by some kind-hearted neighbours, willing in her sorrow to forget their own joy and comfort the afflicted. She has just learned how the father of her children, their sole support, has met with a watery grave, and she is now alone and desolate. And then, on the next succeeding Sabbath, how the altars blaze with lighted tapers and thank-offerings for mercies received and appreciated. You may smile, you may sneer, call it idolatry and Popish; but the thankoffering of a grateful heart, even through a mist of superstition and error, will ascend to the throne of grace, and the outpourings of the heart, though man may, He will not despise.

There is a marked change in the pronunciation of the villagers on this coast; the language still more resembles our own. "Will'ee drink a glass milk?" was asked of us (words abbreviated) by old Abellona's daughter, on our first entrance—and the old woman called her "Mary" instead of Maria,' as the name is pronounced by the Danes—and a "slow"— and Mary herself answered "Yus." Later the driver replies to a question, "Three"—not tre, a solid *th*— "waggon come after os:" broad language like that of our own peasantry.

The sale was now over, and we prepared to depart. N.B. The crockery, nickel silver, &c., sold for higher prices than they had originally cost at the Sheffield warehouse where they had been purchased.

CHAPTER XLI.

The Agger Canal — Food of the peasants — The girl who trod upon bread.

AGGER CANAL.

The weather was too rough for us to return by boat; so the boer-carriages were to drive us to the ferry on this side of the Agger Canal. We passed by the "North Sea," which will soon disappear under the heavy breakers now beating against her sides, and then over a plain of driving sand—not above the horses' knees, however, otherwise it would have been insupportable—for the space of some miles. "I recollect," said one of the gentlemen who accompanied us, "when this sea of sand we now cross was one of the most fertile meadows in Jutland." The canal was at that time closed, and the whole coast shut out from the North Sea by a range of lofty klits; the post-road from Agger to Lemvig then ran by the shore's side.*

---

* It was in the month of February, 1825, that a violent storm, such as had been never known since the memory of man, broke on the western coast of Jutland. The North Sea, raging with a fury quite unprecedented, burst over the klits, laying them low, carrying sand and destruction over the adjoining country, and reopened the Agger Canal, which gave ingress to the Liimfiorde, closed upwards of two centuries. It was not, however, until the year 1834 that the first vessel passed through into the open sea. From that time it became more used, and, in the year 1856, 1710 vessels passed through it, in and outward bound, the channel at that time drawing eight feet of water. In consequence of the mild winters of '58 and '59 the passage is now reclosing, and at present is reduced to four feet of water.

The Agger peasants live chiefly on fish. Like all Normen, they are lovers of sausages (pøtse) and other "salaisons." A wedding-feast here consists of four courses of fish—very common fish, too, for they devour dog-fish and all sorts of nastiness. For meat they care not, neither for bread. Pity, they say, "to grind and bake good corn into loaves, which might be turned into brandy."

This indifference to bread is not in accordance with the religion of the Danes, for they say, "We must not even lay the Bible upon bread." And when in Zealand a peasant drops a piece of bread, he takes it up quickly, and, kissing it, begs pardon of "Our Lord" for having treated carelessly "His good gift." Many, too, are the stories related by the old as warning to the children "not to profane the blessed bread."

A young girl in service near Flinterup, in Zealand, one day received permission to visit her aged mother, and her mistress gave her five loaves to take as a present. So the girl dressed herself as fine as a peafowl, and, coming where the road was impassable on account of the mud, to avoid dirtying her shoes, laid down the loaves as stepping-stones, in order to pass over dry-footed. But as she placed her feet upon the bread, the loaves sank deeper and deeper, till she entirely disappeared in the bog and was seen no more. The girls of the village still sing a lay about "the bad girl who trod upon bread to keep her shoes clean." *

---

* Hans Andersen has made this legend the subject of one of his charming tales. The same feeling as regards the " holiness of bread " appears to have existed in Bornholm ; and it is related that a woman, A.D. 1592, who " took its name in vain," having declared to a beggar-woman that she had none to give her, was punished by finding the

We passed the Great Canal in a pilot-boat, and then drove across the smaller one, now entirely closed "to the public."

This caprice of the waters is not, however, of modern times, for we find by history that in the year 1050, Harald Haarderaade, escaping from Svend Estridsen, was compelled to transport his fleet across the sands into the North Sea, over the banks which still bear the name of Haraldseid. Some few years later Knud the Holy passed with his fleet, destined for the conquest of England, safe without impediment to the North Sea. The first closing of this passage is supposed to have been caused by the sinking of a vessel in time of war to prevent the entrance of the enemy into the Liimfiorde; the sand, taking this obstacle as a point d'appui, closed around it, and gradually caused the stoppage, which lasted for centuries. We continue our course, rather wearisome, through the pretty village of Agger by the Flade lake; pass by the new church—old one long since embedded in the sand. How slow the man drives!

---

whole of the batch then baking in the oven turned to stone. One of these loaves was preserved for a long time in the museum, and the Czar Peter was so much astonished at the fact that he carried off a crumb by way of curiosity.

CHAPTER XLII.

Battle of the Giants — Patriotism of a peasant — Sequel to the story of Hamlet — Protection against flying sand — Magnus Munk and the still — Gipsies the outcasts of society — The dragon and the wizard — Appearance of the Black Pest — Depopulation of the Ale Mose.

LEMVIG.

July 15*th*.—READY to start this morning, when a message came from the mairie, begging us to wait an hour and our friends of yesterday would accompany us as far as a chamber called King Rosmer's Høi. We assented, and started, a large party, on our way to Neessund, to meet the steamboat. We pass by the solid church of Heltborg (giant's castle), which stands directly opposite to that of Karby (once Karl-by), in the island of Mors.

In days long since gone by was fought a terrible battle between the heroes of Thy and the Karls of Mors. They pelted each other across the water with huge masses of granite, which there lay in heaps, until the introduction of Christianity into the North. The stones were then turned to a good account, and the churches of the above-named villages built with the materials. On the few which remain the peasants still discern giant finger-marks.

We stopped at King Rosmer's Høi, a chamber similar to that we have already visited near Frederikssund,—not quite so lofty, but the size of the stones is marvellous, and there are two small cabinets-de-toilette, one on each side of the principal room, which is more remarkable. After all, Rosmer was no smaa konge, but a Jarl—there were none north of the Liimfiorde. A duke once—Duke Toke, or Jokke (to play the fool)—but the title he did not like.; his only son Odenka became bishop, and possessor of two-thirds of the lands of Vendsyssel, and his sons were all bishops after him.

Of Jarl Rosmer himself we know little. There is a ballad about him: he reigned over Thy, Mors, and Salling, about the ninth century, and was said to have been contemporary of King Gorm.

At the shore of the Nees-sund we take leave of our friends, and embark upon the steamer, which sails down the Liimfiorde. We have again a village of Dover hard by: Limes, too, in profusion: are in the waters and off the manors of the Kaas, poor Mary's "Baron Cowes," one of the few ancient Jutland families still existing. We sail by the island of Thy. Flat are the coasts on each side; later the Liimfiorde becomes wide and extensive like a real sea. The ragged klits which separate the waters from the ocean again appear in sight. We turn to the left into a branch fiorde, where, snuggling at the foot of a range of green hills, in a little bay of its own, so comfortable and protected, a very haven of delight to those who come from windy Thy, appears the place of our destination. We drop some small coin in the tin money-box placed on the skylight for "docks folk," and are quickly landed on the pier of of Lemvig.

The descent into the town of Lemvig is sharp and precipitous, and the town is visible to the eye only when you arrive, so that the old saying runs—"Take care you don't come to the water before you get there." You see the lights shining on the other side of the Liimfiorde long beforehand.

It was in the war of the seventeenth century that a Jutland peasant was constrained by force to conduct a party of Swedes across the moors to the city of Lemvig, where they were about to raise a " contribution." Now the peasant, before starting, declared that he would never betray his country, so he led the troop by a roundabout way, and it was dark before they arrived at the border of the Liimfiorde. " Shall we not soon arrive?" exclaimed the captain of the troop. " Ten minutes' gallop and we are there," replies the peasant; " see, those are the lights shining in the distance—en avant!" and plunging the spurs into their horses' flanks, the whole body sprung forward, and fell headlong into the waters of the Liimfiorde.

On the following morning (it was Christmas-day), when the people came out from church, they found the shores of their little bay scattered over with corpses washed up by the tide; among them the body of the peasant, who was known to them; and later they heard how he had sworn never to aid or abet the Swedes in their design upon the purses of his countrymen.

GUDUMKLOSTER.

16th.—It was six o'clock this morning when we quitted the little town of Lemvig—Læmwich, as it is written in King Valdemar's Jorde Book — a most enviable little place, where cherry and rose trees train along the walls, and avenues of horse-chesnuts flourish straight on their stems. We now say " adieu" to the Liimfiorde —not quite, for she turns up occasionally: when least expected, appearing like a white silver film in the horizon, between the numerous tumuli with which this country bubbles, to-day rendered more bumptious still by the presence of innumerable hay-cocks. The crops here look well—buckwheat and rye. Potatoes too are magnificent—far finer than those of windy Thy. The ancient tomb-mounds do good service to the farmer: they break the fury of the blast and protect the young crops. The corn is finer behind one of these little eminences than in the open plain. Thy, too, though fertile enough when under cultivation, has the disadvantage of a limestone bottom, burns more easily, and suffers much in time of drought; her very turfs are inferior to those of the rest of Jutland. Our way runs by Gudumkloster,—"Good as a monk of Gudum" ran the proverb; and I am only too glad to repeat anything in favour of the Church when in my power. We will pause one moment, and again turn to Amleth, whom we lately left, shortly after the murder of Fengo, in the island of Mors.

Amleth now speedily arranges his affairs, and then prepares to return to England to visit his father-in-law. But this time he will go as a king should do, so he causes a shield to be fashioned of curious workmanship, on which he has engraved all the deeds of his manhood, and scenes from his childhood upwards, the murder of his father, the late marriage of the queen his mother, his own mad pranks, his journey to England, and his marriage with the daughter of the English king.*

---

* Fearing that the vivid description given by Saxo of the pictorial decorations on the shield of Amleth may give rise to some erroneous idea as to the state of art in these early days, I must explain that these representations were nothing more nor less than "Hällristninger," or figure-drawings—runes of the fifth century. The only specimens

He causes all the shields of his followers to be richly gilt, and, after a prosperous voyage, arrives at the court of his father-in-law. He is joyfully received by the king, and presented by his wife with a pledge of their mutual affection, a son and heir.

The English king inquires after Fengo, and for the first time hears of his death. Fengo was his ally, and these two were bound together by a solemn promise to avenge each other's death, even if they spilt the last drop of their blood in fulfilling their oaths. His feelings are divided between his oath and affection for his daughter, added to which, he highly esteems his son-in-law. He conceals his feelings, greatly tormented by his oath, until the queen dies. He then determines to get rid of Amleth by some underhand means, and thus clear his conscience. So he sends him on an embassy to Scotland

---

existing in Denmark are one or two figures on a rock near Heltborg, in Thy. In Sweden they abound on the rocks of Bohuslän. A ship (*a*) much resembling the comb termed by French hairdressers "demeloire" —up on end—represents a voyage; a tree a forest, &c. &c. Battles are sometimes more fully described. I give specimens:—

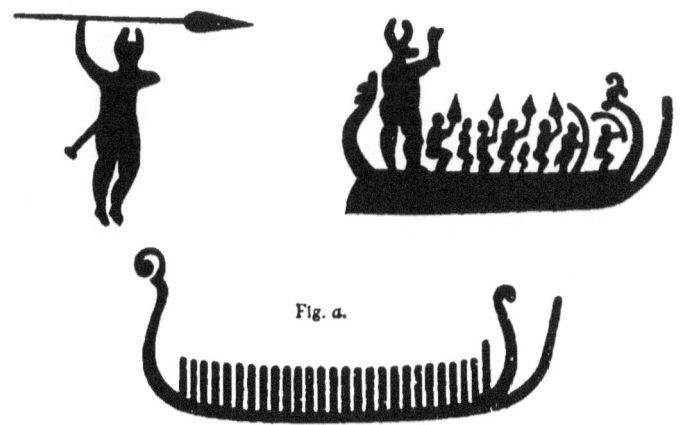

Fig. *a.*

to demand for the king the hand of the Scottish queen Hermentrude in marriage, being well aware that this sovereign not only loved the life of a maid, but also slew all those wooers who approached her court on a matrimonial speculation.

Amleth, on arriving in Scotland, sits down with his followers by a river's side. The Scottish queen is aware of his arrival; a spy passes the guards, and, while Amleth slumbers, removes his shield and the bag containing the letters from the English king, and carries them to his royal mistress. The queen, on seeing the shield of the sleeping prince, at once discovers, by the devices engraved thereon, who he really is. She reads the letter from the King of England, and, after Amleth's own fashion, changes the characters, so that Amleth is ordered to demand her in marriage for himself. Hermentrude does this because she hates the old king and prefers for her husband a handsome young warrior like Amleth. She causes the spy to return to the camp and replace the shield and bag where he had found them.

Amleth had discovered his loss, but feigns sleep; catches the spy, awakes his followers, and at once goes to Queen Hermentrude, by whom he is most graciously received. She praises his noble deeds, and is quite astonished at the mésalliance he has committed in marrying the daughter of the English king, a princess born of slave parents. "You should have married me, who am neither poor nor low, and worthy for you to live with—of pure royal blood—who can make a king of him whom I marry; accept, then, the hand as yet refused to everybody, and which no one has as yet demanded without loss of life." Amleth, nothing loth, consents. She embraces him; and the nuptial ceremony over, they both depart for England on a visit to the Court. He is there first met by his former wife, who, after reproaching him with his want of faith, tells him, "I have good cause to wail; still my love is great; I cannot hate you; therefore will I still live in harmony with your second wife, though my son will hate her as you hated your stepfather Fengo. Beware of my father, he seeks to kill you; put no faith in his promises." The English king comes out with two hundred armed warriors to meet him; but Amleth, forewarned, causes his people to wear under their gala-clothes their chain-armour. When he enters the portal of the castle the king draws his sword, and endeavours to slay him; but Amleth receives only a scratch, and flies. He sends a messenger to explain the affair. The king, however, is not pacified. A battle takes place, in which many of Amleth's followers are slain. Reduced in numbers, he causes the dead to be collected and fastened on to the chargers they mounted when alive. The enemy are by these means deceived, and Amleth comes off victorious; the English king is slain.

Amleth now returns to Jutland, accompanied by his two wives; and here first begin my illustrations of the "Prince of Denmark's" story. Not far removed to the right from the city of Lemvig, near the sea-coast, lies the village of Ramme. It was here, according to tradition, he first established himself on his return to Jutland; for he found the country in revolt. The queen, his mother, had taken part with Viglet, the pretender, who, in his absence, had usurped the throne.

You may still observe the grassy remains of an ancient encampment, such as we call in England a

"Danish camp," constructed for defence against an enemy attacking from the eastern side. This mound is called Ramme, and also goes by the name of Amleth's Castle. Our hero has now his choice before him—either to acknowledge the usurper, or fight his way against an unequal enemy. Honour tells him to follow the latter course. At first he is successful, and drives Viglet back with great slaughter into Zealand, as the ridge of tumuli by Møborg still attests. Viglet returns the following year. Amleth, prepared for the worst, is anxious before his death to procure a fitting husband and protector for Hermentrude (of his English wife we hear nothing). She however insists on accompanying him to the battle, declaring it is only a faithless wife who fears to accompany her husband when in danger. The battle now runs northward. Amleth is defeated by his enemies, and slain on the heathery moor which extends wide and brown before our eyes. You may observe a ridge of "høis," not far from a small white church. There, under the loftiest, he lies buried, with due honour (so tradition says); and the høi still bears the name of Amleths or Angels Høi, as the moor itself is well known to every peasant-child under the denomination of Anglands Mose.

Alas! for Hermentrude—"La donna è mobile," as the song goes; and she was not in this respect superior to her sisters. Amleth once slain, she accepts Viglet; as old Saxo, the monk, has it—not I—"So soon fate turns round the promises of a woman; for what a woman promises in her mind can never be depended upon. Many change for as little as this; they promise easily, but seldom keep their faith "—following up this sentiment with something so uncomplimentary to the fair sex, I cannot take upon myself to translate it. Saxo winds up with a flourish of trumpets about Hamlet and his virtues, comparing him to Hercules, and deploring the untimely fate of a prince worthy in his eyes to have ruled over the whole world.

With Gudum we leave cultivation, dip down into a dell, and out again—all brown moor and heather. Dells or dales they are here called—we have Longdale, Stourdale, and Friesdale. These dells have little rivulets of their own, busily turning the mills on their bank's side. The trout rise among the water-lilies, yellow still; and the meadow-sweet is now in its full luxuriance— "engdronning," or meadow-queen, they here call it. Each flower in this primitive country has its own story. The heartsease is here termed " Stepmother "—to understand why, you must turn your flower upside down. Then before you stands a fat, portly petal, clothed in garments of brilliant colours: turn her round; you see she has two green petals (of the calix) to her bodice. On each side of her are ranged her own daughters in gowns of gaudy stuff—same colour behind and before, with one green point apiece. Then come two elder girls in dresses of brown or dull purple, very dowdy. Look, too, at their bodies behind, poor things; they have only one point between them; obliged to sew it on and cut it off alternately—these are the stepdaughters. We again pass by the Liimfiorde, not far from the little town of Struve, where we landed for five minutes yesterday —a small village, frightened and bustled out of its propriety by the expectation of the arrival of the new Jutland railroad in its little harbour. It really does not know what to do first: a new quay it must have—church it has already, a very respectable one. So it commences new houses; has transformed its privileged kro into an inn, and reminds me of a Danish drawing-room on loverdag (Saturday), or cleaning-day; all bustle and mess —furniture in confusion, half turned out of window.

The women wear a queer costume in these parts—a shawl tied tight round their heads, with a gag across their mouths, a preventive against flying sand—like that worn by Dorothea Queen of Christian I. in her portrait in the Gallery of Frederiksborg. Their dresses, as their head-gear, are of homespun tartan.

HJERM.

We arrive at the cleverly-vaulted village church of Hjerm, where we stop to visit the last resting-place of Mogens Munk, the leader of the Jutland nobles against Christian II. He is buried here,* and his monument of sandstone engraved with an inscription in ancient letters. On his coffin lie his helmet, sword, and cuirass; but the vault is now closed to the public; for some years since occurred a most ridiculous incident. Somebody, accompanied by many learned men, and especially by a clever anatomist, Dr. D., proceeded to Hjerm church to make a descent upon the coffin of Mogens Munk. "Don't open the coffin," exclaimed the deacon; "let the dead lie still." They proceed to the vault; Dr. D., measure in hand, prepared to mark down his latitudes and longitudes, to take a cast of his skull, and write a treatise upon the subject—to prove the character of the defunct, by his bumps and the form of the cranium, diametrically opposite to what history describes. The lid is uncovered, and what meets their

---

* 1558.

astonished eyes? Not Mogens Munk, but an illicit still for the fabrication of corn-brandy. Next day came the excise. The still had disappeared; but on further search it was discovered on the top of the pulpit sounding-board.

Decidedly the first Protestant clergy made up for the celibacy of their predecessors. One ecclesiastic is here portrayed, together with his wife and eighteen children. We are in a new beat as regards English names: there are the Feldings, Jermiins, and the Stranges; among other noble worthies lies the last descendant of the house of "Grib," over whose extinction there is great lamentation on the epitaphium. Christian III. gave to Olaf Munk, ex Roman Catholic bishop of Ribe, the Kloster of Tvis for life as an apanage (foundation of poor Prince Boris), and there he lived and died. And now we make for Holstrebro, a pretty little town not far off, where we stop to dine, and then proceed on our journey towards Ringkjøbing.

HOLSTREBRO.

We approach the coast, leaving to the left that vast expanse of uncultivated heath and moor which runs through the centre of North Jutland, the Ale Mose, where, towards the village of Rind, the gipsies chiefly herd: "Natsmandsfolk," as they are called—night-men; not from their profession, but from the darkness of their skins. They first made their appearance in the sixteenth century, when many hordes came over from the East, and enjoy here as elsewhere a most unenviable reputation. They are looked upon by their fellow men as a sort of outlaws, accused of setting fire to houses, being beggars and thieves. The profession they ply is that of chimney-sweeps. They skin the dead beasts which die a natural death, and perform offices other men refuse—rakke-arbeide, it is termed. When young they are said to be tractable; but when once they rise to manhood and marry, they relapse into the bad ways of their brethren. They are allowed to attend no festivals; no man would seat himself beside them. In the town and country kros wooden cups are kept for their express use — rakke-glas they are called. In some countries the public executioner was ennobled; in Denmark he enjoys the office of "city scavenger," and his seven underlings are rakkers. In the churches of Deiberg and other villages there are separate pews set aside for their occupation, called rakke-stole. Some years since a prisoner of the gipsy tribe was induced to teach their peculiar language to the chaplain of the prison of Viborg, who later published a grammar in the Rotvœlsk tongue, as it is called. On his dismissal from jail he was instantly murdered by his former associates.

We had brought a letter for Professor Tang, proprietor of the mansion-house of Norre Vosborg. We found him at the inn at Holstrebro, together with Hans Andersen; so we accepted his kind invitation to pass a couple of days at his manor-house, some three miles distant from Ringkjöbing. It was seven o'clock when we left Holstrebro. Our road runs across the wildest heather-scenery — scarcely a village, scarcely a farm. It will take us some four hours to drive there; so I amuse myself by looking over the map. We are not far from Borbierg, whose village church was built under most singular circumstances. Holy, very holy people in vain endeavoured to raise the walls. As fast as they built them up, the devil again cast them down. Tired out, though much against their inclination, they enter into a compact with his satanic majesty; sign and seal that he is to receive as his own property the first bride who enters the church by the east porch, and leave them quiet; but the holy men are sharper than Old Nick, for they build a western porch, which he never thought of; and up to this very day no bride has ever come in by the eastern gate, nor would she for her bridegroom's weight in gold.

THE ALE MOSE.

As you travel for miles along the Ale Mose, and nothing but heath, heath meets the eye, you would imagine that this tract of land has been for ever uncultivated; but such is not the case; for among the wild mose, now alone inhabited by the gipsy and the lapwing, may be discovered, from time to time, ruins of cottages and remains of furnaces, where once the blacksmith plied his trade—swords and weapons are laid open by the turf-cutter: it is easy to perceive that civilization has here once been, and long since passed away. It is now five hundred years ago since, in a swamp adjoining a small village on the mose, there dwelt a dragon—a very harmless dragon, provided always he was left undisturbed. The people, however, suffered greatly from rats, and one day there appeared a wizard who offered for nothing to rid them of the plague, provided there were no dragons in the neighbourhood. Now the people were so anxious to get rid of the nuisance, they lied, and assured him there was nothing of the kind ever heard of thereabouts; so the wizard, confiding in their word, sat himself down, and, having first cut a circle in the heath, and kindled a fire in the midst, began to read from his book Cyprianus, commencing at the last page, backwards: the rats ran into the fire and were all burnt. Then in came the dragon. When the wizard saw the dragon, he turned pale, exclaiming, "I must now die; you false men, you have deceived me, but you will not live yourselves many years. You are accursed, and your village will become desolate!" Then the dragon folded his tail round the wizard, dragged him into the fire, and they were both consumed together.

It was on the eve before Christmas, in the year 1348, that there dwelt in this herred near the sea a rich nobleman, Eskil Juel by name. A stranger knocked at the door of his castle, begged for shelter and permission to remain the night. But Eskil replied, "No, I will not give house to a vagabond. We keep feast and festival with our friends on Christmas-eve, and will not be disturbed. Go to the parish priest: he has a large house; he drinks deep, and will let you stay till to-morrow." Now it was the old custom in those days for the priest to perform a midnight mass on the eve of Christmas, such as still exists in old Catholic countries. When the villagers arrived at the church they found it closed, and no lights. "It is a shame and a sin," they cried, "for the priest to sit drinking in his house; no doubt he has forgotten the service altogether." So after waiting till near dawn they went to the parsonage to see what was the matter; and if their suppositions proved true, to upbraid the priest with his conduct. When they arrived at the house they saw but one faint light glimmering through the window, and on the floor lay dead the priest and those who were with him in the house, all save one old woman, and she still breathed. "A bad guest," she gasped, "has Eskil Juel sent to us this Christmas-eve. All here are dead, and I am dying fast." Then the man ran back, and told his fellow-villagers what a bad Christmas was in store for them. When day dawned a great ship was seen stranded on the sand-banks; all on board were lying dead, their faces black, the stranger alone had reached the shore. None however sickened that day; but at night the pest began, and spread in a few days over all the land: it lasted for one year and some months, destroying more than one-third of the population of Jutland. It was a terrible year that of 1349— no sun, but a heavy mist over all the earth. At last, towards the second spring, the mist dispersed, the sky again appeared blue, and the pestilence was stayed.

But the villages of the centre of the land, that long expanse of mose now desolate, called the Ale Mose, suffered the most; the few inhabitants who escaped the scourge emigrated to the sea-coast, and from that time since the country has been uninhabited. So the prophecy of the wizard came true.

We now turn off at the village of Ulvborg—Wolf Castle—rather an ominous appellation in these dreary parts of Jutland; but wolves no more exist here than in our own provinces of England. Towards the middle of the last century they were common enough; they tore the cattle, and did much damage. The last of the race was killed, in the year 1811, somewhere by Estvadsgaard in a forest near Skive. Wild boars too are quite extinct. In 1694 Christian V. is said to have killed sixteen in one day's chace.

Vosborg now appears in the distance, and a crossroad over the mose leads us towards it. It stands alone, isolated, surrounded by trees. The North Sea roars in the distance; all is wild and mysterious. It seems as though we are about to invade the hold of some robber-chieftain, not to visit the demesne of a peaceable member of the Danish Parliament. We arrive, drive through an ancient gateway into the second court, whiz again round a corner into a third, are landed on the stone steps, where the dame châtelaine stands, with her youthful daughters, ready to receive us on our arrival.

CHAPTER XLIII.

Legend of the English prince and his bed of gold — The luck of Vosborg manor — Little Peter the cow-driver — The industrious Nisses — Long Margaret and her eight murders — Private tutor of Prince George of Denmark — Story of Havelock the Dane — Customs on Christmas-eve — The corporal and his little child.

VOSBORG.

July 17th.—IT is a queer old place, Vosborg, with its triple range of vallums and its moats, the first of which, on the western side, quite out-tops the house; in former days a protection against marauding bands; in the present more peaceful times, against the equally troublesome west wind. The château, like most of these ancient manors, is of different periods: the oldest wing dates from some five hundred years, and here, too, we are again en pays de connaissance, for within these walls was born Niels Bugge, leader of the ever-revolting Jutland nobility against Valdemar Atterdag. He never enjoyed the rites of Christian burial; but from the drops of gore which fell trickling from his body upon the sands at Middelfart sprang the plants of the red cabbage, which alone are there found growing on the shore, and still mark the spot of his assassination.

It was in Niels Bugge's time that near Vosborg took place the well-known shipwreck of the English prince, still sung, set to music, one of the most popular ballads among the peasantry of this country. Who he was I cannot ascertain; but he travelled like a "real prince:" not swung up, like Prince Alfred, in a vulgar hammock, but with his "real bed of gold." He came to grief on the lands of Ridder Frost, a very bad man, who not only plundered him of his goods and chattels, golden bed included, but allowed him even to be sacked and insulted by his "kokkedreng," cook's boy.

"Oh!" exclaims the unlucky prince, blubbering like a schoolboy—

> "Oh! had I ne'er fallen in Frost's hands,
> But come to shore on Bugge's lands,
> Sir Niels would have sent me both knight and svend,*
> Now robs me Sir Eskil's kokkedreng."

When this news comes to the ears of Sir Niels Bugge, he despatches to his assistance his two sons, and recovers among other things the celebrated golden bed from the hands of the robber Frost; invites the prince to his castle of Hald, gives him a fresh outfit, and sends him back to England loaded with honours. The English prince was not of an ungrateful disposition, for he leaves his golden bed behind him. The altarpiece of the church of Holstebro is carved from the oak of the vessel in which he was wrecked, the head of his golden bed is preserved in the church of Sal, while the foot forms the altar-table of that of Stadil—where you may see them both if you have any curiosity. This old château of Vosborg, like most of the Jutland manors, has its mystic number on which its fate depends. Vosborg always passes away in marriage or by sale in the third generation. From the Bugges it passed to the Vendel Bos;† on to the Podebusk, or Putbus,

---

* Retainers.

† An early illustration: Bo Henderson, of the household troops of Knud the Holy, stood firm to the fortunes of King Niels, and from a

some of Lille Tove's German relations who came over to look after the loaves and fishes of Denmark.* Then passing over the Juels, Langes, and the Winds—one of whom was a celebrated mineralogist, and first discovered the silver-mines of Kongsborg; he lies buried in Tronyem Cathedral—we come to Svanevedel, the last of whom sold his soul to the devil; then to the Leths, from whom it passed to the grandfather of the present proprietor. We are now in the third generation, a blooming family of six daughters enliven this mysterious mansion, but no son—no heir. Vosborg will again fall into the possession of some other name by marriage. The story of the Tang family is too interesting to be passed over in silence. I have it from the mouth of the proprietor himself, who is justly proud of the industry and talents of his forefathers.

It was in the early part of the eighteenth century a family of Vendel peasants emigrated to these parts, and settled on the lands of the domain of Vosborg.

Hemet Leth was at that time lord of the manor, a bad extravagant man, always in want of money, and oppressive over those who depended on him. Tang was the only man who dared to remonstrate with him on his injustice, and who possessed any influence over his mind. Vosborg is not far removed from the Nissum Fiorde; the sea-water at the spring-tides runs up to the outer vallum, inundating the intervening meadows with its flow.

Vendel peasant became ennobled, and ranked among the most illustrious of the land.

* One of the family, Wenceslaus, really was rightful Duke of Rugen, but unjustly disinherited; he and his family were prayed for in the churches of their native isle for generations after the usurper had gained the ducal power.

It was the custom each succeeding spring for the peasants of the domain to drive up their cows and turn them loose into the meadows, to eat off the salt grass—a good alterative it was considered for the cattle—the fields themselves benefiting by the operation. One morning, young Peter Tang, a boy of eleven years of age, while driving his beasts to grass, meets by the bridge of Vosborg an old woman seated on a waggon laden with apples.*

Little Peter as he passes by holds up his hands, childlike, and begs an apple from the old woman, who refused, crying out, "You little miscreant! you ask an apple from me, a poor woman, when in your own hand you hold a golden one of your own!" † Later in life these words of the old woman often crossed his mind, and encouraged him in his industry and perseverance. Peter is now eighteen years of age. The Jutlanders were less slaves to their landowners than the peasants of Zealand; still they were subject to the feudal conscription, from which, with the good will of the lord, they could purchase freedom by the payment of fifty dollars. So old Tang goes up to the manor with a bag containing the necessary sum, and begs to purchase the freedom of his boy.

"No, no," replies the lord of the castle, "your son is a fine clever lad, and in these days good soldiers are wanted. I can't let him off."

The peasant saw well enough that it was something else his lord wanted, so determined to know his terms.

---

* Apples were not then cultivated in this part of Jutland; so the Holsteiners and people from the East sent up their refuse to sell to the peasantry, who were glad to purchase them in exchange for eels.

† People's good fortune was always foretold—afterwards.

"Well then, give me that little meadow of yours, and I will sign the freedom of your boy."

Old Tang's heart waxed heavy, for he had himself reclaimed this meadow from the waters; but though the loss was great to him, he loved his child better: a paper is drawn out, signed and sealed; young Peter is free, and sent to a professor to complete his education, for his father determined to apprentice him to a merchant at Ringkjöbing.

At the age of twenty-five appears the name of Peter Tang as one of the richest merchants of the city of his adoption. High in character, he married the fair daughter of the burgomaster, Marien Kier. His fortune still continues augmenting until the year 1778, when Christian Leth, the son of his old lord, dies childless, and the manor of Vosborg is for sale; but no one will buy it, the times are hard, and the season bad. Peter one day, after his store is closed, walks down, stick in hand, to the château.

"If," says he to himself, "the three old limes at the entrance of the second court are still standing, I will then purchase the château; if they are no longer there, I give up the idea." The limes stood erect, fragrant in full blossom, as they now are; and on the following Monday Peter Tang, the boy who twenty years before drove his cows over the bridge to the salt meadow, became Lord of Vosborg. But the aged mother of the last proprietor, widow of his old oppressor, still dwelt therein; so Peter, who bore no malice, visits her, and consults her what to do.

"Let me," she replies, "die where I have always lived; but first make the roof water-tight, for I cannot sleep for the rain. You shall give me a home, for I am penniless; but I will aid you with my counsels and experience; and while you are absent about your commercial affairs will manage the estate for you."

Peter consented, so the noble lady and the peasant worked together hand in hand, and Vosborg was put into repair—new farm-buildings built—you may see them now. Old peasant Tang was still alive; and Peter's first act was to return the meadow exacted to procure his freedom; but his father refused to accept it. "Keep it," he said, "you deserve it." The poverty of the peasantry at that season was fearful: succeeding years of bad harvests had produced a famine over all Europe—those terrible years which preceded the first outburst of the French revolution. Peter receives no money from his peasants; he sends ships to Dantzic and Amsterdam to procure corn to keep them from starving. The second year is worse than the first, and Peter's heart fails him—the purchase of Vosborg will prove his ruin. He now brings over potatoes for their subsistence, but they do not much like them. Matters come to the worst—at last improve, and all prospers.

Some years later, old Peter now, but hearty still, walked, as usual, stick in hand, over from Ringkjøbing on the Saturday, after closing time, to stay till Monday at Vosborg. While standing on a hill he observes a narrow strip of dark-green foliage among the meadows; he turns to observe it; finds it to be a ridge of potatoes, preserved by an old woman, and planted since the time of famine. From this ridge dates the introduction of the potato-plant into the west provinces of Jutland. At the death of their father the five brothers and two sisters found themselves possessors of eight noble châteaux and herregaards which together united amount to more than a Grefskab, or county. Peter Tang, the rich merchant of Ringkjøbing, was grandfather to Professor Tang, the present proprietor of the manor.

To imagine for one moment that an ancient habitation like Vosborg could be without its ghosts and its traditions in a country like Jutland would be monstrous.

First on the list come the Nisses, who dwell in one of the small bridges hard by; they are good little fellows, and, beyond teazing and tormenting the milkmaids, never do any harm to anybody. It was the custom (and is sometimes now) at the three great festivals of the year, Christmas, Easter, and St. John's day, to place some pots of porridge outside the doors ready for their supper. When the old bridge was pulled down, several of these little earthen vessels were dug up among the foundations: they were quite empty— no remains—leaving people to imagine the little fellows had not only eaten their suppers, but had also enjoyed them.

These sprites are grateful, too, and never forget a kindness; for a great many years ago there came a heavy fall of snow; it lay so thick upon the ground, high as the moat which surrounded the château, no one could leave the house. The cattle were all safely housed in the farm-buildings, with the exception of six calves, who were lodged in a shed in a field some way off. After a fortnight's imprisonment the thaw came, and the farm-labourers set forth to remove, as they imagined, the frozen remains of the starved animals. Great was their surprise to find the little creatures not only alive, but grown fat and flourishing, their stalls clean and well swept. The Nisses had taken care of them during the fortnight the snow lay upon the ground. But then, as the boers remarked, no wonder the Nisses looked after them, for the first time the calves had left the stables the axe had been laid across the threshold, and that always brings good luck.

The stories about the Nisses resemble those of the German tales. They answer to our brownies—are particular about where they take up their abode, and with whom—never with anybody less than a farmer. The cottagers and poorer people have only a familiar spirit; and when a woman churns more butter than her neighbours, when her hens lay more eggs, it is set down to her "familiar." Query, if this familiar might not be explained by the two words *industry* and *order?* As for a Niss, he generally takes up his abode in the loft or under the bridge which spans the moat; is a good friend to the household, but quarrels everlastingly with the watch-dog. If affronted he changes his abode, and going out after twilight accosts the passers-by—" Will you take a little boy into your service, who asks no wages; nothing but a pot of porridge on New-Year's Eve?"

Then, too, there is the White Lady, who marches about the house, with her Paternoster in hand—no vice in her, she is only pale and sad; but Long Margaret, she's the person; the very idea of her will make your blood run cold. It was in the year 1770, or thereabouts, that Long Margaret, or, as the peasants called her, "The Egyptian," wandered about the moors and heaths in the neighbourhood of Vosberg; she told fortunes; was looked upon as a witch, appearing at all times when least expected; no one liked her, though she was supposed to be quite harmless.

She was well known to the surrounding neighbourhood, at that time more thickly populated than now, for many of the ancient herregaards have since disappeared. Towards the fall of the year '69 rumours became rife of murders committed; of young girls being found dead on the road-side, their throats cut, and their hearts torn out. The greatest consternation prevailed: the authorities and the police were on the alert; but as the bodies were unrifled of the gold and silver ornaments usually worn by the peasant girls, no clue could be given to the perpetrators of the deeds. No one ever suspected Long Margaret.

Seven of these murders had been already committed, when one day a pedlar girl, carrying her wares on her back, in passing down one of those very "dells" we drove through on our way to Hobrø, was suddenly seized by the long bony arms of the old Egyptian woman, cast on the ground, and an unsheathed knife presented to her throat. The girl screamed and struggled with her antagonist. "Don't struggle so, little girl," remonstrates the old crone: "one little prick and all is over!" The poor child was gradually growing faint, when two labourers driving their cattle along the valley, attracted by her cries, came to her assistance. Long Margaret escaped; but was later taken prisoner. "Oh!" she exclaimed to her captors, "had I only but devoured my ninth heart I should have been far away beyond your reach!"

On being questioned by her judges she coolly informed them that she meant no harm; but, finding herself growing old and infirm, she was anxious to transform herself into a night raven, and fly; that, according to the laws of necromancy, to procure such a boon she must first devour "nine raw bleeding hearts," taken hot from as many maiden breasts—symbolical of the nine hearts of Denmark, representing the nine syssels or counties of Jutland. She had already devoured her seventh, when the unlucky cries of the pedlar girl brought from the herdsmen the assistance which ended in her capture and condemnation. Long Margaret was not, however, doomed to the stake, as such a witch should have been—none were ever burnt in Jutland after the end of the seventeenth century—she merely lost her head like common mortals; and they neglected to bury her remains in a moor, with a stake in her inside, as they ought to have done; for she is said occasionally to make her appearance, and walk in the long passages of the wing of the château where she was imprisoned at Vosborg.

Second-sight is as common in Jutland as in the Highlands of Scotland, particularly as regards "the foretelling of fire." Bad luck to the owner of a mill whose conflagration is foretold by a "wise woman;" it invariably comes to pass.

What excellent portraits you meet with in every private house in Denmark, and more so in Jutland than elsewhere, setting aside Juel, who really, by the number one comes across, must have painted with both hands at once! This may, however, be easily accounted for by the number of pupils who studied in the atelier of every great Dutch master. Finding at first little or no employment in their own land, they were glad to make their "tour du monde," as the artisans do that of

Europe. It is difficult to say where they did not extend their travels to, for in the Ethnological Museum at Copenhagen exist several paintings of South Sea Islanders, executed by a pupil of Rembrandt.

These young artists found good occupation for their brushes in the never-ending epitaphia of the churches, as well as in the family portraits in the old manors, and private houses of the provincial cities of Jutland. There are few of the better portrait-painters who have not worked for the space of some years in Denmark—Mieris, Denner, Schalken—unluckily the names of the artists have seldom been preserved.

At Vosborg we have many portraits, chiefly of pastors and their wives, in starched ruffs and most military moustaches: among them one by Carl van Mander, of Christian Lodberg, Bishop of Ribe, and private tutor to our own Prince Consort, George of Denmark.

Many of these early Protestant worthies led a queer life of it, giving, like many of their Romanist predecessors, la farine (of their existence) au diable et le son au bon Dieu. Christian, son of a peasant in the province of Thy, was sent to school, and showed great talents early in life. His studies completed, he set out on his travels alone, and for want of cash served in the Spanish army at Naples, in the wars which succeeded the insurrection of Masaniello. He later fought under the Great Condé, and on his return to his native country took orders. By means of powerful interest he became appointed tutor to Prince George, whom he declares to have been most amiable, but he never would or could learn anything. He accompanied the prince on his travels through the various courts of Europe for the space of four years, during which time he kept a most minute journal of all they saw, and the events which took place at the different courts they visited. When he departed for England poor "Est-il-possible," who had no memory, begged of his tutor the loan of the manuscript, "For," said he, "I shall never know what to talk to the foreign ambassadors about when they ask for audiences, or recollect who to inquire after, unless I am able to refresh my memory."

So the worthy tutor, now bishop, lent his journal to his dull-witted pupil, and never got it back again; a fact to be regretted, as a four years' tour through Europe, with all the minute details of visits to foreign courts in the seventeenth century, would now be of immense interest. Probably it is hidden away somewhere among the royal archives.

A very strict bishop, too, this vieux militaire became. He in his charge writes strict injunctions to his priests not to appear when "travelling" in secular clothes (which might be read with advantage by some of our own parsons one meets in shooting jackets on the Continent)—not to have intercourse with those who call themselves "diviners"—profess to discover stolen goods—never to bless "necromancers," recalling to their memory how a certain priest, "Niels in Henne," who was accused of causing ships to be wrecked for his own advantage, had been burnt as a wizard, to the great scandal of the clergy, not many years since.*

---

* Not only were the parsons accused, and suffered from accusations of witchcraft, but ladies of high rank lost their heads. Christian IV. hated witchcraft from his heart's core. In 1608 he caused to be beheaded Mrs. Bridget Rosenkrantz; and again, in 1621, in writing about the indictment of another suspected lady, he says, "Concerning this young lady, she must be strictly examined, and in no way spared; when you can get no more out of her, cut off her head." She

This warrior Bishop of Ribe was a maternal ancestor of the proprietor of Vosborg. His wife is really too ugly to look at—painted by the same master. The clergy, however, of later date seem to have evinced better taste in the choice of their help-meets.

The farm of Vosborg is the most considerable in all Jutland. We are more in the grazing line here—beeves for the English market—but somehow or other, when in the library, poring among the old tomes, I forgot all about the farm.

We were talking over the English names, of which so many are to be met with in Denmark, when a lady, who devotes herself to teaching in the poor schools of Copenhagen, told us of the intense interest taken by the school children during the Indian war in the fortunes of Sir Henry Havelock, our British general.

The morning the news of his death arrived she found the whole of her school dissolved in tears, weeping their very hearts out, for they looked upon him as their own countryman—the very Havelock the Dane of the popular ballad—the lapse of nine or ten centuries being nothing to an infant mind. Sir Henry was more grieved over by the children of Denmark from this early nursery association than by those of the British Empire. The story of Havelock* is by the earliest

---

was condemned to be executed, 9th January, 1623, and the proceeds of a legacy of 500 thalers of "decollatæ virginis" is still enjoyed by the university of Copenhagen.

Peter Bognførre, curate of Bjergby in Vendsyssel, was accused of having bewitched the parish priest of Asdal, who was suddenly seized with a fit of stammering whenever he entered the pulpit. He was later summoned before King Christian, condemned to death, and burnt at the stake.

* THE STORY OF HAVELOCK THE DANE.

Ethelwald, King of England, had an only daughter, whom, at his death, he confided to the care of Godrich Earl of Cornwall. The

French poet known, Geoffroi Ganier, 1147, and styled Le Lai d'Avalok.

Labour in this country is scarce, and every summer crowds of the German peasants come over like our

---

Princess Guldborg was very beautiful, and when she attained the age of twenty, the time when she was to succeed to the kingdom of her father, the false earl determined on making his own son king.

At the same period the King of Denmark died under similar circumstances, and bequeathed his children, Prince Havelock and his two sisters, to the protection of Godard, who, as the story says, "was the greatest scoundrel ever born besides the traitor Judas." He put the children for three years in prison, where they suffered from cold and hunger; at last he put the daughters to death, and Havelock would have shared their fate had he not on his knees renounced his right to the crown of Denmark. But Godard soon repents his clemency, and gives him to his servant Grim to drown. He carries Havelock home to his hut tied up in a sack, to be thrown at night into the sea; but a wonderful light over the boy alarms Grim and his wife; they discover he is the son of their king, and determine to save him. Grim flies from Denmark with his family and Havelock: the wind carries the vessel to England, where Grim lands at the entrance of the Humber, " in Lindesey, at the north side." Here he builds a house and lives by fishing. The place was called Grimsby, and it is a curious fact that the town of Grimsby, founded by Grim, enjoyed in early days exemption from payment of the Sound-duties at Elsinore. Havelock assists Grim in his work, and in a year of scarcity goes to Lincoln, where he is employed by Earl Godrich's cook.

When the earl sees Havelock he determines to marry him to the Princess Guldborg, and thus fulfil the promise he had given her father, to get for her the strongest and handsomest man in England. Fearing treachery from Earl Godrich, Havelock and his bride leave Lincoln for Grimsby. Grim was dead, but his five children are well off, and receive them kindly. Guldborg is told of the royal birth of Havelock (in a dream), and "when from joy she awakes her husband with a kiss," he tells her a singular dream he had had himself, which Guldborg explains as foretelling he should be king. Havelock, accompanied by Grim's sons, goes to Denmark, where he is recognised by Ubbe, who declares in his favour. Godard is taken and condemned, and Havelock proclaimed King of Denmark. He returns to England, conquers Earl Godrich in a battle at Grimsby, and is proclaimed King of England. King Havelock rewards those who had done him service: Grim's daughter, Gunhild, he marries to the Earl of Chester; the cook, his old master, he creates Earl of Cornwall; and Ubbe becomes Stadtholder of Denmark, &c. &c.

Irish haymakers to aid in the gathering in of the harvest. The peasants here have a pretty tradition: "That as the clock strikes twelve on Christmas-eve the cattle all rise together, and stand straight upright in their stalls." On that day, too, the cows in the stables, as well as the horses, are fed with the best of everything—hay, corn, and beans; and all is made tidy before four o'clock. As for the watch-dog, he fares better than anybody. The housewife goes into the courtyard, removes his chain, and, bringing him to the house, first cuts off from the long brown loaf a slice of bread, which she gives to him, saying, "Here's for my huusbond, and here's for me;" and next she cuts off one for each of the children—"Here's for Mette, and here's for Hans,"—and then chops one into three pieces for the "trillinge,"* of which there is sure to be a set in the cradle. When he has finished these slices she gives him his rightful supper as well, adding, "Now, good dog, you shall run loose this night, for in a season when there is peace and good will upon earth you will surely harm no one." Nowhere is this good old custom of keeping Christmas kept up so pleasantly as in Jutland, where even the little birds are not forgotten, for a small wheat-sheaf is laid in the garden over-night on Christmas-eve, that they may also eat, be full, and rejoice.

We walked where Skamm church once stood—all is a desert—nothing will now grow there—for it was once a convent.

No one in Jutland loved to remove the first stone of

---

* I greatly approve of the justice of the Jutland "huustru" in dividing the portion of the "trillinge." If children come in a lump they should be made to count as one in the division of the property.

a sacred building, for he who did so was accursed: when once the mischief was done, you might continue the work, and no harm come to you. Now, the materials of Skamm church and cloister were most tempting to the lords of Norre Vosborg; but no one would risk his soul's weal, and remove the first stone of the ruined chapel. At last a young man, who had served in foreign parts, excited by liquor, went out in the dead of night, brought in a huge stone, and cast it in the court of Vosborg. When sober he was seized with terror and remorse: and hanged himself the same night. No suicide can enjoy the rites of Christian burial; so his corpse was fastened across the backs of two cows, who fled towards the mose, where they sank in, and were all immersed together; and the holes are there still.

Now, however, the lords of the manor pulled down the chapel with safety, but no one dared touch the altar-stone; for there sat a huge black dog, and howled piteously at all who approached; so the altar-stone lay for many a year, till the war against the Swedes in the seventeenth century, when troops were quartered in the castle. One evening as they sat before the fire in the great hall, a private related to them this story; and a corporal who was there, who feared neither God nor man, declared the devil might have him if he did not bring home that altar-stone; and, what's more, he would take his little daughter with him. The child trembled, and cried, "Oh, father, leave me!" but he dragged her on; and when he saw the dog on the stone he cried out, "Come forth, you black devil!" Then the dog, growing greater and greater, seized the man with his teeth and between his paws, and the corporal cried, "Child, pray for me, and I will give you a new gown." So the little girl commenced the Lord's Prayer, the only one she knew—it was not her father who had taught her that, but the scullion, a poor peasant girl, of the castle. As she prayed fervently the dog grew less and less, and at last sunk down into the stone and disappeared. From that day the man turned over a new leaf, became pious and well conducted; the little girl got her new gown; as for the altar-stone, it remains there now, and you may still see it, as we did, untouched.

CHAPTER XLIV.

The bells of Thim — Gyldenstierne of Thimgaard — Poorhouse of Ringkjøbing — Old rat of Hee — Threshing to the sound of music.

―――◆―――

HEE.

July 18*th*.—WE quitted our kind entertainer this morning at ten. The Professor was already off early to an agricultural meeting on the road; and after much leave-taking and thanks for hospitality, we started, as fast as our host's four horses could carry us, on our road; first stopping at the kro at Hee, where we found not only Mr. Tang, but our old acquaintance Count Schulin, the amtman, all busily engaged discussing some new improvement in the fabrication of butter—very unnecessary, for, talk for ever, they will never make it better than they do in Jutland.

They have an abominable custom in this country, that of selling the old gravestones from the churchyards, when the families are extinct: it is downright sacrilege, and is the only case in which the love of "bon marché" has got the better of the hereditary superstition of the natives. Here the three steps of the kro are formed of three separate "In piam memoriams," — cherubim, hourglasses, and floriated crosses, trodden under foot. The same custom exists at Thisted. In the town street at Holstrebro a pile of ten were lying in a corner of the church cemetery, some really of considerable beauty, waiting to be purchased. It is a villanous practice, and a disgrace that the Government should allow it.*

We turned in to look at the granite round-arch church of Hee, built by Bishop Hay (as his name was then spelt) in the twelfth century—a granite model of the cathedral church of Ribe: when the parish of Ro was suppressed they carried the church of Noe and built it up against Hee. Later we pass on our road that of Thim, celebrated for its stolen bell, the finest toned in all Jutland.

THIM.

It was in some war with the Swedes that Peter Gyldenstierne, struck by the tone of these bells, determined to obtain them by some way or another. So he consulted all the villagers how to get them down without injury to the church-tower. No one could, or rather no one would, assist him, till a countryman presented himself before him, saying, "Provide for my wife and children, and I will show you how to manage the matter." Peter consents; the peasant causes two lofty hillocks of sand to be erected, and then cutting the chains lets the bells fall down gently, one after the other. The plan succeeded, and the man claims his reward. "Yes," answers Gyldenstierne, "I will perform my promise and provide handsomely for your wife and children; but for yourself, a traitor to your country, you shall take the place of the bells." So he strung him up to the church-tower. One bell arrived in Jutland safe, and was hung up in the tower of Thim church; but the second came to grief, and was ship-

* I understand a law is about to be passed forbidding this custom.

wrecked off the coast, by the Nissum Fiorde. It fell, however, tongue uppermost, and lies imbedded in the sand; when the tide is low on a summer's eve, its music may still be heard by the fishermen who ply their crafts on the water; such music, so beautiful, they say the like was never heard. As for the other bell, her tones are sad and melancholy: no wonder— she wants to come down to her sister.

Thimgaard was a splendid castle, but has lately disappeared, and is now in the hands of peasants. King Frederic II. here often visited rich Peter Gyldenstierne, who dearly loved all pomp and state. The twelve stones on which his twelve retainers, in gorgeous liveries, stood bowing to the ground each time he quitted his house, still stand in their ancient places.

Peter Gyldenstierne was grandson to the cousin of Torben Oxe, who caused poor Dyveke's stone to be removed from the church of Elsinore, and placed at the entrance of his manor of Thimgaard, to be "spat upon" by each peasant as he went by the gate. When Thim manor passed into other hands the stone was sent to Copenhagen, and stupidly placed among the Runic stones of the Round Tower.

RINGKJØBING.

We leave the Nissum Fiorde, about to be drained on the Haarlem principle by English capital, under the direction of two engineers. Without wishing to prophesy evil, I pity the shareholders and their money, dependent on the caprice of the North Sea and west wind on this most incomprehensible coast of Jutland. We have a village of Hammet not far off; and now we approach Ringkjøbing, near which, an island in the fiorde, lies the green Holmsland, with its two white churches, the most fertile meadow-land in all the surrounding country.

Very small this town appears as we drive on, the capital of a county, too. We reach the square. The hotel stands before us, an old carved timber house, its windows shaded by a row of ancient clipped elms. "Well," exclaims one of the family, "here is a picturesque old inn, the first we have yet come too: do look too at the iron-work of the bell—a rose, and that wreath of leaves and border—how charming!" only it does not ring.

Tuesday, July 19*th.*—We are quite glad of a rest; and there is nothing in the world so charming as a hostel of the olden time, externally. As for the interior, I am not quite so sure of the fact: scrub those old worm-eaten boards for ever they will never look clean; and as for the beams, only walk across the room and the dust pours down from the ceiling—better in water-colours than in reality.

There is not much to see in Ringkjøbing—indeed nothing at all. Its palmy days are over. The opening of the Agger Canal destroyed its commerce, at one time (in the days of Peter Tang) considerable, with Holland and other countries; but we were glad of a couple of days' rest, and passed them very pleasantly in the society of our friends Count and Countess Schulin and their charming family.

Having nothing particular to do, I accompanied the Préfet to the town-house, and visited the new prison—airy, clean, and ventilated to perfection, quite a pleasure to be incarcerated therein—and then visited the city "fattighuus," which you must not confuse with an "hospital or almshouse;" it answers to our "union," and is the property of the commune, who, as in England, are compelled to support their own poor.

It consists of a long one-storied building, divided into good, airy, well-sized rooms, two beds in each. The married people are not separated; in one chamber lay an aged couple, whose united ages must have amounted to well nigh two centuries, bedridden both, on a sea of feather-beds, of exquisite cleanliness, gradually burning out the remaining oil of their expiring lamps together, side by side, the younger members of the community attending to their wants and comforts; but when their agony draws nigh they remove from under their heads the "feather" pillow, otherwise their death would be hard and their struggles long. Then there was a work-room, where aged women were busy spinning flax and carding wool; and the kitchen in which they dine together—in the morning, coffee and bread and butter; for dinner, a soup and one dish of meat; of an evening, tea and smør brod. A range of hams hung round the ceiling beams. The workhouse is not popular, and no one comes in unless quite obliged. The inhabitants are allowed each Sunday four hours' leave of absence, and generally, I am sorry to say—so the superintendent told me—return intoxicated, not with joy, but with liquor. And now, says the matron (opening a door), here is the room in which we lay them out when dead; see the trestles all ready—how very nice!—everything so convenient.

I dare say you imagine we were eaten up with rats at our old hotel. You are quite mistaken—not such a thing to be met with in the country between Skjern-aa and Stor-aa, if you hunt for ever; and I'll tell you how it occurred, for less than a century ago the whole land was overrun, and Ringkjøbing most of all.

There arrived one day in the port a vessel from Finmark in Norway. The captain came on shore, and confided to the care of a merchant a sack of clothes, to be left till called for in his warehouse.

On returning after an absence of some days, he finds his goods nearly destroyed by the rats. The merchant declares it is not his fault—we are overrun with them. "Would you like to get rid of them?" inquires the stranger. "Indeed it would be a blessing," answers the merchant. So the stranger takes a book from his pocket, and begins to read aloud. From his tone you might have imagined it to be the 'Church Service,' only he commenced at the wrong end and read backwards. No sooner had he begun than all the rats in the town, all the rats from the farms, water and land rats, come running as hard as they can go, helter skelter, tumbling into the fiorde and drowning themselves. All the world stood amazed; at last they arrive more slowly; and now at the end comes an aged rat, so old, so rheumatic he can hardly crawl. "Are you the last?" inquires the wizard, for such he must have been. "Last but one," he replied: "no one remains but my father's brother, the old rat of Hee, and he'll be here soon." And come he did—an old rat, white as snow: dragging himself to the water-side, he plunged into the fiorde, the last of his race, since which time none have ever been met with in this part of the Amt of Ringkjøbing.

This evening, after dining with our friends, we walked out into the fields near their house, to witness the process of threshing the rape in the open air to the sound of music. A small threshing-floor, with eight men hard at work beating with all their might and main; behind, a pile, mountain-high, of the refuse straw, or whatever they call it. A cart drawn by one horse, mounted by a bare-legged urchin, brings up the material, which is tumbled over on to the floor; then, as it falls, the fiddle strikes up a slow melody of marked time, not unlike the well-known air of 'Roy's Wife'—bang, bang, go the flails in correct continued measure. Then when the heap is battered down he suddenly changes to a more cheerful strain, strikes up a Scotch reel, or something very like one. Bang, bang, go the flails in a crescendo movement, the threshers bursting out into a loud chorus every now and then, shouting out like the dancers of the Highland fling. This music relieves the weight of their labour—the labourers seem to enjoy it, and work away con amore.

The harvest-home was to have taken place some two days later, at which period there is much dancing and "storr gambell," as the old ballads express it, which may easily be translated by the most ignorant of Scandinavian language as "great gambols."

The peasants dance a sort of reels interspersed with the most intricate figures. According to the old custom, one of the party sings the couplet of a ballad, something like "Liden Kirsten," or "Dronning Dagmar lies sick in Ribe,"—most deadly lively; the rest of the party join in chorus and then dance, after the manner of Brittany.

July 20*th*.—We commence by a country cultivated in stripes—potatoes, corn, and buckwheat—followed up by a long expanse of heath; pass to the right Deiberg, where the gipsy tribe possess their own peculiar forms; red kro in succession to red kro, till we arrive at a network of running streams near the village of Edgvad by Tarm-kjær, in one of which stumbled the horse of King John. He broke his leg, and was carried in a litter to Holstrebro; from thence he was removed to Aalborg, where he died. A very dull road on to Varde, a small town of no consequence. Yet it had once its own event, for here in 1534 was captured by surprise Skipper Hermann, boon companion to Skipper Clemens, by John Rantzau, and the revolution extinguished in the southern part of Jutland more successfully than it was in the northern counties. But we have two miles further over the bank to Strandby, where we embark for the island of Fanø. Plenty of partridges here. We meet a yoke of oxen dressed out in straw collars, with star-like points, like a Brahmin idol. We reach the ferry—boat arrives after an hour's delay—are carried out to sea in a boer's cart, and then embarked; the luggage arranged, our cart has to unload the boat, filled with fresh-dried stock-fish, the produce of the island: haddock, cod, and skate, all neatly done up into packets. One hundred and five are counted out; then another carriage arrives: we embark some peasant women, in their quaint costume; the men tuck up their breeches and wade out to save their skillings—just a little too deep—the tide is rising, so they scramble in wet and uncomfortable. In half an hour we disembark at Fanø.

CHAPTER XLV.

Island of Fanø — Voluminous petticoats and black masks of the peasant women — Their Oriental character and Dutch cleanliness — Queen Thyre wrecked off the Isle of Man — Amber-gathering.

ISLAND OF FANØ.

July 21*st*.—MAY be you have never heard of Fanø: it lies situated nearly opposite to the little seaport town of Hjerting, from whose harbour in summer season runs a beeve-bearing steamer to the coast of England, with supplies for that most voracious of gastronomic whirlpools, the London market. Fanø is a long narrow piece of land, not unlike a high-heeled bottine in shape, delicately pointing its toe under the direction of some fashionable maître de ballet.

Of late years it has less the resemblance, or rather is the ghost, of a bathing establishment, frequented by quiet humdrum people, seekers of health, not pleasure, who lodge in the two small hotels of the place. Disembarked at a certain Jørgensen's, where we found clean comfortable quarters and good food: you might have eaten your dinner off the floor, had it not been for the sand. It is quite refreshing to again meet with the Dutch cleanliness we had quite left behind on quitting the Liimfiorde, making always an exception for Varde.

Fanø is one of the few places which sticks to its ancient habits and costumes, and has remained stationary for the last thousand years. The costume of the women is highly curious. We are now in the land of petticoats—not crinolines, but good, substantial, coloured woollen petticoats—of which the fair inhabitants, and very fair they are, wear an indefinite number, from seven upwards, according to the solemnity of the occasion. They tell of a bride who appeared at the altar almost fainting under the weight of her thirteen—but she was "somebody"—such a wedding, the old people said, had not been seen for many a day. Thirteen petticoats reminded them of the times of their grandmothers when they were young.

As we crossed over last night in the ferry-boat a peasant girl stood leaning over the cargo talking away to the watermen, her back turned towards me; so I inspected her "bearings." Her outermost garment was of green woollen, bound round with black velvet gathered in flat plaits round the waist; then came a blue, afterwards a red, which she should have worn outside, for it looked very smart. On arriving at the red she moved, so I had to cease my researches, but commenced again later. Well, the red was followed up by a brown, then came a yellow, then a second blue—dingy blue, quite right to wear it undermost—then came—never mind what—and lastly a pair of legs, very neat-turned ankles, clothed in purple worsted stockings, with no feet to them. She wore a black velvet jacket, ornamented with filigree buttons, and a foulard twisted round her head.

But the oddest custom of all is that of wearing a black mask, similar to those worn at the bal masqué, minus the bavolet, when working out in the fields. The men are occupied on the high seas, or fishing; on returning, they eat, drink, and sleep, never leaving their beds till they set off on a new expedition. It was the same at Skagen and at Agger. The women perform all the heavy work at home—but not at the expense of their complexions. Anything more ludicrous cannot be imagined than a troop of these black-masked creatures returning home, driving their cows from the downs. It seems to affect the ewes, too, for we met several new-born lambs white as the driven snow, with black masks exactly like their mistresses.

The children are very handsome, and the girls, at the cottage windows, prettier than anything we have come across for many a day. They have quite an Oriental type of countenance—long eyes, dark, fendu à l'amande, aquiline nose, fine and delicate mouth, a dark but brilliant complexion; even the fashion of the masks (though our grandmothers of the eighteenth century never walked or "rode" out without wearing these "loups," as they were then termed) give the impression as if they were some remnant of customs imported from an Eastern land; and what with the Varangians and early connexion with Turkey, it is not at all impossible that it may be so.

The village we are now dwelling in is that of Nordby; not desirable as a residence; it is too like Skagen, all sand to walk upon, or rather wade in. The second village at the extreme end of the island is called Sønderbo. On arriving at Nordby we were surprised to find straw laid down in every direction. Very refined, remarked one of the party, quite like Belgravia; some Fanø bride, no doubt, just brought to bed of a son and heir; when, as we proceeded on our way, the straw increased in thickness, and the wheels glided softly over it, we discovered our mistake—it was scattered on the sandy road to prevent the cart-wheels sinking into the ruts, a most admirable arrangement, and not an expensive one; it proved to be that of the sand-reed,* with which the dunes are planted, serving the double purpose of binding the sand-hills and improving the roads.

The land in the neighbourhood of this village is in good cultivation. People talk a great deal of nonsense about "sandy soil, nothing will grow in it;" everything almost seems to flourish in it if tried. The evergreen oak, the fig, the mulberry, prefer it; the buckwheat, corn, and rye thrive; and as for the potato-fields, it is a pleasure to look at them. The only manure here used in quantity is the dog-fish and other coarse fish cast upon the strand or taken in the nets of the fishers.

It was an eight miles' drive to Sønderbo, a village more Dutch-like in its character even than its sister: the houses have a peculiar, neat, trim appearance, and the gardens, each of them surrounded by a hedge of what people in England call the "tea-plant," which thrives here to perfection, and resists the fury of the wind—whose leaves, may be, furnished the beverage supplied for our breakfast this morning.

Most of the houses are decorated with figure-heads, some with very antique carvings, relics of ill-fated ships wrecked off this most inhospitable coast.

I looked in at some of the cottage doors. The interiors responded to the rest of the building—a grand display of crockery—old Delft plates—and in the centre of each rack, shining bright as gilded gold,

---

* Arundo arenaria.

one of those old repoussé plates once used for serving bridal cakes at the wedding feast, but now, my informant said, quite old-fashioned.

A tradition of Fanø relates that in days of yore Queen Thyre Danebod was wrecked off this coast, and on her arrival from England first set foot on Danish ground in the adjoining "Isle of Man," spelt just like our own island of the Irish Channel, which was once also a Danish possession.* Here on her first arrival from England, mark, was Queen Thyre wrecked, which leads us to suppose she was, as old Saxo Grammaticus declares, a daughter of King Ethelred, though the Danes now deny it—old Gorm was much too sensible to lug women about on his expedition against King Alfred. In gratitude, a "thankoffering" for her preservation, she gave sundry fields to the church of Man : fields covered with buildings, so they say, which are to this present day called Manø Hølade ; to the church of Fanø she presented a font of granite. We entered the

---

* In 1266 Magnus, son of Hakon, King of Norway, concluded a treaty with Alexander III. of Scotland, by which he yielded to him, in perpetuity, the Hebrides and the Isle of Man, with the patronage of the bishopric. The prelates of the Isle of Man had no seat in the British House of Peers, for, till the Reformation, they acknowledged as their metropolitan the Archbishop of Tronyem, and had until the turning over to Sweden of the kingdom of Norway, and may, for what I know, still have, a right to a seat in the Stor-thing of that country, though, as may be imagined, the right was seldom exercised. Endless were the negociations entered upon between the Scottish and the Danish sovereigns as regards the islands of Sodor and Man, and it was some years before the whole affair was amicably arranged by the marriage of the Princess Margaret to James III. So careful, however, were they of their rights, that a clause was entered into the marriage contract, by which the princess in case of widowhood is forbidden to marry the King of England, or any subject of that nation, that they (these islands) may never fall under the power of the English sovereign. We got them, however, after all.

church, a modern building, erected after the taste of the inhabitants; and there it stands—circular, misshapen, and rudely hewn—quite old and primitive enough to have been the gift of Queen Thyre. But Queen Thyre does not seem to have been the only person wrecked off this isle, if you may judge from the flotilla of little boats suspended to the beams of the village church. Many are very ancient, and some are as late as the years '45 and '53. The Lutheran Church does not reject, it appears, these thankofferings of the shipwrecked mariners.

The people here, as they do at Skagen and other sandy places, cultivate the melon; but the working of amber is their staple trade. Quantities of it are picked up off their coasts. Whether the laws are as arbitrary as on the shores of Pomerania, where amber is a royal monopoly, and gibbets were planted on the beach-side ready to string up the offenders who should pilfer the royal waifs, I do not know; but they work it well and with taste. We returned home to a late dinner, and start to-morrow early for Ribe.

CHAPTER XLVI.

Ribe Cathedral — The anchorite Bishop — Sacred theatricals — Ribe "ret" — Sumptuary laws — Bridal trousseau of the eighteenth century — Ragged schools of the middle ages — Death of Queen Dagmar — Queen Agnes at Ribehuus — Funeral of Marsk Stig — The robber's bride — Legend of Tovelil — A Tinghuus — The werewolf and the nightmare — The night-raven and the basilisk — Monument to the heroes of Fredericia — Farewell to Jutland.

———◆◇◆———

RIBE.

Friday, July 22nd.—We again cross our ferry. Horses ordered in advance, but not ready; the boer-cart fetches us in the water, and lands us at the kro—strax. Strax —how I abominate that word! The carriage is however there, but when that is loaded, and not before, do they harness the horses, and when the horses are at last harnessed then they make out the "time seddel." And the postilion? coming strax, gone to dress himself. Why, it's the very old man who's been loitering about with a pipe in his mouth, as composed as if he was going nowhere. We are off, a tiresome, dull, uninteresting drive of twenty English miles. Let no one ever take the west coast of Jutland, from the Liimfiorde downwards; it does not repay. We have amused ourselves well enough with visits to our various friends, and a good dose of historical associations—history mixed up with locality and legend, as it should be. Danes, wise in their own conceit, are apt to consider they do the world a service in disproving the traditions

CATHEDRAL, RIBE.

of centuries; but they find out nothing new; upset old associations, deprive their history of its romance, which, if not true, is at least, as the proverb says, "ben trovato." The weather is piping hot, and our horses, fresh from the fields and not in the best condition, are suffering in consequence. We bread them at one kro, hay and water them at a second, always keeping to our chaussée time of five miles an hour. Then the tower of Ribe Domkirke appears in sight. Another kro—more water. "There," says the old postilion, "look at that river; here we are in Jutland." On the other side Slesvig, or, as the Danes delight to call it, South Jutland. The world and his wife are now a haymaking; such forks, too, as they are!—our own Plantagenet portcullis with a handle tacked on it;—it seems to make very good hay all the same. We at last arrive at Ribe, cross the river by a wooden bridge, and, driving through her narrow quaint old streets, lodge at an hotel on the Place opposite the cathedral.

Ribe, as you all of course know, is one of the most ancient cities of Jutland; for somehow or other we are in Jutland still. She forms a little well-watered oasis in the duchy of Slesvig, what we call a peculiar in England, in the same manner as the Pope holds Benevento, in the centre of the kingdom of Naples.

The great lion is her Domkirke, without exception the finest church in Jutland. Like most of these northern edifices, its exterior—a mixture of granite, sandstone, and brickwork—is not highly attractive. After a lapse of time the colour of the brickwork pales, while the sandstone and granite darken, the original contrast is lost, and the whole becomes a smudge. The lofty square tower is imposing from its height. The interior has been lately restored, and is very interesting from the uniformity of its style, the earliest round-arch period. The cathedral consists of nave and double aisles, the outer one of a later date. Under the clerestory window runs a fine Norman arcade of triple arches, surmounted by the shark-tooth ornament. We mounted to inspect them, and found large spacious loggie, with vaulted roof. The columns which support the nave are square. Then comes the choir, to which you ascend by four steps, with lofty dome, separated from the transepts by the light carved stalls, and then by three steps more you reach the round apse, which terminates the building. Here is placed an altar with gilded cross and candelabra tripod—taste of the Empire, merging into the classic of Christian VIII.'s time under Thorvaldsen's reign. They should all be sent to the right about, being highly out of character with the building they are destined to adorn. The contrast between the dark granite and the white walls is good, but the apse spoils the whole effect of the building by its poverty and glaring whiteness. The church, however, viewed from the right of the altar, is very effective, and may rank high among the cathedrals of the north, an architecture apart from that of England, France, and Germany. The art of ancient glazing is entirely lost in Denmark, and the windows of their fine ecclesiastical as well as of their domestic buildings are entirely spoiled by the modern square panes of glass, arranged without any attention to the date of the edifice.

The cathedral church of Ribe is built on the highest ground of the city, called the Liliebierg. This eminence did not, however, preserve it from the effects of the great inundation of 200 years since, when the water stood five feet in the nave, and live fish, says a monkish calendar, were caught in the refectory of one of the monasteries. As for its antiquity—Anscarius himself is said in 850 to have built there a very small church; but the first stone edifice was founded in King Niels' time, and all authorities admit it to be the most ancient cathedral in the kingdom. Two kings sleep within its walls—Erik Emun,* brother of Knud Lavard, and King Christopher, youngest of the unlucky offspring of King Valdemar the Victorious; but their monuments, if ever they had any, have long since disappeared. An alabaster stone covers the remains of the latter, but no inscription is visible. In the chapels of the transepts are still to be seen the granite archways under which the altars once stood—chapels dedicated to the last-named sovereign and his Queen Margaret.

The sentiment of "Nolo Episcopari" does not appear to have been carried out in the Papal days of the diocese of Ribe, as it is in our modern Anglican Church. Once the canons of the cathedral could not agree in their choice of a bishop; so they addressed themselves to a poor and humble monk, Peter of Raa Ager, an anchorite, and begged him to indicate to them an honest man, and they would swear to accept his nominee. "Since ye, my very good masters, will have me, poor simple man that I am, to appoint your bishop, Peter of Raa Ager

---

* A sovereign who, not approving of collateral branches too nearly allied to the succession, put to death his own brother Harald, in revolt, it must be owned, against him, and his eleven sons—one, Olaf, escaped in woman's clothes, and became King of Norway. On the other hand, Erik revenged promptly the murder of Knud Lavard, deposed King Niels, and ended by ascending the throne in his stead. A fine battle they had for it; five bishops and sixty priests were numbered among the slain.

shall be the man. I have always heard that he who bears the cross, crosses first himself." And he became Bishop of Ribe.

The monument of the last Popish prelate, old Bishop Munk, stands imbedded in the wall of the outer arch, in all the pomp of mitre, crosier, and episcopal robes. Here reappear the three roses of the Munks, and a star of Gyldenstierne. He married a lady of that family, and embraced the Protestant faith to please King Christian (to say nothing of the convent of Tvis). Whether it be matrimony or the Reformation, never did portly ecclesiastic look so thoroughly overcome by his feelings as he does on the tombstone erected to his memory. We have also Hans Tausen, second Protestant Bishop of Ribe—first his portrait, in an ermine tippet, sour as verjuice; and then comes his epitaph, well worn by the feet of passers by, but now imbedded in the wall. It is to be hoped he did not compose it himself—"I. I. I.,"—for it is a very conceited one.

Then we have no more monuments of general interest, no new names, save those of Holt and "Ostvald," our Scottish Oswald, on an old well-worn stone. We mount the tower, a necessary evil in a flat country if you wish to know its whereabouts. Passing through a narrow carved oak doorway of Bishop Munk's day, bearing his three roses, we mount ladder upon ladder, and then through a trap-door we arrive in open air again—country flat as a pancake, green as the Emerald Isle; running streams surround the tower on three sides, the North Sea in the distance; meadow as far as eye can extend—nothing but meadow. In front towards the city stands a mound, the site of historic Ribehuus. As regards øprors, Ribe seems to have been lucky in the middle ages, less worried than most places; but she made up for her exemption by the plague of fire and water, to say nothing of the black pest. She bore, however, these matters jauntily, for in the year 1577—the year betwixt an "over-swimming," a black pest, and a conflagration—the comedy of 'Susanna and the Elders' was played with great applause by the Rector of the High School and his pupils. These sacred theatricals continued until very late in the North of Europe. In 1712 the 'Creation' was played before the Swedish king at Malmø, but the machinery got out of order, and the rose refused to blow.

Though Ribe possessed Gray Brothers and Black Brothers, she could not vie with Viborg in sanctity; so she took a peculiar line of her own, and piqued herself on her police and her justice. "Ribe Ret," as it was called, although most wholesome and effective in suppressing crime and misdemeanour, was considered so severe, it became a proverb, "that they only sent those to Ribe for justice who were ripe for hanging;" and the old saying ran—"Thank God, my son! you did not come before the justice of Ribe, cried the old woman when she saw her son on the gallows of Vaarde." In Ribe, too, was erected a gallows of stone — a gallows of aristocratic pretensions, on which no one but a "born burgher" was allowed the privilege of hanging.

Nothing could be more arbitrary than these "by-lovs" (municipal laws) of Ribe. A burgomaster was allowed to invite twenty-four couples to his wedding, with their daughters, and twelve young men to dance with the girls. Should the young ladies preponderate, so much the worse; they must sit still. Only six dishes for dinner, and so on in proportion to the rank of the family. Should they disobey this law they were to be fined one mark Danish to the king. This was a wise precaution, as it was found necessary to discourage the taste for extravagance which pervaded all classes,* nearly to as great an extent in the celebration of weddings as of funerals.†

Little wine, says an author of the 18th century, was consumed in early days; for at the celebrated marriage of Erik Ottesen, grand master of the realm, at which King Christopher and his Queen Dorothea were present, but half a cask was drunk, whereas now twenty pipes of Rhine wine were oft cleared off, without counting that of France for the common people.‡ As for the trousseaux, they would have satisfied a Parisian élégante of the second Empire. The list of that of Tycho Brahe's grandmother is a book in itself. Not only did she bring linen enough, damascened and in piece, to last a century, but all sorts of finery for her

---

* The Danish sovereigns did all in their power to repress the extravagance of the nobility. Frederic III. issued sumptuary laws to the effect they were not to wear pearls and gold on their hats and clothes, and, when they gave parties, they were not allowed to serve other than cold dishes to their guests; "warm food and delicatessen" were strictly forbidden. Christian V. dined every day off a loin of roasted veal, washed down with Rhenish wine, of which a jug was placed by the side of each person present.

† When Lars Ulfeld, brother of Corfitz, whose picture hangs at Frederiksborg, married a second time, all the family made him presents of silver plate to the amount of 5137 ounces: Hoffman, who gives this list, remarks,—"There was more profit in marrying then than there is now."

‡ When the Sagas talk of wine, they mean brandy-wine. The nobles contented themselves with the beer and hydromel of the country. "Drink as much as you will," was the hospitable saying, "for the cask has a sister." In ancient times a ton of hydromel was the fine for every day a nobleman should absent himself from the diet at Odense.

husband, among which is enumerated "a pair of gold-laced inexpressibles," with silk embroideries. But "Ribe Ret" extended even to the "barsel," a ceremony at which burgomasters had no right to interfere. A lady might invite thirty of her female friends to assist—maids or matrons—no more; once there, they were not allowed to potter in and out, disturbing the sick woman, but were compelled to stay until all was over.

The numerous pious foundations appear to have been excellent; and if good Lord Shaftesbury imagines that, although he has established ragged schools in England by his philanthropy and energy, he invented them, he is mistaken; for here in the middle ages a similar institution existed for "fattige poge," or poor homeless vagabonds, to be picked up in the street anywhere; then came the Reformation, and the poor poges got swept away in the general haul of ecclesiastical revenues. No wonder. When prelates and mitred abbots, when abbesses and nuns, rent the heavens with cries of sacrilege, who would listen to the wailings of the "fattige poge"? Still, there was much justice in King Frederic's mind, and many an aged woman now finds shelter and repose at Ribe, in the cloister attached to some suppressed convent. We to-day visited one of these establishments, and found the old people in the ancient monastic garden, seated in the summer's sun, and others, rheumatic perhaps, fearful of wind, under the splendid lime-tree in the cloister yard. The Danes may have fallen from their political grandeur, if you will, but they have fallen on a feather-bed.

We extend our walk to the site of Ribehuus, now a huge mound, surrounded by a sedgy moat, a mound of which the inhabitants are still proud, as connected with Queen Dagmar. You recollect the old ballad:—

> "Queen Dagmar lies sick in Ribe.
> In Ringsted they do expect her.
> All the ladies in Denmark
> Stand round about her couch."

Awful affairs, these royal accouchements. No wonder she died: stifled, I dare say, as poor Marie Antoinette nearly was in after days. Her death occurred in 1205, and now, after a lapse of six hundred years, her name is as popular among the peasantry of Denmark as ever. The nuptials of Dronning Leonora were also here celebrated; and again, after the murder of Glipping, it was here the assassins entrenched themselves, having seized the castle from the hands of Tage Muus (mouse), its governor. They had first tried Skanderborg, but Queen Agnes, already informed of the bloody deed, drew up the drawbridge in time, and, standing in the balcony, holding her two children by the hand, listened to the exulting taunts of the Grand Marshal. "You have laughed at me, Queen Agnes! You have jeered at my grief on account of my wife, and now I have burnt your house."

The spirit of the youthful Menved could not tamely brook the insults addressed to his royal mother; boiling with rage, he exclaimed, "You, Marsk Stig! you self-made king! as sure as I am King of Denmark, you shall lead the life of an outlaw, and the moors alone shall be your bed!" His brother, little Christopher, roared and cried.

Marsk Stig was taken aback by the words of the child, but, soon recovering himself, he replied, "Thou art my king, and I may be an outlaw: but I will make many a Danish mother grieve for her son, and many a wife widow yet!" He then saluted the royal party and retired. As we have before related, he seizes on Hjelm, turns pirate, is excommunicated by the Pope, and dies an outlaw. As he is not likely to appear much more upon the scene, I may as well relate the story of his funeral, celebrated in verse and chronicled in the memory of the history-loving Danes.

Towards the close of the 13th century the servant of the priest of Hindsholm in the island of Funen was, towards dark, busily employed in cleaning hops, when a farming man arrived breathless, declaring he had seen a funeral enter the church—a rich funeral, followed by a train of warriors. Much alarmed, for they knew the church to be closed and the keys safe in the priest's house, they imagined it to be a phantom rising from the sea.

One of the maids, who was betrothed to Mads Jyde, a grim warrior of Marsk Stig's band, declared she was not afraid; she would go and see herself what it really was; so she fetched the key, and when she arrived at the church-door she found the building filled with armed men, the vizors of their helmets closed; her own "huusbond," *i. e.* the priest, her master, there, with his hands tied behind his back, compelled, by threats of a drawn sword, to read the funeral service. Alarmed, she conceals herself, and, the service concluded, the men break open an old vault, and deposit the coffin therein. The priest is dismissed, an oath being first exacted from all present never to reveal what they had that night seen. When the warrior-band has departed the maid-servant comes forth from her hiding-place, and examines the vault where the coffin of the new-buried corpse is laid; she finds it but carelessly closed. The girl remains until morning, when, after some exertion, she manages to unbar the door of the vault, and discovers within it a new coffin over which was laid a violet velvet cloak powdered with silver stars of seven points.

"Well!" thought she, "it is a pity to leave this here to rot and spoil;" so she rolls up the cloak and then recloses the door.

Years pass by, and Mads Jyde returns from the wars to claim his bride. The marriage is celebrated with the usual rejoicings and festivities, and in the evening the guests conduct the new-married couple to the nuptial chamber. The first object that meets the eye of the bridegroom is the violet cloak with silver stars laid across the bed. "What is this?" he exclaims, pale with agitation; "tell me!" The bride, in her innocence, relates her story, concealing nothing from her husband; he blows out the candle, kisses her on the cheek.

The following morning the villagers arrive early to serenade the new-married couple, but no answer is made to their greeting. Ten o'clock strikes; midday is past, when, alarmed, they determine to break into the bridal chamber; the door yields to their efforts—a fearful spectacle meets their eyes. Across the bed lies extended the body of the bride of yesterday—a corpse. One fearful wound in her breast has done the mischief; the dagger still remains undrawn—the bridegroom fled. Mads Jyde had dearly loved his mistress, but he had better loved the memory of his outlawed lord, and respected the oath he had sworn at his funeral in the village church of Hindsholm.*

Ribehuus was entirely destroyed in the Swedish war of the 17th century. Among its governors was the celebrated Erland Kalf of the last Valdemar's days. In the wars of the Succession he sided with the Slesvig Dukes, brothers of Queen Hedvig, who, delighted at his desertion of their opponent's cause, handed over to him two important fortresses; but a sentiment of remorse now seizes him, he again returns to his allegiance, bringing with him the castles committed to his charge. "Capital beast that!" exclaimed King Valdemar, always inclined to be facetious; "he ran away a calf, and is now come back a cow, with two fine young heifers!" Not bad for a royal joke.

We had brought letters for the family of the clergyman of the cathedral, who were most kind and hospitable, and did all in their power to make our stay agreeable. This evening we accompanied them to the annual haymaking festival of the town, held on the opposite side of the river, about two English miles at least from Ribe. The beau-monde of the ancient cathedral town were all present, and there was a great

---

* There has been a grand dispute as regards the place of the interment of Marsk Stig. In the church of Stubberup is an ancient stone, with a copper plate on which is inscribed,—" A.D. 1292 (repaired by Kirsten Hardenberg, 1656) died the noble and well-born Marsk Stig Andersen von Hjelm, and lies here interred;" but this was put up by one of his descendants. He left a son (he was, I know, married), Stigsen, as he was called, who made peace with the king, and enjoyed the highest favour. He married a Miss Bugge, sister of our old friend Sir Niels. His death is thus related:—" Marsk Stig owned Bjørnskor. Once, when hunting in a strong heat, he fainted, alighted from his horse, and sat down on a stone in Torup field, where he died.

deal of fun going on among the hay, dancing and singing in chorus of national airs: very pretty were some of the modern ones. The ancient Danish music is awful: lugubrious to a degree not to be described—worse than that of the Spanish muleteer. In England we speak of the "tune the cow died of," though what the melody was which caused so disastrous an event is as yet a myth. My firm belief is that the unfortunate animal met with her death from the imprudent singing of some old Danish ballad within her hearing. I walked about bouche béante with wonder and admiration, staring at the town meadow, a present of Erik Menved to the city: one sea of haycocks, eight English miles square, without any separation, barrier or hedge; green grass, fine as velvet!

To quit Ribe would be impossible without alluding to the well-known ballad of Tovelil—not the Tove of Gurre, but the Tove of the first Valdemar, the Fair Rosamond of Danish story; victim, like Liden Kirsten, to the jealousy—in this case just, it must be avowed—of Queen Sofie, one of the most unpopular queens of early Danish story.

"Merry did they dance in the castle-yard:
Then danced the queen with her maidens nine;
And proud was Tovelil, the damsel fine;
But King Valdemar he can love them both.

O hear you, Tovelil, mine own heart's dear,
I would the queen would die in this year:
Heaven would it grant my wife were dead,
Then you should wear the crown so red!

Be silent, oh king, the queen stands near;
To your idle talk she lends her ear."

And so it goes on. Queen Sofie now sends for Tovelil, and asks her what she is talking about? Tovelil replies,

Nothing—about the knight who demands her hand in marriage. Concealment later becomes useless, and Sofie again taunts her. "What did the king give you?" she inquires. Tovelil, now bold—maîtresse en titre—replies:—

> "He gave to me as fine a gold band
> As ever was seen around the queen's hand;
> For I to him two sons did bear;
> For this the king he loves me dear.
> Knud and Christopher ride never far
> From the king's side when he goes to the war."

Sofie now meditates revenge. She orders a "bad-stue," a vapour-bath (probably an introduction of her own from Russia), to be constructed, and begs Tovelil to accompany her to bathe. She however declined; "she bathed yesterday;" but later she is induced to enter to prepare the bath for her lord. Queen Sofie closes the stove, and heaps wood upon the fire:—

> "There is no water, there is no soap;
> For the love of Heaven, oh let me out!
> Then could all hear along the street
> How Tovelil died so hard a death."

The queen now walks down Ribe street, and, meeting Knud and Christopher, cries out, mocking:—

> "Here come you, Christopher; here come you, Knud·
> Go both, and take your mother out.
> Run down the street, and hear her cries,
> For Tovelil in the bad-stue dies."

The sons spur their chargers, upsetting the queen sprawling in the gutter, all in her "scarlet red." They burst open the door, but too late:—

> "Her sons they hear no more her groans:
> The fire has burnt to her very bones."

And when they take the body of their mother from the bad-stue, she was—

"As a goose roasted for Christmas."

"But King Valdemar he can love them both"—not the goose—but Tovelil and Queen Sofie.

Such was the fate of the Danish Fair Rosamond, roasted to rags in a vapour-bath.

TØRNING.

July 25th.—We leave Ribe betimes for Hadersley, first stopping a mile from the town, at the village of Tørning, beautifully situated in a picturesque valley, by a mill, to visit the Tinghuus, the most ancient in the kingdom of Denmark. We might have saved ourselves the trouble: the Tinghuus is now no more; the great salle is divided into cottages; some of the panellings, painted with the arms of the earlier sovereigns, are still visible. The Ting has been of late years transferred to the adjoining kro, where politicians can quaff ale and discuss politics at the same time. Here arose the first dispute between King Christian and the peasantry of Slesvig, in consequence of the motto to that sovereign's shield being hung up written in the German language instead of the Danish. They tore down the wäpen; a revolution was nearly stirred up. The king, however, on the application of the peasants, allowed another to be painted, and the obnoxious motto removed, "for," said they, "we are not Germans, but of South Jutland."

In the northern provinces of Jutland these Tings were held in the open air; we frequently came across hillocks called "Ting Høis."

You would imagine we had done with ghosts and mermaids, church lambs and churchyard horses, trolles, nisses, and Hyldemoir, &c. &c.; but this very day two more diabolical characters—the werewolf (loup garou) and the night-raven—appear on the scene.

The werewolf, one of the earliest superstitions of ancient Scandinavia, is said to be the offspring of a woman who, by the aid of some rite—chloroform?—brings forth her children without suffering. In this case all the sons become werewolves and the daughters nightmares. The werewolf bears a human form during the day, but you may always know him by the "meeting of his eyebrows," and at night-time he assumes the shape of a three-legged dog. But if you suspect a person to be such, and accuse him, he becomes free at once from the evil.

It is related how a man, who had been a werewolf from a child upwards, late at night drove home with his wife from a festival. On the road, when he felt the time of his evil draw nigh, he alighted, and gave the reins to his wife, saying, "If anything comes to thee, mother, you have only to defend yourself with your apron." He then left her, and presently the woman is attacked by a werewolf. She beats it with her apron, which the monster seizes in his teeth and carries away. When her husband returned he held in his mouth a torn-off piece of his wife's apron sticking between his teeth. On seeing this, she cries, "Lord! husband, thou art a werewolf!" "Thanks to thee, mother, I am now free!" he replied, and from that time the evil never affected him. The nightmare is a female werewolf.

A peasant had a betrothed bride who was a nightmare without knowing it herself; she came every night to her bridegroom, who was soon made aware of her evil, for he remarked that she entered through a little hole which was in an oaken window-post. So he prepared a stick to fit into the hole, and, when she had come the next night, he fixed the stick in the hole, and she was forced to stay in the room. Then she instantly regained her human shape, and kept it. The peasant married her, and they had many children. Many years had passed quietly away, and they were both advanced in years, when it happened one evening that the husband thought of the stick, which was still fixed in the hole of the oaken post. Then he jokingly asked his wife if she knew how she had once entered the house, and, as she knew nothing about it, he told her, and even took out the stick, that she might see by what entrance she had come in. The wife peered through, but while standing there she became suddenly quite small, slipped out through the hole, and vanished for ever.

Once upon a time there was in Jutland a queen who was a great admirer of horses. She had one of which she was especially fond, and which occupied her thoughts both while awake and in her dreams. Often at night, when the groom came into the stables, he perceived that the horse was uneasy, and thence he concluded that it had been ridden by the nightmare. One night he took a pailful of cold water and cast it over the horse, and the same moment he saw the queen sitting on the horse's back.

The night-raven is a more mysterious creature still, being a "conjured ghost;" to become one was, as you recollect, the wish of Long Margaret of Vosborg.

In the spot where such a spectre has appeared, a pointed stake must be driven into the earth, which will always penetrate the left wing of the "night-raven," and make a hole in it. The night-raven emerges only from the ugliest sloughs and moors. First, it begins to cry beneath the swamp, "Rock! rock! rock! up!" and when it is once out, it darts away, crying, "Hey! hey! he—y!" Then it lights upon the earth, at first resembling in shape a cross, hopping along like a magpie. Soon it flies away towards the east to the "holy grave," which if it can contrive to reach, it comes to rest. When it passes over our heads, we must take care not to look up, for if any one look through "the hole in the left wing" he becomes himself a night-raven, and the bird is released. It is a peaceful animal, and does no harm, only it seeks to fly further and further towards the east.

Lastly, we have the old legend of the basilisk. When the cock is seven years old it lays an egg, from which comes forth the basilisk, an ugly monster, which kills people solely by looking at them. The basilisk can only be killed by holding a mirror before it, for it cannot survive the sight of its own ugliness.

We have really now done with hobgoblins and supernatural monsters of all sorts; but if you require any more information on the subject, you may search for it yourself in a Danish book written by David Monrad, and aptly termed 'Heathenish Christianity.'

FREDERICIA.

We found Haderslev as we left it, in full fair time. We again passed through Kolding, whose castle-ruins appear to have suffered from the effects of the last winter, and Hannibal, on his watch-tower, now bends forward, considerably out of the perpendicular. From thence to Fredericia, a beautiful drive along the fiorde's banks—a recompense due to us for our ugly seven miles journey of this morning. The town of Fredericia is a fortress of some consequence in the Danish dominions. It has had its affair with the Swedes, independent of its exploits in the last war, too fresh in the minds of the world in general to require relating. Its present interest consists in the two monuments erected to the memory of the Danish heroes who fell fighting in the cause of their country at the battle which bears its name: they are the work of Professor Bissen. One, a bas-relief, erected in the public cemetery, is as beautiful in design as admirable in execution; the subject, two soldiers bearing a dead comrade in their arms for interment from the battle-field. Unfortunately, it has been injudiciously placed too near to the churchyard wall, so that you catch, on arriving from either side, the rounded backs of the bearers en biais, which presents a most ridiculous appearance, and have to cross over to the opposite side of the road to judge of the general effect. It is, however, fine as a work of art, and adds much to the reputation of the artist by whom it was designed. Fredericia is restoring her church—red and white—in its ancient colours. Some carving on the pulpit is worthy of Grinling Gibbons, all fruits, flowers, and shells.

The small boat which is to carry us across the blue waters of the Little Belt waits. Tide and wind contrary; but an hour will soon pass away. We can watch, as we sail along, the richly-wooded coast of Funen. We can gaze on the actineæ—actineæ of a beauty unrivalled floating along in their course. Only look at them, in their filmy parasols of transparent white, hemmed with a deep feathery fringe! how they collapse! how they again reopen! The one resembles a star-fish in a balloon, gauzy transparent; the other has four eyes, if eyes they be. And now we ride on the Belt. Middelfart, with her imposing church, her trees, and her shipping, are near. Syren-like, she attracts us to her shores. Well, there is a charm in beauty, but the Syren must be powerful indeed, her fascinations great, and her potations drugged, who can ever cause us to forget the pleasant time we have spent, the hospitalities we have received, during our six weeks' wandering among the fiordes, the moses, the wild and original scenery, of that most historic of all provinces the ancient kingdom of North Jutland.

CHAPTER XLVII.

The island of Funen — Red cabbage of Sir Niels Bugge — Ploughing ghosts — Odin and Odense — Murder of St. Knud — The traitor Blakke — Funeral of Kirstine Munk — Dormitorium of the Ahlefeldts — The lady who danced herself to death — The pet cats of Mrs. Mouse — King John and his family — The Lear of Odense and his daughters.

ISLAND OF FUNEN.

July 26th.—WE land at Middelfart, and, whilst our carriages are preparing, wander down to the shore-side. The "red cabbage," sprung from the blood of Sir Niels Bugge, was not, however, there; perhaps we may next time be more lucky. Then on to Odense, twenty-four English miles, over a road straight as the crow flies, a hill always before you, and, when you are at the top, another. The land is rich and highly cultivated, but you sigh after the expansive wastes of Jutland. It is divided into small fields—like England were the hedges of quickset; here they are mostly of lilac. This division was rendered necessary by the dishonesty of the inhabitants. "Cursed is he that removeth his neighbour's landmark," we all know, but we are ignorant of the punishment assigned hereafter to those who commit this crime. The Fionese declare that the ghosts of the culprits are compelled to plough the fields from which they unlawfully removed the stones, to all eternity; and in the villages of Ryslinge and Lørup they may still be heard of a night speeding their ploughs for the benefit of no one. Across a hill, too, called Graabjerge, the peasant will tell you it is dangerous to pass after nightfall, for the unwary pedestrian may suddenly find a red-hot rein poked into his hand, and be compelled to plough as long as the tortured spirits care to repose themselves. In this case there is but one resource : kick off your shoes—sabots, if you wear them—and, when you turn back, shove your feet quickly into them, and take to your heels.

ODENSE.

Oh for the meadow of Menved! its eight square miles of haycocks! Stuffy, oppressive Funen! We may grow used to it, but at present we despise her "prettiness" from our hearts' core. At last comes Odense—not a bad town, with long streets and fine churches. A canal alone connects it with the fiorde. Despicable place! A city—capital, too, of a Danish island—and no water save a murmuring brook! No historic interest can ever make up for such a disappointment, so the sooner we are off from the clean but noisiest of all noisy post-houses the better.

Don't inquire the etymology of the city's name, and rashly plunge into the vortex of real Odins and false Odins. It won't pay. The statue which once stood on the so-called Odin's høi has long since disappeared. Let us turn at once to Knud the Holy, of whom we have heard so much—not Knud, flushed with the hopes of victory, about to sail with his mighty fleet to wrest his rebellious province of England from the Normans— not Knud prosperous lord of the castle of Sjorring, which we visited together one windy day—but Knud in the fair isle of Funen, with a few followers, a fugitive from those most oprør-ious of all subjects the Vendel boers. On his journey none succoured him, save one, and that one a granite boulder. The weary king, on his way from Middelfart to Odense, sank down from sheer fatigue on the rock which lay by the wayside. Touched, says tradition, by the sorrows of the unlucky monarch, the hard granite softened, and the king enjoyed an undisturbed repose, as on a bed of down, till the morning dawned, and he continued his journey.

Among his suite was Earl Esbern, called Blakke, or the "red-haired," from his shining locks. Knud loved him much, but he proved a traitor. He assured the king there was no danger; that instead of passing across the Great Belt he might repose at Odense. When the king was in the sanctuary of St. Alban's church—English St. Alban's, a favourite saint of our own Great Canute and founder of the edifice—Blakke persuaded him the Vendels had returned to Jutland, so he slept quietly together with his two brothers. Blakke then called to the peasants, "Go round and shoot the king through the window." They did so. Knud was kneeling before the high altar, with his brother Benedict, when a javelin, hurled through the window, laid him low. The king, feeling his end was nigh, prepared, his arms folded, to meet his death with dignity. He prayed for his enemies; but he was very thirsty, and demanded to drink; thereon a young man ran to the fountain in the market-place, and, filling an earthen pot with water, gave it to the dying king, passing it through the window on his spear; but an old peasant with his axe struck it down. The king looked up; their eyes met, and a few moments after the king expired. That man was never again tranquil; the dying gaze of the king, so patient and so sad, for ever haunted him, and he died shortly afterwards in great agony.

It is related in the same Chronicle how, while the small but trusty band of the king defended his person, the false Blakke killed the good Benedict, brother of the king. Blakke himself was slain in the fight; and when the battle was over, these two were found lying side by side. The blood of the prince flowed in a long stream of reeking gore along the pavement to the right, that of the traitor to the left: even in death their life-blood would not mingle.* About the year 1100 Knud was canonised, and his body is interred within the church which bears his name, in a splendid shrine above the high altar. His brother Benedict is allowed to repose by his side. You may see them now, each in a carved oak box, Benedict's by far the smartest. He and the Holy Knud remain, no longer regarded as relics and holy, in a chapel of the building, and their mouldering legs, once the admiration of thousands, may still be discerned, half powder, through the glass apertures of their coffins. There is no image of St. Knud here extant, but in the village of Branninge, by Ribe, you may see one, a very ancient carved figure, in the full armour of the day, his head covered with a monk's cap.†

---

* Blakke went backwards and forwards between the king and the rebels, always on horseback; hence the proverb, when speaking of a traitor, "He rides on Blakke's horse." The children in Skaane still play at a game called "At sto Blak eller Blakke," in allusion to his perfidy. He was brother to King Svend. See vol. i. p. 114, note.

† Peter Pagh, Bishop of Odense, was the first to introduce the portrait of Knud the Holy into the arms of his diocese, 1339. He composed, indeed, a very complimentary stanza in Latin on the subject—not without a false quantity, though, for which I should have been put in the bill by Cookesley at Eton,—saying how he had introduced a lily into his shield. Alnothus, an Englishman from Canterbury, who lived in Denmark for twenty years, wrote St. Knud's Life, and dedicated it to King Niels, his brother.

Adela, his widowed queen, wanted, on her retirement from Denmark, to carry off these precious relics to Flanders. Had she persisted in the execution of her whim, she would have met with the same fate as the saint himself. Deprive Odense of her "apothek" and head doctor! Furious, the inhabitants resented the idea. "Did he not cure every disease? A most skilful oculist, he restored sight to the blind! For rheumatics, he had no equal! and for the purification of the blood, never talk of 'la moutarde blanche,' when St. Knud is to be got at!" Though a saint, he had his spécialité, and particularly prided himself on his success in all cutaneous disorders.

So Queen Adela, who had no particular fancy for being poked with a javelin, retired to Flanders, and left St. Knud to the adoration of the multitude.

His church is a fine building of exquisite proportions, spoiled by the modern fittings and loggie of the last centuries, used by the monarch and the heir-apparent (who generally held the post of governor of Funen), as well as by their guests; for Odense has had a world of fine company in her days of splendour. Our own George I., among the number, in the old Electress's lifetime paid a visit to Denmark, to Christian V.—came to see his old aunt the dowager queen—always kind to the Palsgrave family. But Odense is out of fashion now; her palace untenanted. Next on our list of royal folks appears Erik Lam; he turned monk. I've no patience with your "rois fainéans" who turn religious to get out of this world's troubles. It is not religion at all—all sneaking, nothing more nor less.

Then comes King John, whose splendid sepulchral slab, removed from the extinct church of the Gray Friars, lies imbedded in the wall—a fine specimen of its period: the king arrayed in his royal robes, and good Queen Christina, who here died 1521, standing by his side; between them their youngest son, Prince Franciscus,* a small boy, in full costume, with golden chain, to which hangs a pendent rose, some old Pope's present. Within the same vault, but no monument erected to his memory, lies Christian II.,† together with his father and mother, at last at rest. Hard by stands the coat of arms, in carved wood, of young Prince Franciscus, bearings of the house of Oldenborg;‡ observe the sup-

---

* No prince of the house of Oldenborg had ever before received the name of Franciscus; and people wondered greatly at its selection. He was named in honour, said King John, of holy St. Francis; for on that Saint's day not only was he born, but his father received the news of peace having been concluded between himself and Sten Sture.

† At his funeral appeared a rich merchant from the Netherlands, who demanded a large sum of money which he declared he had lent to the deceased king during his banishment. King Frederic II. answered that all his debts must be paid by his children, brother-in-law, and those nearest in kin, and not by the country; and that this answer might stand good for all the creditors, who, as you may imagine, were never paid.

‡ On a field or, two bars gules, is the cognisance of the house of Oldenborg, concerning which "smudge," as it is termed, there hangs a story. In the year 1090 the Count of Oldenborg, while in the Holy Land, for a conspiracy against the Emperor Henry IV. was condemned to engage in single combat with a lion. In the Müller collection is preserved a curious old engraving of this story. The count, armed cap-a-pie, stands in a stone jail-like court, surrounded by high walls, over the top of which appear the heads of the emperor with the empress (Matilda), bishops, counts, ladies, all anxiously feasting their eyes on the fight. But the Count of Oldenborg is a man of genius. He has in his hand the lay-figure of a man—very like an acrobat of modern days—which he holds out on his shield, and presents to the lion. While the imprudent beast seizes on his prey with his teeth and claws, the count plunges his sword deep into his heart. The blood flies out over the hand of the victor, who, first wiping his fingers on his gilded shield, produces the two red smudges which he afterwards bore as his arms by order of the emperor. In olden days the house of Oldenborg adopted as their supporters, on the

porters, wild men not yet moulted, well coated with hair—hair, however, we all know, will not last for ever, and the savages of the Danish arms have, like the rest of the world, become bald.

Before we close the list of royalty, observe that velvet coffin—plain, simple coffin—a Duchess's coronet, C. M. the initials—worthless Christina Munk. We have visited her birthplace, assisted at her marriage, her disgrace, her death, and now she lies interred, or rather exposed, in the chapel of St. Knud's church of Odense—requiescat in pace! Christina had the good luck to die at the moment when Ulfeld and his wife were at the height of their power—so on her death-bed she was attended by the Hof-Preacher of General Wrangel, as well as by the king's doctor. Her coffin was brought to Odense, met outside the town by the nobility, and buried in the presence of her children and grandchildren all arrayed in white clothing. So after all she was interred as a countess, and not as Mrs. Christina of Boller.

We will first enter the splendid chapel of the Counts of Ahlefeldt,* a really noble dormitorium. Look at the banners—the armour—the coffins—all gilt and engraved; nothing in death and dust can be more magnificent. Thirteen warriors of this house fell in

---

right an armed knight presenting in his hand a lay-figure to the lion, who forms the left side supporter. The houses of Austria, Carafa, and many others, have adopted this story of the smudge, but without any right.

* The Ahlefeldts of more modern date derive their descent from the daughter of King Christian and poor bullied Vibeke Kruse. Very well brought up, too, she was; for Dr. Laurits Jacobsen, in his Journal, notes, 29th April, 1647, "Have I this day, by the king's order, examined Miss Lisbeth in her catechism;" and later the king expressed his good pleasure at her grounding in her Christianities.

the Ditsmark combat, when the sacred banner of the Danebrog was lost to the Danes for ever.

Observe that figure of a lady in a dark brocade dress and tight corsage, with choking ruff. No beauty—Lady Margaret Skovgaard is her name, a lady of great possessions. She was young and fair, and loved the revel and the dance. At a ball at Odense she danced with twelve successive knights—branles, corantos, and what not;—dances not like our calm meandering quadrilles of the 19th century. She danced, and would not stop, till she could no more, and fell exhausted, dead, at the feet of the twelfth knight, her partner.* He—for the age of chivalry was not yet over—caused, at his own expense, this stone to be erected to her memory, and, like the rivals Capulet and Montague, had it richly gilt. "Stuff and nonsense!" cried fourth Christian, when he saw it (he was elected to his throne in Odense); "bring me a tar-barrel. Take a brush and tar the jade all over. I am not going to have my devotions (Christian's devotions!) disturbed by her gold and glitter." But Christian counted without his host, old Time; for, after a lapse of more than two centuries, the tar is peeling off, the gold reappearing, and perhaps she will again rival the gingerbread of the country fairs in her glittering finery. Scandalous people declare that the Lady Margaret had refused to lend money to Christian during her lifetime: it was on this account that he revenged himself. For the credit of St. Knud, all coffins are closed to the public, even

---

* In the description of Sanderumgaard, once in her possession, I was considerably disgusted to find the following remark: "If Margaret Skovgaard did die from over-dancing, she was, at any rate, turned seventy years of age."

that of Mrs. Muus, wife of the first Protestant prelate of the diocese, who, in order to prove she was above the prejudices of her "race," caused herself to be buried along with her four pet cats, each grimalkin clothed in grave-clothes of white satin, with a little black velvet cap and feather placed upon his feline head—a story much in favour of the celibacy of the clergy, if bishops' wives made such fools of themselves.*

Wednesday, 27th.—I have done my best to like Odense, but can't. I have mounted the lofty tower of St. Knud's church, and am not enthusiastic about the view, though anything like the steepness of its ladders I never came across. In the church of Our Lady is the splendid altarpiece, brought from the long since destroyed convent of the Gray Brothers, executed in the town of Odense, about the year 1520, by Claus Berg,† whose name deserves to be handed down among the artists of his age. It was a present from good Queen Christina ‡ to that fraternity, a body much patronised

---

* Christian Povelsen, last Prior of St. Knud, in Odense, in his Journal, says that, in 1532, came King Frederic I.'s letter, that all the silver ornaments in the church were to be given over to the king, even to the "chalice, paten, and pix," at which the prior appears considerably disgusted.

† Claus Berg, the artist who carved the altarpiece of the Gray Brethren, was, as he himself states, of a burgher family, an "armiger" from Lubec. Queen Christina, who resided at St. Clara's convent, sent for him. He entered the queen's service, and had under him twelve servants, as well as pupils, whom the queen paid monthly, and who were dressed in silk clothes trimmed with lace. The queen also stood godmother in 1504 to his son, whom she called Franciscus, and paid for his schooling in Rostock.

‡ Queen Christina much affected Odense as a residence, even after her husband's death, when she retired to the convent of St. Clara. In her book of expenses the entries are numerous. She looked after King John's little bills and paid them for him. "I gave ten marks to the bookbinder's wife, where the king used to bathe, as I have given her

by the early members of the Oldenborg family. In the lowest division, ranged on each side of the figure of Christ, stand King John and his family ; the likenesses, if the portraits of the day are to be trusted, are admirable. To the right bends King John himself, followed by his sons—Christian II. the fac-simile, beard and all, of the portrait of Christiansborg, a ruffianly-looking fellow, and his younger brother, the youthful Francis. On the female side, Queen Christina ; then young Elizabeth of Austria, the fair spouse of neglectful Christian.* And,

---

no money before :" though, when the king went to bathe, his servants followed him, and were allowed a tun of beer to drink whilst he was in the water. Queen Christina does not seem to be a woman of great expenses. She enters " Paid to the washerwoman for her bill of the last half-year the sum of 6 marks "—1s. 3d. English. She paid drink-money to the servant who brought her from England a swan—coals to Newcastle. Her farrier's bill amounts to 30 marks for one year. When Queen Christina returned from her two years' imprisonment in Sweden, she brought back with her a certificate that she had lived nobly and chastely during the time of her absence, signed by the Archbishop of Upsala and twelve noble gentlemen. Such was the simplicity of the times! She died in Odense, and was buried in the dress of a Franciscan nun.

* To do Christian justice, with all his imperfections and his bad conduct as regards Dyveke, he seems, in writing at any rate, to have been an attentive husband. "Les paroles s'envolent, mais les écritures restent," says the French proverb ; and in the lately published correspondence of King Christian a constant good feeling prevails between him and his fair consort Elizabeth. In the first letter of the collection he urgently implores of his " kere frue " to abstain from the drinking of Rhine wine as injurious to her health, but to use the red vintage of France in its stead, of which he will procure her the best to be had. Very prettily he writes, too, on the occasion of his children's birth,—nothing can be nicer ; then, too, he adds a postscript to announce the safety of Sigbrit, the maîtresse mère and prime minister, after the ducking elsewhere alluded to, concerning which I have no doubt Queen Elizabeth was less anxious. She, on her side, in writing from Berlin — where her brother-in-law Joachim, inhospitable old fellow! plainly lets her see he grudges the expense of keeping her—expresses her longing to be once again reunited to him. Then later,

last, another Elizabeth, known to readers of Carlyle—Elizabeth married to the Elector of Brandenburg—Protestant-ways inclined—caught by one of her numerous daughters tripping in her creed, receiving the communion in both kinds. "I'll brick her up," roared her husband, in his ire. Elizabeth was too good a Lutheran not to hate bread and water; so off she sets, with not a change of linen to her back—mends her broken axle-tree with her veil—travels night and day till she gains the dominions of her neighbour the Protestant Duke of Saxony, and never returns to her husband more. Joachim declared he meant nothing; but as his wife was well out of his reach, it was all very fine—she for one never believed him. There she bends — nice-looking, with plaited tresses—the only representation of her extant in the Danish dominions.*

---

as matters grow worse, their communication becomes more and more frequent : les petites misères de la vie humaine are all forgotten ; they are bound together by one interest—their own and that of their children.

One serious tiff Christian did have with Elizabeth, and that appears the only one. He secretly put to death her chamberlain Maximilian, who had come with her from the Netherlands, and of whom he is supposed to have been jealous. He also turned off her grande maitresse and her confessor.

All King Christian's letters to his consort are written "paa papir," not parchment, and sealed either with red or grønl vox.

In 1526 dies Queen Elizabeth, and is buried in her native city of Ghent, and the last we hear of her is the account given of sums paid to Jean de Mabuse, who is charged with the erection of her monument.

* Such a writing as went on in the family at the period of her escapade and for some time after was never known, but can be all seen in the correspondence of King Christian. Old Joachim writes to his beloved brother-in-law, and expresses his utmost astonishment at so unheard-of a proceeding. "He can't understand it; she had no grounds to fear; why should she suspect him of bad motives?" Then comes a correspondence with the Duke of Saxony, to and from, asking and pro-

I am perfectly aware that Palnatoke, founder of the Hvide family, whom we have had before at Marienlyst, uproarious like the rest of the warriors in Harald Blue-Tooth's time, got himself slain somewhere by here; and I have read a description, to which only Froissart or dear Miss Strickland could do justice, of the feudal homage done by the Dukes of Holstein, John and Adolf, to our good King Frederic, in 1579. Anything so smart as they all were no one can imagine. But the noise and the dust of Odense, nothing will ever make up for it.

Though Augsburg can boast her Fuggers, Odense can boast her Bagers; but in this latter case I am afraid virtue becomes its own reward, and the Bager family ranks not high among the counts of the Danish dominions. Olaf Bager was a rich merchant, and a man of noble and generous sentiments. He lent money to his king, the second Frederic, who when he visited Odense never failed to sup at the house of his friend and subject.

Pudding and sweets, as you well know, are served anyhow in the northern climes, in the middle of dinner, as the cook or housewife wishes it. One night at supper King Frederic praised highly some conserves of apricots. "What a bouquet, too, they have!" exclaimed the king. "Wait," replied Bager, "till the dessert; I will give you some incense which will smell far sweeter."

---

mising her protection. King Ferdinand writes a stiff letter to Christian, requesting him to use his influence in sending his sister back again to her husband. *He* does not approve of such proceedings. Then young Joachim writes to his mother, and implores her to return to her afflicted family, and tries his best to move his uncle Christian also; but the Protestant duck is not to be snared back to her nest by any flattery. She's safe where she is, and intends to remain so.

The supper over, an incense-burner, laden with perfumed cedar-chips, was brought in, on the top of which was laid a mass of papers.

"Will your Majesty deign to light the pile?" requested Bager, offering a match. His Majesty did so most graciously, and with quiet satisfaction saw reduced to cinders his own bonds for sums so enormous he had little hopes of defraying the debt. This is historical; but here the Danes were not first, for Fugger lived in Charles V.'s reign, some years previous. Time rolled on, and Bager had a numerous family, some twelve or fourteen—you may see them all upon his epitaphium. He portioned his daughters, got ruined later, and had, like King Lear, to come to his children for help and refuge; but they treated him badly. "He had much better," said they, "have kept his bonds, instead of ruining himself for his sovereign's sake, and becoming a burden to his family." So Olaf, sick at heart, determines to try a ruse. He goes round to his various friends and merchants with whom he had once had dealings, and returns with a heavy coffer, which he deposits in a place of safety, well closed with wrought-iron lock and key. He has, he says, received gifts from some, from others the payment of debts long due. The contents of the coffer he intends to leave by his will to the child who treats him best.

A change comes over the spirit of the ungrateful offspring; it is now who shall treat the old man best—all love and filial affection. So Bager, laughing in his sleeve, ends his days in peace and comfort. He can make no distinction at his death; all have been kind to him, "his dutiful children;" the contents of the coffer are to be equally divided amongst them; it is heavy enough for all. Olaf Bager is conducted in pomp and honour to his last abode, followed by his sorrowing descendants. The will is read—the coffer opened—and lo! they discover what? a heap of stones—a just requital for their undutiful behaviour.

The schloss gardens form the favourite promenade of Odense. Here the military music plays in the evening. But notwithstanding its position as a capital, its patron saint, its cathedral, and its bishop (there was a dance at the bishop's last night), we were very glad to mount the carriage, and move on along the tiresome chaussée, its dulness alone relieved by an occasional picturesque old church nestling among the trees. At last we again see the waters of the Great Belt in the distance, and drive into the little fortified town of Nyborg.

CHAPTER XLVIII.

Funen continued — King Christian II. and the ape — Deathplace of Ellen Marsviin — By-laws of Nyborg — Women to be buried alive — Laws of adulteration — King Hans' invitation to his daughter's christening — Story of Kai Lykke and the Queen — The rival Nisses — St. George killed the dragon in Denmark — Svendborg, the Pig Castle — Gaas made archbishop — Island of Thorseng the apanage of Count Valdemar — Portraits of the House of Oldenborg.

NYBORG.

August 3rd.—WE have passed some days at Nyborg, too glad to recruit our minds and bodies in the comfortable post-house—an inn of times gone by—not all picturesque and dry-rot like that of Ringkjøping, but a house built with good large rooms, before the world began to economise space; very cool and comfortable. So our eight days fled rapidly by; we strolled on the rampart heights, we bathed in the waters of the fiorde, boated and fished occasionally, and thoroughly enjoyed ourselves.

Nyborg is not a town of vast pretensions to antiquity; it dates its origin from the "New Castle," long since gathered to its sister "borgs." Valdemar the Great (though he did beat poor Liden Kirsten to death) was a very good son of the Church after his own peculiar manner, and, like many worthy people of the present century, very fond of proselytising. He preached Christianity church-militant-wise, fire and sword, among the heathens of Rugen. Prislav, own brother of pagan

King Nuclet of the Wends, embraced Christianity, and King Valdemar gave him as a reward his sister Catherine in marriage, with Lolland as her dower. Her son Knud founded here his castle of Nyborg; he did not, however, enjoy it much, for he turned monk for very peace's sake, and Nyborg fell into the hands of the crown. King John much loved this royal residence. Here were born Christian and Protestant Elizabeth of Brandenburg, who considered twenty-two years of incarceration quite locking-up enough for one family. The days of canonisation were over, and she had no fancy to be a martyr.

Scarcely had Christian opened his eyes to daylight when an adventure occurred, which, had it terminated fatally, would have saved him a world of trouble. The new-born princeling lay asleep in his cradle, when an ape, who formed part of the royal establishment, stealthily entering the nursery, lifts him from the cradle and carries him in his arms, laughing and chattering, to the housetop. The consternation of the royal household was extreme, but they acted wisely; left the monkey to his own devices, who, after a time, tired of the office of dry nurse, returned his charge uninjured to the place from which he had taken him. The same story is told of one of the Leinster family and also of Oliver Cromwell.

In later days Nyborg, with its grand and lofty tower, followed the fate of other royal buildings; it was pulled down for its materials, not by that old clothesman the second Frederic, but by the bigamous fourth Frederic to build up his trumpery palace of Odense.

Not being in an excursionising mood when at Nyborg, we merely extended our walks to the adjoining manor of Holckenhavn, a château beautiful in itself as well as in its situation, and undegraded; it was once termed Ellensborg, and was built by Ellen Marsviin, as the iron cramps, bearing the letters of her name, announce, date 1616.

It was here that, some twenty-four years later,[*] Ellen ended her long and successful life in her 78th year. We visited the chapel—splendid in its carved oak fittings; and there on the wall's side hangs the portrait of the foundress painted at the age of 77—no longer Ellen fair and dimpled as at Rosenholm, nor Ellen over-blown as at Nørland, but Ellen an aged woman— a fine, strong, green old age—in the costume of the period, with a peaked hat like that of Mother Shipton— a most interesting picture. At her death—she lies buried in the village church of North Broby, with her husband, Ludvig Munk—Ellensborg passed to Christina Munk, and again to her daughter fair Eleanor Ulfeld; then came confiscation, and the glory of the Munkites was at an end.

By the side of old Ellen are two full-length portraits, those of Corfitz and Eleanor.

Every town in Denmark piqued itself on something in the good old days, and Nyborg appears to have vaunted loud and high its salutary by-lov—bye-law we still call it in England—so severe, its very existence would have made me let my house, " plier baggage," and fly even to Odense. Such a sumptuary law against the wearing of swords at parties—such a chopping off of hands for next to nothing—Star Chamber a joke to it. The women, however, were treated with becoming respect, for in one article it is enacted "that every

---

[*] 1649.

qvinde" detected in stealing or being in connivance with a thief shall be condemned to be hanged, but the sentence, on account of her "woman's modesty," to be commuted to being "buried alive."

As for the laws of adulteration, the punishment was death; but, in case of detection, the offenders were allowed to decide the matter by arms. Fancy a London grocer and twelve of his shop-boys engaged in single combat, in the precincts of the Green Park, against twelve adulterated householders, called upon to avenge the housekeeping grievances of their outraged housewives. In addition to the losing of heads, whippings, and such like, all adulterated goods were declared to be confiscated, and were solemnly burnt in the presence of the injured citizens. Such a decree might be found advantageous even in the present day.

These bye-laws were just, had they extended to all classes; but the magistrates themselves were exempt from their severity: for, says the old Danish rhyme,—

"When the mayor of the city sells ale and wine,
And the magistrate he kills the sheep and swine,
When the baker weighs himself his bread,
The citizens might all as well be dead."

It is evident corporation monopolies were not approved of.

In a letter existing from King Hans to Bent Bilde, Governor of Nyborg, he writes:—"We intend, please God, to visit church with our dear wife the Sunday next to St. Olaf's day, and have our young daughter christened. And we beg you to be present at that time and the same day with your dear wife, and enjoy yourselves with us and several friends whom we have invited."

GLORUP.

August 5th.—We are off for Svendborg this morning, a drive of sixteen miles, but stop half-way to visit the manor of Glorup, the country residence of Count Moltke, famed for its English gardens. English gardens are to be mistrusted even in Denmark, where the climate assimilates somewhat to our own. The velvet turf is always wanting—turf of ages—never to be replaced by sowings of common grass. Dissect for your amusement a small die of our finest sheep-fed English sward, compressed to dwarfdom; you will find nearly one hundred varieties of plants in the small square; it is the work, the progress of years of vegetation, not to be produced by an annual crop; added to which, did they possess the turf itself, the Danes would never understand how to take care of it, or allow the time necessary to the gardener for bringing it to perfection.

Glorup is a fine old place, with lime-avenues of half a mile in length, unrivalled even in Denmark. A long oblong fishpond, all in character with the old-fashioned building. As a whole it is beautiful, but ruined by an Anglomanic taste badly carried out. The house was built by the celebrated Walkendorf, minister to Christian IV., and arch enemy of Tycho Brahe, whose ruin he plotted from the day of the "dog scene" in the isle of Hveen. His portrait is in the village church, together with early tombs of his ancient house. Stone carvings of mermaids and mermen support the vaultings of the roof, a strange device, as these marine monsters were held in the utmost horror by the Church of old. In the ballad of Agnete, when her merman comes to the English church to fetch home his spouse, it is sung—

> "When the merman into the church-close treads,
> The small saints and angels avert their heads;"

but they were English saints, and knew how to comport themselves.

We pass on our day's journey not far from Lykkesholm, once the possession of the house of Lykke—Lykke the gorgeous, as they were rightly termed, for none were richer, nobler, and more magnificent than the hero of my story. If ever you visit the Royal Library of Copenhagen, ask for the Müller collection, and there, among Denmark's nobles, you will find the portrait, after Thornburg, engraved by Haas, of a young man, slight in figure, graceful in form, with long hair cut short over the forehead. The features are not perhaps strictly beautiful in their regularity; the charm must have lain in the expression of his eyes and the brilliancy of his complexion. This is the hero of my story—Kai Lykke by name, the handsomest (smukkeste) and richest young nobleman in all Denmark. His beauty became a proverb, and the old rhyme ran—

> "Every fair damsel in Denmark did pray"—

What they did pray I shan't repeat, for it was very bold of them, and they ought to have been ashamed of themselves.

Well, Kai Lykke, handsome, young, and rich, was badly looked upon by the prudish Hanoverian Queen Sophia Amalie. He had already been called over the coals for a letter (still preserved) in which he says "the queen stands in intimate connection with her lacqueys." This was perfectly true, for she was very familiar, and gossiped with her men-servants. The storm, however, passed over, on his declaring he merely alluded to her "condescending manners." Later Kai Lykke marries, but at the same time writes a love-letter to a clergyman's wife, in which he declares "the most noble lady of the land could not resist him:" puppy, if you will, but the women had made him so. The parson's wife shows the letter to the queen, who, firing up, declares him to be guilty of lèze majesté; that she is the person alluded to as "the most illustrious lady of the realm." So Kai Lykke is summoned to appear, but makes his escape as fast as post-horses can carry him; not a woman in Denmark who would not have forwarded his escape. The indictment is made out, but the letter is not produced in court, out of respect to majesty; Kai is condemned to death "unanimously," his thirteen estates confiscated to the crown, the sum of twenty thousand dollars being allotted to his wife.

But Kai is far away; the queen, rabid at the escape of her victim, causes him to be executed in effigy, attired in the picturesque costume of our Cromwell's time— jerkin, lace collar, and long boots—the most gentlemanlike costume of any era when free from Puritan savour: so the right hand of the mannikin is chopped off, the body broken on the wheel, then decapitated, exposed, and later shown for money by the headsman, who made a good thing, for all the women of the country flocked to see it.

Kai Lykke's house still stands in Christianshavn, near the canal, and is now used for some official purpose. Of his ultimate fate I know nothing. The epitaphium of his wife, preserved among the engravings, did not excite my sympathy—an uninteresting wishy-washy woman, with little twiddling corkscrew curls ranged around her face. An angel is represented as opening the heavens, and beckoning her with the consoling words—"The stars open, and you shall then regain above what you have lost below."

A two hours' drive—same sort of country—very English, pleasing, and compressed—orchards and hops—cottage-gardens, still gay with summer flowers, the "Bright-star," * "Night-light," † "Steel-cap," ‡ and the more poisonous "Knight-spur." § The peasant children sit, as in England, at the cottage doors, stringing chains of the "Thousand Joy" (tusynd fryd), as they here term the daisy.

Not far to the right lies the village of Ryslinge, a very bad neighbourhood from all accounts, where the ghosts are still heard ploughing at night-time, and apparitions torment the affrighted peasantry. In the last century a farmer was so afflicted by their spiritual torments he addressed himself to the parish priest, himself a wizard, how to lay them. Very wise was the advice given—"Leave the ghosts in peace, they will die out by degrees, and, after a time, will only appear once in a century." This same farmer had the luck to house the parish Niss, who dwelt in his "high-loft," patronized by every one except the watch-dog, who could not bear him. This Niss was a great thief, extra-parochial; he stole corn from the adjoining hamlet of Lørup, while the Niss of that parish returned the compliment. The farmers at last held a Ting, and it was decided some one should be set to watch:

---

* Lychnis: Pragtstierne.   ‡ Aconite: Stormhat.
† Œnothera: Natlys.   § Larkspur: Ridderspur.

but no one liked to watch the Nisses; it brings ill luck. At last the blacksmith was induced, by the promise of a sack of wheat from each farmer of the two villages, to lie in ambush among the branches of a willow, the boundary of the two parishes. After a time, he saw from his hiding-place approach the Niss of Lørup, and then that of Ryslinge, each loaded with a sack of corn: they met under the willow-tree. "Hallo!" exclaimed the Niss of Ryslinge, "you rascal—to rob my master!" "And you, you blackguard, what are you about, stealing the parish corn?" Then they fell to fighting, and after a little time the Niss of Ryslinge took to his heels. "I got the best of it," said he of Lørup, looking up into the tree. "Yes," said the blacksmith, but he gave you the last blow." On hearing this the Niss threw down the sack of corn, and ran after his antagonist. The blacksmith then jumped from his tree, picked up the two sacks of wheat, and came home to the village to claim his reward.

We again get glimpses of the sea, a fiorde, the island of Thorseng before us; we descend à côte; down a hill and up again, and are disembarked at the only hotel of the place—the post-inn of Svendborg.

SVENDBORG.

August 6th.—Our post-gaard, most conveniently situated for "changing of horses," looks nowhere; the place is full of bathers, and the house noisy. The town itself, perched on a hill-side, must tell better from the island of Thorseng, on the opposite side of the fiorde; but nothing more soft, more pretty, can be well described than the wood-clothed banks, extending towards Christiansminde. Our first stroll did not however run that way; we betook ourselves in the opposite direction, seduced by the tower of a milk-white church rising from the woods which embower it: St. Jørgens it is called. Here the wicked Danes declare that St. George fought the Dragon. Our English St. George! a great fib! as all men know the combat took place somewhere near Tripoli. Dragon or no dragon, it is a lovely spot the village of St. Jørgens. There has been in former times an hospital attached to the church, and the view from the cemetery is charming. We stopped to gaze at the old square court of the præstegaard, the entrance-door shaded by two limes of glorious growth; and were in full admiration of its picturesque appearance, hay-loaded cart and all, when the son of the pastor came out, and begged us to walk in the garden and see the new house his father had lately completed. The old gaard was to come down. It was an excellent modern house —of greater appearance, and not ugly; no house in Denmark is ever ugly—with its high-pitched roofs and gables, but a sad exchange for the old limes, the square court, and the parlour-windows on the other side, with the open balcony commanding the blue waters. "Chacun a son goût, et tous les goûts sont respectables;" so say the French.

These villages of Funen, with their abundant fruit-gardens and orchards, remind me of Calvados, and sometimes of our own more primitive hamlets of Devonshire, by the coast-side: it is rare elsewhere to meet rich cultivation and sea combined. The peasant-women too wear an eccentric cap—not like the Cauchois, but much frilled behind — and such a bonnet! like a japanned coal-scuttle, formed of glazed and painted carton, bent: you may purchase them flat in the shops.

This is a splendid place for bathing, and the establishments — floating baths, with cradles for non-swimming females — well-arranged and airy. Jelly-fish the only drawback: beautiful to gaze upon, but most disagreeable to the touch; added to which they sting — not anything dire, but a prickly, disagreeable sensation.

Svendborg rather piques itself on its godfather King Svend; though in old documents of the middle ages it is more frequently written Sviin, or "Pig Castle." Orthography, we all know, was very faulty until the present century; and the same name, be it town or family, you frequently find written in ten or fifteen different manners. Still the inhabitants appear to have been so touchy on the subject, and somebody, to clench the matter, composed some doggrel, which he caused to be hung up in the church, that I almost believe there to have been some truth in the assertion.

A town planted on a hill is always picturesque. It is something pleasant to overlook your neighbours' chimneys; and when the buildings are of ancient date, queer and rambling, with storks' nests and fruit-gardens, it adds to the charm. As you pass down the street you may read — if Danish be, like the French of Paris to Chaucer's Abbess, "to you unknown" — in the Latin tongue many a wise saw, many a good old proverb, inscribed above the doorways, coeval with the buildings themselves. Old saws, proverbs, and such like, are now esteemed vulgar; but many a good principle, many a domestic virtue has soaked into the mind of man as well as womankind, solely from the fact of its being placed for ever before their eyes. Svendborg was a loyal town to the house of Oldenborg, and Christian III. evinced his gratitude for her fidelity in 1535:

"What can I do," he asked of her head magistrate, a priest, one Hans Gaas, "to reward your faithful services?" "How," answered the magistrate, humbly, "can a poor goose (Gaas) like me have done service to so great a sovereign?" Nothing like humility in this world: the Geese became ennobled; and Hans, Archbishop of Tronyem.

THE ISLAND OF THORSENG.

August 8th.—We pass through the post-gaard garden, luxuriant in trees laden with unripe apples, to the detriment of the stomachs, I should imagine, of the tribe of babbling children who dwell within—seductive too with skittles and swings; turn into the road through a gate, and by a sharp descent gain the little jetty where the ferry-boats already await the passengers for Thorseng. A ten minutes' sail brings us to shore. The sun is high in the heavens, and we have a long walk before us. Svendborg looks better from the other side. Then too you have St. George's church and wood, and Christiansminde as well; but our first excursion leads us to the church-tower of Bregninge, the highest point in the island, from whose summit you gain a panoramic view of all the Danish archipelago—Lolland, Langeland, Funen, Ærø, and half a dozen other Øs, small fry, unknown to the world in general—all very flat, very green, very blue, and satisfactory to those who care for bird's-eye views, without a background beyond the gray horizon.

This isle of Thorseng, flat though it be, is fair and fruitful, the possession of the noble house of Juel, descendants of the gallant Admiral Niels Juel, whose tomb we visited in the Holm church of Copenhagen. A pleasant walk along the water-side leads to the residence of the lord and master—smiling villages, with gardens, woods, hops, and orchards—a prosperity to make the heart joyful. Valdemar Slot, it is called—a huge pile, with gate-houses spacious enough to furnish a residence to any moderate-minded man, built by the fourth Christian, who gave it, with the rich broad lands surrounding, to his eldest son Prince Valdemar (by Christina Munk), that good-looking fellow who hangs in the Royal Gallery of Copenhagen, painted by Carl van Mander. He appears to have been a spoilt boy, as most handsome children are, and later in life ran wild, causing his father some trouble. Christian writes word to his son-in-law Corfitz Ulfeld, in a letter dated 14th September, 1643: "Count Valdemar Christian leaves this to-morrow on a journey through Denmark. God grant him a happy journey! He has cost me much money. Pray Heaven this may be the last! If you don't make him careful, he will soon spend all the money I have given him before he comes to Copenhagen, notwithstanding he has got here all that he wanted; besides which he owes the tailor 20,000 specie." An extravagant dog was Count Valdemar. He endeavoured to persuade Corfitz to go security for him, and "back his bills." So, to keep him out of scrapes, his father sends him off on an embassy* to Moscow, and negotiations are entered into for marrying our scapegrace to the Russian Princess Irene; when all was

---

* The very same embassy to which Count Horn, whose epitaphium we admired at Kiel, was appointed secretary.

arranged, Valdemar refused to be baptised according to the Greek Church after the Muscovite manner. On his first introduction into the Czar's presence, by way of seeking favour with his future father-in-law, he kissed the sceptre. The Russians declared that from henceforth he became the vassal of the emperor. When Valdemar discovered this, he determined to leave secretly; accompanied by three of his attendants, he tried to escape through Poland. On arriving at the gate of the city after dark, he was recognised and stopped; and, after a pitched battle between his servants and the Muscovites, was taken prisoner, and kept secure until the death of the Emperor Michel, when he was set at liberty. On his way home he carried off a young lady from Warsaw, deserted her, and she drowned herself in the Sound at Elsinore. After Ulfeld's rebellion, disgusted at the coldness with which he was treated by his half-brother Frederic III., he joined the party of his brother-in-law in Sweden, and died in Poland, an officer in the Swedish service.

Valdemar Slot is an ugly pile of brickwork externally, much degraded, and now, alas! in Chancery, a lawsuit between two brothers. It is however worthy of a visit, with its gallery of portraits, one of the most interesting in Denmark, but fearfully neglected, being unappreciated by the possessors. In one of the great saloons are hung those of the early sovereigns of the house of Oldenborg, from Frederic II. downwards, all on horseback; each horse, however, follows that of his predecessor, giving the whole the appearance of a royal carousal or merry-go-round.

It was Frederic III. who, as "cadet du sang," commenced life as Archbishop of Bremen—a world of trouble his father had to get him appointed.* There he is; most ecclesiastical too he looks—as like a bishop as the Duke of York did of Osnaburg—à cheval, armed cap-à-pie, distinguished alone from his brethren by the starched plaited ruff of the Lutheran clergy. His duties cannot have been onerous, though to me the wearing of the frill would have been worse than all the penances and fastings of the Romish Church. We mount the staircase; on the landing-place hang all the family of the fourth Christian—heavy, drunken Prince Christian, who made way for his brother the bishop and his wife Madalena of Saxony, she with feather-fan in hand and lapdog by her side; Prince Valdemar, the possessor, though he never resided there, a fine boy—a child to be proud of, as indeed all Christian's were. And those fair ladies with golden powdered hair, high ruffs, and somewhat uncovered, looking-glasses and pearls. Who be they? "Those," replied the conductress, " are the twelve frilles of King Christian." Powers above! twelve! Lump together all the demi-monde of that immoral court —all the Kirstens, Karens, Vibekes—you can never number twelve; but they are very pretty women, much superior to the portraits of Rosenborg. I must take the liberty of vindicating three from this sweeping verdict: those three exquisite creatures who hang below belong to another period, somewhat later, and are, if I mistake not, authentic copies of some of our English beauties of Hampton Court. One I imagine to be the Princess of Orange, Mary Stuart, daughter of Charles I. —she was good at any rate; a second, highly rouged, not

---

* The best portrait of Frederic III. is that by Wuchter, with Kronborg in the background, engraved by Haelwech, gone the way of all Danish pictures—burnt in some conflagration.

unlike the haughty and imperious Castlemaine, whom I have already met with in Rosenborg; the third, a lady of King Charles's court, surpassingly lovely. Not to linger, we have, among many others of interest, Queen Louisa of England in all her youth and beauty. What majesty! what a presence! Her portrait is not rare in Funen. Then there is Niels Juel, first as a boy—hofjunker to Duke Frederic—in red jacket and silver buttons, something like that worn at a Spanish bull-fight; again repeated, surrounded by his victories, as Admiral, Knight of the Elephant, &c., a table with the names of his vessels, his captains, lieutenants, and officers, down to the lowest grade. But of all the portraits of the Juel house, there is one most charming, a lady of the last century, missal in hand, coming out of church, the light of a setting sun falling on her dress through the mullions of a Gothic window, one of those effects of light so much loved by some of the Dutch painters; the master unknown.

My opinion is that to see these islands in their fullest beauty we should have visited them in the month of May, in the new-born luxuriance of early spring-time, before the harvest is gathered in and the green fields become stubble. In these northern climes the summer is bright, but short. The months of May and June, though the days are prolonged till midnight, and twilight is only a cloud passing over the fair face of nature, yet are but of thirty days, and soon fly by. Could we extend the year to fifteen months, one more summer quarter, it would be a great convenience.

We had another excursion to make from Svendborg before leaving—to the pretty wood of Christiansminde, which we gained in a boat, and on—a pleasant walk—to

Bjørnemose (no bears there now), the picturesque château of Baron Bille Brahe—somewhat bare, but backed by woods and fair gardens, a residence fitted for modern occupation and the enjoyments of the present age, well placed on the extreme end of the Svendborg fiorde. Visit it, if you are ever at Svendborg, and return, as we did, by water.

CHAPTER XLIX.

The Island of Lyø — Capture of King Valdemar by his treacherous vassal — Kirstine Munk and her children — Horns of Wedellsborg — Marksmen of Middelfart — Snoghøi in Jutland — Brahe, the King of Funen — Island of Thorø, and Balder's stone — Ellen Marsviin married again ; turns cattle-dealer — Her game of cards with the king — Island of Langeland and the giant Rud — Sir Otto Krump's defence of Tranekjær.

ISLAND OF LYØ.

August 10th.—WE had imagined a steamer to Assens, but find it goes alternate days, and to-day we must sleep on the opposite coast, at Aarøsund, in Jutland. We pass by the island of Thorseng, terribly in the way; it blocks up the beautiful Svendborg fiorde, while it adds but little to the view. Coasting by St. George's wood and village, a very archipelago of small islets, Skaarø, and half a dozen other Øs, make their appearance. They are all flat and uninteresting, and the banks of Funen itself nothing to speak of. At last we enter a fiorde, and the little town of Faaborg lies before us, distinguished from her sisters by her praiseworthy attempt at a quay, and avenues planted along its side. Faaborg might become a watering-place, and prosper, if it only would have lodging-houses by the water-side. We unload some pedestrian students, pipe in mouth and valise in hand—I should not like to walk through Funen, or indeed Denmark, much too flat and dusty—and then proceed. Steam past Bear Island; and now, after turning the

T 2

Knollen Point, another green islet appears in view—islet celebrated in Denmark's early history. A sad celebrity too it bears; for from the event which there occurred dates the downfall of her country's greatness.

In the ballad of 'Dronning Leonora,' King Valdemar exclaims—

"Full well we recollect the hunting of Lyø." *

It was on the eve of the 7th of May, in the year 1223, that Valdemar the Victorious, and his elected son Valdemar the younger, reposed after a hard day's hunting, not far from a fountain which still bears the name of Kongens Kilde. Soundly they slept in their tents, little imagining the danger by which they were menaced. Suddenly, in the dead of the night, they are attacked and seized by the armed bands of their vassal Count Henry of Schwerin, and carried prisoners to the fortress of Lenzen, in Altmark, where they remained for three years.† In vain the pope threatened, in vain other sovereigns solicited their liberation. Valdemar at last obtained his liberty by having first surrendered his conquests, and renounced all future claim to their possession. Old Hvidtfelt thus quaintly describes the unfortunate event :—

"They sat in the tower in irons and strong chains for three years, at which every man, both princes and people, were greatly surprised that so insignificant a

---

* The High House—det høie huus—so often spoken of in the island of Lyø, and which is now part of the priest's gaard, is of later date than Valdemar, for he slept in the open air.

† When Count Henry of Schwerin went on a pilgrimage to the Holy Land, he confided the countess to the charge of his sovereign—Queen Berengaria was dead—and it was to revenge the seduction of his wife by the king that Count Henry undertook the expedition. The Princes Erik and Abel remained as hostages for seven years.

count could imprison so powerful a king and his son without a blow being struck in their behalf, or the spilling of blood."

Well might the world be astonished that the pusillanimous Danes did not rise as one man, and lay waste with fire and sword the country of Schwerin. The excuse they assigned was, that their sovereign would have been removed to some more distant fortress, and his liberation rendered more difficult to procure. But Henry of Schwerin was but a petty count, and had the Danes acted with proper pluck they might easily have invested his dominions. It is more probable that the øprorious nobility of those days were glad to be free from the control of a sovereign who, while he had added to the national glory of their country, ruled them with a rod of iron, and repressed with a firm hand their unlawful enterprises.

We steam past the little island, which still retains its "réputation giboyeuse"—hares and partridges abound there ; it is now the property of Baron Holstein. Leaving Assens to the right, we enter the little harbour of Aarøsund. "You will have to sleep at Haderslev," said a passenger ; "no possible inn at Aarøsund." But my faith in Jutland kros is strong ; and we found one, where, had we had leisure and time at our disposal, we would willingly have lingered some days—a long one-storied house, built near the fiorde side : sitting-rooms opening on the sward, with garden and large timber-trees, seats underneath, and bathing-cabins not far removed. There is no doubt we are again in Jutland: the air is pure, bracing, and fragrant—quite different from the soft, mild atmosphere of the islands. A brother traveller, affected with what he called "the falling-sickness"—epileptic fits—was suddenly attacked towards early dawn, causing great consternation in our quiet kro, otherwise we should have slept like princes, for our linen was of the finest texture, white as the driven snow, smelling strong of iris and lavender; our beds were covered with couvrepieds of old embroidered silks— wreaths of jasmine on a sea-green ground—drawn in our honour from the hidden recesses of an ancient carved wardrobe some three centuries old or upwards.

WEDELLSBORG.

August 11th.—The steamer would wait for us one small half-hour, did we wish it; but the mail arrives in time, and we are ready on board. We disembark at Assens, and wander about the town while horses are preparing. Nothing remarkable in Assens; she is busy restoring her fine old church, and does it well. A little wool trade too she possesses of her own: beyond this ask nothing—one small Danish town is own twin sister to another.

We drive on to Wedellsborg—Grefskab, or county, of Count Wedell—another of those Danish paradises by the water-side, imbedded in woods. The house is of no architectural pretensions, but most comfortable to live in. Among the numerous portraits is one of Christina Munk, with her three eldest daughters *— small girls. First Anna, betrothed to Count Rantzau, who was drowned before his marriage in the moat of

---

* Elizabeth Augusta, wife of Hans Lindenov— a fourth daughter of Christina Munk—was the ancestress of the Wedell family, and mother of the bad Baroness of the "windy waste" near Aalborg. She gambled away all her possessions, and, after great poverty, lived on a small pension given by Christian V.

Rosenborg, and she died of grief. Sophia Elizabeth, a child of great beauty, who married Count Christian Penz. A woman of spirit, a great flirt too, she was—so much so as to scandalise her royal father, who writes word how "Sophia Elizabeth is to be reprimanded on account of her flighty behaviour with Christian Penz," just too when he was so busy about her grandmother, good Queen Sophia's funeral. She secondly married Holger Wind, who at the time of Ulfeld's disgrace deserted her: so in her anger she returned his portrait with the eyes "clawed out," just to show him how she would have served him had he been within her reach. Lastly Eleanor. The three little girls are dressed exactly like their mamma, in buckramed farthingales, scarlet red, and starched ruffs, gold powdered hair. Prince Valdemar, just out of bed in his little shirt, and a small dog, complete the group. Corfitz and Eleanor Ulfeld in their early days, before trouble and sorrow had thinned their locks and wrinkled their youth and beauty. The Wedell family descend from a granddaughter of Christian IV., and in the family chapel of the church of Wedellsborg you may see this king's portrait suspended to the walls, dead on his "lit de parade," somewhat like a chandelier, in a scarlet pelisse fastened together with bows, his legs swathed up in fine linen or muslin with a bow at the end.

It was near Wedellsborg that two of those splendid Scandinavian horns were discovered; one, the finest specimen, is here preserved, and hangs in the dressing-room of Count Wedell; the other was forwarded to the Museum at Copenhagen. And now, after taking leave, we proceed on our journey, and, before arriving at Middelfart, stop to visit the far-famed manor of Hindsgavl, where in former times a royal castle of much repute stood; but, "jetons les souvenirs aux orties," we do not require them here; for such a scene of loveliness as is presented to the eye from the manor-gardens is seldom to be witnessed. The wooded shores of Jutland, the indentation of the coast, the island of Fœnö and her "calf," combined with the blue waters of the Little Belt—the prettiest cerulean cincture that ever girt a fruitful isle—all combine together in smiling colouring and beauty.

The old castle had the honour of being burnt and sacked, together with Middelfart, by Marsk Stig,* who to these islands became a great scourge—too well he fulfilled his promise to the youthful Menved, laying waste, burning, and destroying; and then Hindsgavl, after passing through a deal of war and bloodshed, was finally blown up and destroyed by the Swedes in the unlucky war of the 17th century—a "genteel" ending for a Danish fortress.

N.B.—The farms of the island of Funen are very extensive, though not quite on the same scale as those of Jutland and the Duchies. The rat-charmer of Ringkjöbing must be sadly wanted in these parts, for in one manor we visited the proprietor kept upwards of sixty cats.

MIDDELFART.

August 12*th*.—We find Middelfart in full gala. Stuhlwagens arrive from the earliest dawn; something is about to happen it is evident: so we inquire. A grand popinjay match comes off in the wood near Hindsgavl,

---

* 1290.

followed by a rustic ball, to last all night, and late next morning too perhaps.

We wander to the scene of action. The shooting is fair enough—nothing like the Tyrol marksmen, but the "hane" comes tumbling down occasionally. We could not, however, remain, for we had friends at Snoghøi, on the Jutland coast, and were engaged to pass the evening there.

I have described so many herregaards, that it may be something novel to visit a real Danish villa, and a prettier specimen can nowhere be found than that of Snoghøi. Planted by the ferry-side, a long low house, with well-proportioned rooms, built for comfort, not for state, terminated by a large, square, open loggia, embowered in clematis; its look-out, Middelfart, most picturesque of all towns when viewed from the Little Belt and the adjoining forests. Behind rises a hill, laid out in the prettiest of gardens, an arboretum of rare shrubs and forest trees, pines and araucarias. The whole have been planted by the proprietor, M. de Riegels—twice planted; for in the war of '49 and '50 Snoghøi was the scene of strife and bloodshed; her fair plaisaunces destroyed, and rendered uninhabitable to the family for three years. Now all again is smiling; a rock-work of cannon-balls alone chronicles the previous devastation of the property. While we strolled in the hanging gardens of the villa, brilliant with summer flowers, the youthful members of the families fished from a punt in the waters of the Belt, whiting and flounder their prey.

The moon rises red and tawny—just like the opera; but we are in honest respectable Denmark, far from the land of Cherubinos and Almavivas. When people say "Buona notte" here they mean it, and don't go skrimmaging about after dark, but go to bed with a good thick duvet covering a-top of them, be it July or even the dog-days, and sleep and snore in their short couches till the next morning.

It was late, nigh midnight, when we quitted Snoghoi and our kind friends, and again embarked for Middelfart. We had breeze enough this time, but a side one.

The waters of the Little Belt sobbed bitterly against our boat side as we floated along. "You are going," cried a little wavelet, as I bent over the stern side, watching the reflection of the full moon in the silvery waters, "you are again going to leave our shores—you, who above all travellers love and appreciate our wide plains, our old manors, the ancient histories and the legends of our people." But I answered to the wavelet how I hoped to return at some future period, and should never forget the happy days we had spent in her ancient manors and her windy provinces; how I admired her fertile lands, and wished that more capital could be invested in developing the natural resources of the country; but that now, the first sod of her moses once turned, her railroads in progress, much would be done towards the improvement of her agriculture and the enrichment of her proprietors. Now perhaps her gentry would at last discover and appreciate the wealth of the manure rotting idle in their stagnant moats—would cleanse them, as we are about to do our own Serpentine, to the general suppression of fever, rheumatism, and ague, only too prevalent in her inland parishes. And then tack, tack, went the barque, the wavelet leaps up, imprints a briny kiss upon my forehead, and dancing, rolls on, to repeat my answer to her companions—yes, tack, tack, went the boat. Talk of the 'Song of the Shirt,' "stitch, stitch!" write the 'Song of the Sail,' just as odious in its own way, "tack, tack!" shooting off to right or left, as the wind may be, some 200 yards, when you fancy yourself all arrived at your destination. But we are at last arrived, and bid a long, but I hope not last, good night to the shores of old windy Jutland.

BRAHESBORG.

August 13*th.*—We retrace our steps a part of the way to Assens, to stop and spend the day at Brahesborg, the château of M. de Trescow. No doubt who built Brahesborg—Jørgen Brahe, and somebody Gyldenstierne his wife*—iron cramps, holding letters long as those of St. Peter's dome, announce the fact— a custom luckily chiefly confined to Funen, by no means ornamental; he seems to have been somebody in his day, was nephew to poor ill-treated Tycho, and called "the little King of Funen." He appears indeed to have been a very Marquis of Carabas of these parts, —possessor of Brahesminde, Brahesborg, Brahesholm, Brahetrolleborg, and half a dozen others—many passed into other hands, while the some six manors of the present family belonged to somebody else. It's astonishing how property changes hands in Denmark.

Jørgen desired his workmen to build a house which should last till the world's end; it may, for its cellars are vaulted like a fortress of the 19th century; it is, however, more remarkable for simple solidity than for the beauty of its architecture. There was an era

---

* The epitaphium of Jørgen Brahe is engraved by Haelwech.

of ugliness in Denmark, from the middle of the 17th century till the commencement of the 18th—houses imposing from their size alone. The apartments are grand and spacious. The portraits of the sovereigns of the house of Oldenborg give dignity to the mansion; an old loyal custom, now nearly out of fashion. It is astonishing how few of Thorvaldsen's works are to be found in his native land. Brahesborg is an exception; for here we have the Kneeling Ganymede, work of the artist himself. All Denmark is now in full vacation —Sorø and Herlufsholm, Copenhagen, Odense, and the high schools of the provinces; in each manor we find a merry party of youth of both sexes—twelve or fourteen cousins and relatives—spending their holidays together. To those who have dwelt in France, where offspring are scarce, such an assemblage appears quite patriarchal, but the châteaux are large, and the hearts of the proprietors as large as their dwelling-houses are spacious. I have seldom come across more happy, joyous family-parties than during my residence in Denmark. Everything is ample and liberal at the table—well served and no display. The men-servants wait, but, if the family are extra numerous, the women aid in the service. People here all know their position, and are quite above vulgar absurdities.

And now my sojourn in Funen is merely a series of hospitalities received. Holstenshuus, where we passed another pleasant day, the seat of Baron Holsten, not far from Faaborg, more remarkable for the glorious view over the Little Belt and the Danish Archipelago than for its mansion, an old striped house, an autumn pied-à-terre of the proprietor.

At one mile distant from Svendborg we have Hvidkilde, château of Baron Holsten Lehn, the gem of all Funen mansions of the last century. A wondrous fountain, from which it derives its name, casts up its waters like an artesian well by the side of the house, fertilising the plains, the gardens, and refreshing the moat itself. Everything that luxury, art, and good taste can give is here to be met with—gardens and hothouses, fountains and fine old furniture, the rooms fitted up with all the comfort and good taste of a first-rate English country residence; farms of a large extent, poultry-houses, pheasantries.

In the lake hard by has lain hid, says tradition, a vast treasure of gold and silver for 200 years. The Swedes, laden with the pillage of the rifled island, endeavoured to convey it across the ice; a scuffle with the Boers ensued, the ice gave way, and the cart, treasure and all, sank to the bottom.

We are determined to visit no more châteaux; several were on our list, some of historic interest; but each succeeding day starts up some new object So at last, in despair—for the summer glides on; we have no longer the long light nights to travel through as when in Jutland—deaf to temptation, we prepare to leave for the sister island. One château, a gem of ancient days, a jewel of mediæval architecture, I did regret, but it was, alas! uncomeatable, and that was Egeskov, the property of Baron Bille Brahe.

There are dark tales in relation to this mansion, illustrative of the manners even of fourth Christian's period. Laurits Brokkenhuus then was lord of Egeskov—a hard, brutal man, known well for his cruel and revengeful disposition. Among the fairest of Queen Anne Catherine's ladies stood his daughter Rigborg, distinguished

alike for the charms of her person as well as for the
fascination of her manners. Morals, as we all know, in
King Christian's court were at a sadly low ebb; and in
the year 1590 the frail Rigborg gave birth to a son—
Frederic Rosenkrantz, of Rosenvold, the reputed father.
Furious at the disgrace of the family honour, the enraged father of Rigborg demanded that the seducer be
(according to the laws of the day) ignominiously branded,
and undergo a fearful punishment as well as the loss
of two fingers, and that his daughter be immured for
life. Immuring consisted at that time of incarceration
within a room, bricked up like the fanatic recluses of
the Roman Church, a small aperture alone left open
for the introduction of the prisoner's nourishment; no
light. (No wonder poor Elizabeth of Brandenburg
scampered off from old Joachim at the very idea of
such a fate; she had heard enough of it in her own
native Denmark.)

The barbarous sentence on Rosenkrantz was commuted by the king, and he went to fight against the
Turks, where he met his death.

Poor Rigborg! Christian—a roi galant himself—
should have interfered in your behalf, but he did not.
She was safely immured in a small dark turret chamber,
on the second story of the tower of Egeskov, and here
she pined through five long weary years, until one fine
day her father was called to his last account, and she
released by her brothers from her fearful thraldom. As
she did not die during her incarceration, it is to be
hoped her ghost does not haunt the scene of her former
misery; in all probability she had enough of it during
her five years' imprisonment never to return there
afterwards, even in "spirit."

ISLAND OF THORØ.

The small island of Thorø we did not explore, for the weather was still hot, and it would scarcely have repaid the trouble.

Like Lyø and others of the same calibre, it formed a natural deer-garden for the early Danish kings; and in Valdemar's Jorde-Bog is mentioned as good for the hunting of "hart, doe, and roe." In earlier times still, on a site close by the bay, lay a stone called Balderssten, under which they say was buried the giant who is sung in the kæmpevisen:—

> "Balder, his wife, and Rune,
> They had a great fight upon Fune,
> Or some say on Thorø;
> And Balder he beat Rune."

The name of Balder has been handed down to posterity by the song which at Christmas-time is still sung in chorus by the children in many parts of Denmark during the application of the nine blows inflicted on the culprit in the game of forfeits.

> "Blows we now beat three,
> One after the other in time,
> Nor will the sinner to free
> Until he's got his nine."

After the ninth blow he is released. Balder and Rune came to grief about Balder's wife; Rune endeavoured to escape in a boat, but when he was driven into the bay, near where the stone stood, Balder caught him and crushed him with the big flat stone, on which the prints of his ten fingers were distinctly to be seen.

The stone was surrounded by trees, and was in all

probability a menhir, but has now entirely disappeared. Later, Thorø came into the possession of Ellen Marsviin, who here first appears in a new light—no longer Ellen Munk, but as a bride, wife of Knud Rud of Sandholt, one of the richest noblemen in all Denmark, who died in 1611. Here she carried on a great traffic in "staldøxene" (cattle), furnished the king's troops, and well too; for a French writer, in this very year, after praising the appearance of the Danish sailors and the army on board the fleet, adds, "There is no luxury, but a wonderful abundance of good meat, as well as all the necessaries of life." Old Ellen built here a stone house, called Marsviinsholm. She was, however, hard on the peasants, unlike her first husband, Ludwig Munk, who was the model landlord of his age; so her memory is not revered. The people tell how one day she staked the island of Thorø against his Majesty at cards, and lost it. At first Ellen declared it was only fun, that she never played in earnest, but Christian was not to be put off in that way; so she begged to keep it until after crop-time; and, to spite the king, sowed thistles; the land in consequence became so bad the king would not have it. She got into hot water with the Church, to which she had no idea of being a benefactor without ruling and regulating all appointments even down to the gravedigger. She it was who brought the celebrated altarpiece from Delam Cloister to Thorø, on which were the portraits of Christian I. and Queen Dorothea, which were lost on their way to Copenhagen. Eleven years later she gave up the island to the king, to complete the apanage of his grandson, young Count Valdemar.

ISLAND OF LANGELAND.

August 16*th.*—A small boat is engaged to carry us to Langeland; we may be two, we may be four hours, perhaps longer; all depends upon the wind. Down comes a pelting shower, rendering departure at six an impossibility. Had it fallen yesterday—tenth Sunday after Trinity—great would have been the anxiety of the peasants, and woe to the crops, for on that day " our Lord wept over Jerusalem." Our course lies in the opposite direction to that of last week; we float down the narrow fiorde towards Christiansminde and Bjørnemøse, and then turning, twisting, and tacking by Thorseng and its sister isle of Thorø, until you get into an open sea, pass by an islet called Siø and two other little Øs, and gradually float—for the breeze is lulled, what little there is of it—into the harbour of Rudkjøbing. Every town in these parts turns out a something kjøbing. A wondrous giant, Rud by name, lies interred near here, and gives his name to the capital of Langeland. Tranekjær, the seat of Count Ahlefeldt, is the lion of the island, and thither, towards the evening, we bent our way. It was once a château-fort of some consideration in the middle ages, and stands placed on an eminence commanding a view of the surrounding archipelago, &c.

In the reign of King Christian II., Sir Otto Krump—the same Sir Otto we found buried in the church of Mariager—held the strong castle of Tranekjær for the royal party. Among the correspondence of the King is a letter dated Tranekjær, 5th March, 1523: endorsed, by the king's own hand, "Sir Otto Krump's letter to the King's Majesty, in which he writes to say he will to him be 200 thalers." We visited the park, extensive and English-like, and the gardens running down to the lake side, its orchard, and the sward as green as a polished emerald. From the blue waters of the lake rises a small, very small, island, like those we keep for swans to build their nests on. Around the edges was planted a garland of that large creeper,* with a leaf the size of a catalpa, so commonly seen running over summer-houses in England. It grew luxuriantly, its tendrils running down and floating in the limpid waters; then from the centre of this trailing border rose a pyramid of hollyhocks—red, yellow, white, and rose-coloured—dancing and nodding in the breeze: some stand stiff and stately, scarcely reflected in the lake below; whilst others, Narcissus-like, bend forward, longing to catch a glimpse of their golden and roseate petals in the pure mirror.

Langeland is termed un vrai jardin. Well, it may be one, for what I know—its villages, its hop-gardens, its orchards are prosperous, the wild vine is in full luxuriance and flower, its churches in good repair—all tells of a resident landlord who does his duty in that station of life in which he is placed—but somehow I don't care for fertility when travelling; we have enough of hedges and ditches in England; all is prosperous, and, like Alexander Selkirk's complaint of his beasts,

"Their tameness is shocking to me."

So we returned to our hotel, and the next morning drove over to the ferry, where we re-embarked for Lolland.

* Aristolochia sipho.

CHAPTER L.

Island of Lolland — Yule-feast of Olaf Hunger — Wendish families from Rugen — Royal ordinances — Lutheran clergy — Sir Edward the Pedagogue Priest — Shell of the Swedes — Mr. Ursins and our Prince George — Birthplace of Erik Glipping — The Curate of Helsted and the mother's curse — Tale of Sir Otto Rud and King John — Revelations of St. Bridget — The ill-behaved nuns of Maribo — Grave of Eleanor Ulfeld — King Charles "forgets" the loan — Eleanor in captivity and death — The bricked-up lady of Hardenberg.

ISLAND OF LOLLAND OR LAALAND.*

August 17th.—The Danes had told us it was a nasty passage over to Taars, and advised us to steam from Korsör,—which advice was gratefully received, but we followed the bent of our own inclinations. The wind was really favourable; in four hours' time we were landed at Taars, and then had to wait that neverending hour till the horses were procured and ready.

Womankind is admirable in travelling; it rises early and bears fatigue, is easily contented at the inns with bed and board; it will do and put up with anything, except "wait." What are we to do? A whole hour, and those horses never come; infamous!—write to the postmaster, &c. &c. So, for very peace sake, we (for the family is now increased by the arrival of the Philistines, or, in plain English, a black-and-tan terrier called Vic, and two schoolboys from Harrow) throw up a barricade at once against all possible grumblings; we undress, we

* The Danes spell it either way.

swim out to sea, and remain floating in the water; if any one approaches us are "just coming out," and so the hour glides by, the horses arrive, and we scramble out, dress, and reappear just in time to escape scolding, and not keep people waiting.

According to Helvaderus, a chronicler of early date, the flat fertile island of Lolland was first populated some 2000 years after the world's creation by men from Jutland; and at as early a period as the seventh century did a wandering apostle of the true faith, Wilibrod by name, preach Christianity to the Pagans of this remote region,—without success, however, it appears: for it was not until Harald Blue-Tooth tacked on Lolland to his new-founded diocese of Odense, that Christianity can be said to have been there established even in name. Not that the introduction of the new faith profited the inhabitants much; indeed, how could it? a creed forced upon a people by fire and sword, while they still clung in their inmost hearts to the worship of Thor, Odin, and other Scandinavian heroes, whose bloody deeds and wild traditions were more in accordance with the barbarous fierceness of the age than the milder tenets of Christianity.

Terrible were the sufferings of the unhappy islanders during the succeeding century, from plague, pestilence, and famine. Thousands are said to have perished from hunger alone, as well as from the devastations of the epidemic. So great was the scarcity, the bareness of the land, that it is related when King Olaf Hunger (famine was his name) himself sat down on one Christmas Eve to keep the Yule-feast together with his Court, there was no bread, no, not one wheaten loaf served on the royal table. A very dull Christmas, with such poor fare, he must have had of it. Still, among these scourges of famine and plague, churches rose in the land. Three still exist, founded within that unlucky century.

Many of the names still to be met with in the sister isles of Lolland and Falster will sound strange to those accustomed to the Danish tongue—Kramnitze, Tillitze, Corselitze; these are of Wendish origin, Wendish names brought over by the settlers from the heathen isle of Rugen. No sooner did the Christian faith get hold among the people than down came the Wends upon the islanders; they burned, they pillaged and laid waste—just as the Northmen themselves did on our English coasts—till Prince Prislav sat down comfortably in Lolland, with his Wendish followers and his royal bride, and ended his existence. Later her towns were burnt by Marsk Stig, and his pirate-band came in for a good share of the black pest (Digerdøden). Lolland was given in dower, pawned, and taken out again. In certain years there was great plenty—all provisions wondrous cheap; but, as those years followed fast on some great calamity, it may be safely supposed that butter, corn, and fish were cheap, simply because there was nobody to eat them.

The kings appear to have been most exacting, and their lords spiritual, the bishops of Odense, more irritating still. Such laws against the chase! No peasant allowed to keep more than one dog, or to slay even a fox detected in the robbing of his hen-roost. Still, some of the ordinances were of good effect, particularly as regards the fertilisation of the land: by one of these, in the year 1446, every peasant as well as every child in Lolland is forced to plant thirty hop-plants, six grafted pear and apple trees, before the

Volborg-Day, which answers to our St. John's, under a penalty of three silver marks. This command may appear somewhat arbitrary, but it was issued after a year of excessive cold, during which the hop-gardens and orchards of the island had greatly suffered. But to make up for these annoyances, in the year 1399 the waters of the Baltic froze so hard the islanders skated over to Lubec on the solid ice.

To the fearful pest of 1565 upwards of 13,000 men fell victims: among them were numbered twenty-eight parsons, all men of singular learning—so say the chroniclers at least—though I doubt if the loss was great. These early reformed priests were only Lutheran by courtesy; they took so unkindly to the "starched ruff" their diocesans of Odense found it necessary to impose a heavy fine on those who still persisted in the wearing of Catholic vestments; and as for their wives, they dizened themselves out so in gold, velvet, and damask stuffs, that the bishops, losing all patience, issued such sumptuary laws on the subject of their dress as soon settled the business.

I have been dipping to-day into an old book written upon the islands of Lolland and Falster in the earlier part of the last century—one of those works, like our own county-histories, useful as books of reference, full of dry statistics, mingled with queer anecdotes, genealogies, and what not. Among other matters is a short notice of the life of each Lutheran parish-priest from the Reformation downwards. The memoirs of these simple pastors of the reformed faith are interesting, though many of the anecdotes related are absurd, and have a tendency to turn the clergy into ridicule. No one could cite them as shining lights of the Church, far from it. Had they met with a little persecution, as did the Nonconformists in the days of our Stuart kings, their energies might have been called forth; but in Denmark the Church of the reformed faith was, from the first, Catholic, *i.e.* universal. King Frederic II. would allow of no dissent. The first who differed from the tenets of Martin Luther, or propounded new doctrines, "Away with him!" was the cry; and while, in less than a century from the establishment of the Reformation, we find the Anabaptists skipping about the streets of Holland in propriis naturalibus, and, a little later, the Puritans of England cutting off their king's head, the Church of Denmark has remained—stagnant it may have been, but still united. Little has been done on the part of the Lutheran Church to excite inquiry. "Be content with what you know, and don't meddle with matters you cannot understand," is their maxim. But for the most part they appear to have been good, excellent men, kind to their parishioners, charitable, giving liberally out of their modest incomes to those in want and sickness, and in the earlier days to have held a higher and more respectable position in society than did our own "parsons," as described in the 'History' of Lord Macaulay.

From the amusing accounts I have run my eyes over, I could almost imagine Sir Walter Scott had taken as a model for his Dominie Sampson some bookworm of the Danish Church. Absence of mind and eccentricity appear to have been the special failings of these worthy men. One learned divine always conversed with his horse in the Latin tongue, which gave him a bad reputation, for his parishioners looked upon it as "necromancy." When out riding he had all the conversation to himself, as you may imagine, but that was what he liked. He tried it with the pigs first, but they answered with a grunt, which disturbed the thread of his conversation.

In our own country we are universally of opinion that an ex-pedagogue is ill-adapted to form a good parish-priest, more especially when he enters upon his duties late in life. Of a certain Sir Edward it is here recorded that, on his retirement from scholastic duties, he not only flogged his men-servants when caught out in any dereliction of duty, but his maids into the bargain. He lived for the rod, and by the rod; and if he swore by anybody—which it is to be hoped he did not—it must have been by King Solomon. When the bishop of the diocese on his pastoral round lodged at his house, he determined to teach his diocesan humility, so he served him kail and cabbage, while he treated his servants to venison steaks and wine.

NASKOV.

An hour and a half's drive brings us to the city of Naskov. We alight at the hotel. "Why, we expected you by the steamer last week," said the landlady; "had all your rooms prepared and dinner ready." Some busybody had chosen to announce us.

Naskov boasts a fine church, lately well restored; a very fleet of vessels hang suspended amongst the coronas. When Frederic IV. visited the town, and his eyes first lighted on its church-tower, tall and slender, capped with its stunted mail-work of slate, he exclaimed, "Well! never before have I seen a stripling with such a low-crowned hat." Nothing very clever; but the loyal population of Lolland have handed it down from father to son; they repeat it still, as they will indeed do for many generations to come, and look on it as first-rate. To the right of the altar, mounted on the capital of a disused column, stands a huge shell, burst in twain, which came tumbling through the roof of the building in the 17th century, during the celebration of a christening.* Just above the spot where it now lies, the hole in the roof has been plastered up with yellow mortar, to mark the place where the destructive missile found its entry.

Before the restoration of the church took place the mummies of the vaults below were the glory and gain of the verger, now closed to the public for ever. It was a regular Madame Tussaud, a very chamber of horrors. There was Karen Holm, another young lady who danced herself to death, with a smile still on her countenance; the man who died of the black pest, and whose body was tarred over from top to toe, to prevent infection, all black in consequence; true, not to life but death.

If the christening party in Naskov church escaped scatheless from the bursting of the shell, such was not the case with the inhabitants when, at a later period, the city was forced to capitulate, for the terms imposed by the victors were so hard that many years elapsed before the town again recovered its prosperity. Some five years later upwards of 160 houses stood unoccupied. The Swedish king himself appears to have been the most economical guest of the party; the expenses of his board and lodging amounted only to

* 1657.

300 thalers for the space of some days. As for Mrs. Admiral Wrangel, she squeezed out of the inhabitants the sum of three thousand specie for her own "menus plaisirs." *

Among the few men of note to whom the city of Naskov has given birth ranks high a certain divine, George Ursins by name. He is said to have spoken fluently nine separate languages, and composed verses in no less than eighteen. So charmed with his erudition was the royal Prince-Consort of Queen Anne that he desired to appoint him as his "Confessionarius," and offered him the sum of 1500*l*. English annually, as keeper of his conscience.

Learned Mr. Ursins however declined. He preferred his residence in the island of Lolland and the society of his books. Maybe he had qualms of conscience as regards accepting so large a stipend for the care of an empty head. Some satisfaction there may be in directing the conscience of one endowed with natural talents, and turning those gifts of nature in the right way to the best advantage, or in the reclaiming from such error one who has gone astray; but the direction of an addlepate, harmless and unimpressionable, must be a sad and tedious occupation even to the most patient of mankind.

In 1266 the little city of Naskov, too, gave birth to our old acquaintance Erik Glipping, the Winker, as he was called, though those who love not his memory declare his sobriquet to signify "Clipper," derived from a bad habit, in which he was too apt to indulge, of clipping—sweating, we modern vulgarians call it—the

---

* General Wrangel, like the rest of the world, sat to Wuchter during the Congress which preceded the peace. His portrait is engraved by Haelwech.

lawful coinage of the realm.* Forest lands exist—a gift to the city from his mother Margaret of Pomerania; Sprænghest, as she was called. She broke the wind of all the horses she mounted by her violent riding.

Lolland is as flat as a pancake. We leave Naskov, and drive through roads bordered on either side by fields—square fields. When they are oblong, oh! what a blessing! quite a feature in the appearance of the country. Then each field is surrounded, not by a hedge, but hurdles and a row of pollards, willows or poplars.

JUELLINGE.

Not far from Naskov we arrive at Juellinge, a château of Count Friis; most imposing it looks, too, from a distance in its ancient Gothic; but on arriving you discover the Gothic is most suburban in its character. Its gardens have still a faint perfume of old Popish days. We visited the chapel, restored by Good Queen Sophia, whose "hope was in God alone,"— an admirable motto, so applicable to the days in which she lived, when the tenets of the past were uprooted and the future was dimly discerned. She allowed herself to be seduced by fanatics of neither

---

* "Hyt Klipping Fi" was the cry (when he was out of hearing) of the people. In this, however, he was not worse than his successors, for Frederic II., of pious memory, caused the money to be clipped until the thaler valued scarcely more than three mares; the people refused to take them, so he issued an ordinance, read in Nestved on Ascension Day 1564,—"That those who refused to take them should at once lose their heads without mercy;" and, as about this time the mint-master and all his men had died of the plague, his subjects were compelled to put up with what they could get; and, writes King Frederic to his minister Gyldenstierne, "the shops are put to great inconvenience by the want of small change."

side, but went her own ways steadily, unflinchingly, mixing herself up with the rabidities of neither party. Many old carvings still remain. Hanging in the church you will see a picture, representing a man in a clergyman's dress, together with his wife, one living child, and eight dead infants in their swaddling clothes, concerning which the old woman who keeps the keys will relate a story. This man was curate of Helsted, and once refused to bury the corpse of an unbaptised infant. The mother prayed him earnestly, but he refused, using harsh words, "I will not cast earth upon puppies." Then the woman cursed him, and prayed his wife might never bear him a living child. The curse was fulfilled; eight dead children were born one after another, and it was not until he was induced to bury an unchristened child that the boy you see in the epitaphium was born alive.

The chapel of the Rud family is worth a glance. Fine old sepulchral slabs of the 16th century. Whether they be descendants of the giant of Rudkjøping, history relates not, but they were stalwart knights, men of thew and sinew, in their days, connected with all the best blood of Denmark—Fleming, Byng, and Høg, among the rest—as you may see by the border of escutcheons which surround their effigies. Of this family was Sir Otto Rud, a gallant warrior in his day, and much beloved of his sovereign the good King John, for he was a boon companion, and they loved to joke together. One day, as the king was poring over his favourite book, the 'History of King Arthur and his Round Table,' he turned to Sir Otto, and exclaimed, "Where now, in the present day, could I find such knights as Gavin, Sir Ivan, and the rest of them?"

"Nothing more easily, liege King," replied the knight, "do you only, by your virtue and chastity, establish such a court as that of King Arthur, and the knights will be found fast enough." The King collapsed, for at that time there was much scandal about his misbehaviour. "Indeed," adds the chronicler, "when Queen Christina was imprisoned in Sweden, King John appears to have forgotten he had ever been a married man."

KNUTHENBORG.

We now make for Knuthenborg, Grefskab of Count Knuth, situated on the sea-shore, embowered in park and forest. Laaland is flat, fertile, and ugly; but plant a château on the sea-side, surround it with forests of beech, with garden and park and fine timber-trees, it at once becomes a paradise. Such is Knuthenborg, or, rather, will be; at present it is in a state of transition. An older residence, not yet pulled down, a new castle in course of erection, one wing finished, awaits the majority of its youthful possessor. It will be a magnificent place when completed in the style of Denmark's national architecture—for she has a style, and wisely preserves it. We passed a pleasant day in the society of our kind friends the countess and her youthful family.

MARIBO.

It was nearly pitch-dark when we arrived at the town of Maribo. We caught glimpses of a lake, a new-built Gothic town-house, and then whirled into the porte cochère of the Gjæstgiver of the city.

Maribo was given, when it bore some other name,

to the only surviving son of Tove, Knud Valdemarson, as he was called, he whose step-son followed him to the war as squire and then murdered him.

An old document, dated 1417, mentions how on Michaelmas Day the Bishop was summoned to Vordingborg Slot, and there, together with King Erik, Queen Philippa, their nobles, knights, &c., sealed the grant of Ryse Gaard, in Zealand, to found a cloister in Lolland, to be hereafter called "Maribo," in honour of St. Bridget and the Holy Virgin. King Erik it was who completed the cloister after the death of his queen; every man, woman, and child in the country had the honour of contributing to it. Each man for himself and his household paid the sum of 2*d*., and for each child eighteen years of age 1*d*. Bachelors were taxed, old maids were taxed; no one escaped. It was a right royal foundation; the king got the credit of it, and the country paid the expenses.

Scarcely was the convent commenced when there appeared in the heavens every night a wondrous luminary over the forest which Queen Margaret had herself purchased of Jens Grim, and paid for as a site for the building, which was regarded as a clear proof Jomfru Marie wished to take up her abode there; so St. Bridget had to give way and appear second on the list. "Beata Brigita vidua," St. Bridget the Widow—of the Brahe family—was a noble Swedish lady, mother to four sons and four daughters. As soon as her husband died she was seized with a desire to visit Rome, feeling sure that the foundress of Vadstena would be well received by the pope. When sixty-seven years of age she travelled to the Holy Land, accompanied by her daughter the lady Karen.* She died on her return to Rome, in 1373, and was canonized by Urban VI. some years later, when her bones were brought over to Vadstena with great rejoicings. The revelations of St. Bridget in former days held a high reputation in the Church of Rome, particularly those regarding the seven future kings† of Denmark and Sweden, the seventh of whom is supposed to allude to Christian II.‡

At the Reformation the nuns of Maribo, though let down easily, conducted themselves so badly that Bishop Jespersen, Confessor Regius, went down expressly to investigate the matter.

They were accused of letting into their house drunken tradesmen, as well as noblemen, of tearing each other's caps and fighting; not contenting themselves with swearing by ten thousand, they swore by ten thousand dozen devils, using awful bad language; they beat each other, drank spirits, and got so intoxicated they could not stand on their legs; held to the Catholic belief, had "wicked books"—*i. e.* Papistic—and prayed to all the saints in the calendar. The bishop, in despair, issued new regulations, but to no effect; the nuns continued just as bad as ever. Fresh rules, in 1596, were put in

---

* Later St. Catherine.

† The first appears as a "crowned ass," which, to say the least, was not civil; another as a trembling sheep; a third as a slaughtered lamb; a fourth as a ravening wolf; a fifth as a high-flying eagle, &c.

‡ He shall stir up the whole world and the sea, and make sorrowful the simple. It is he shall draw the blood of the innocent, but he shall leave the country, and that shall happen as is said, that he shall sow pleasure and reap sorrow and affliction. Fools shall reign and old and wise shall not be brought forward. Honour and right shall be laid aside until he comes who shall appease my anger, and he shall not save his soul from what is right.

force, with a little better success, and then later the convent was dissolved.

In this deserted church, under a plain stone bearing an inscription and now railed round, sleep in peace the remains of Eleanor Ulfeld. Twenty-three years of imprisonment did she undergo in that fearful Blue Tower to gratify the woman's vengeance of the Hanoverian Queen Sophia Amelia, her sister-in-law.

The story of her griefs tells ill in English history for the reputation of our "merry monarch" Charles II. Eleanor had proceeded to London to procure the payment of 24,000 rix-dollars Corfitz Ulfeld lent in those days of splendour to the exiled heir of the house of Stuart when in Holland. Charles had at first denied the debt, and there exists a correspondence between the Kings of England and Denmark on the subject, which letters were forwarded by the latter to the Swedish Queen Christina, in whose service Ulfeld entered. When Christina read the papers presented to her by Baron Juel, the Danish envoy, she replied, with a freedom of speech worthy of our Queen Elizabeth, "Ulfeld is an honourable man. He says he paid to the King of England 24,000 dollars, and I believe it to be true ; and if the King of England denies the debt, so has he lied. Yes, even if twelve such kings as Charles II. had declared it untrue, so dare I say they have all lied, and I should still believe Ulfeld ;" and she remained firm in her belief of his honour, which was later confirmed by the receipt for the money, signed by the Scotch General the Duke of Montrose. King Charles then declares "it had quite escaped his memory,"—but he never paid ; for on Eleanor's arrival in London, seduced by the bribe of a large sum of money from the Danish queen, she was kidnapped by order of King Charles, placed on board a Danish vessel, and brought over to Copenhagen.

From the moment of King Christian's death Eleanor's star began to fade : her privileges were taken away from her ; she was no longer allowed to drive into the palace yard or dine at the royal table ; in 1657 her title of Countess was taken away. When she arrived at Copenhagen, Queen Sophia Amelia herself, with the aid of the maid, undressed her, and, having deprived her of all her pearls and jewels, caused her to be clad in the coarsest clothing. Eleanor and her maid were brought to trial ; a phial of poison alone was found concealed in her hair, which she had purchased at Dover to use in case of " necessity."

In the Blue Tower she remained, amusing herself with modelling beakers in clay with a piece of bone, for she was allowed no knife, and working other "artful things." Eleanor was the most accomplished of Christian's daughters: she spoke German, French, Italian, Latin, and Spanish ; played on harp and flute ; was a good artist, had a great turn for poetry, and, says a writer of the day, " could sing one Psalm and compose another, and know what was passing in the room at the same time." Most of her poems are addressed to her dog, named " Cavalier," a poor mangy beast, who had been bitten by a ferret, presented to her by the queen, as a " marked insult," when in prison. She was allowed no window to her room, merely a hole in the roof, and no pipe to her stove. One day King Christian V., inquiring what she was doing, was told " making beakers ;" so he asked to see one. On examining it—a sort of tankard, standing on three balls, with a cover—the king discovered some writing underneath; but release her he dared not during his mother's lifetime.

His Queen Charlotte Amelia pitied Eleanor's unhappy fate, and in return for a purse embroidered with beads dared to brave her mother-in-law's wrath, and ordered her a new window and a pipe to her stove. When Queen Sophia Amelia died Eleanor was released by order of the king, who gave her a pension of 1500 thalers yearly. She went, on leaving the prison, to her granddaughter Miss Lindenov's house on the canal, by the Holmskirke, but only remained there three days, for all the town came out to see her; later, she retired to Maribo, where she resided till her death, passing the greater part of her time in embroidering altar-cloths for the church, with verses expressive of her gratitude to her nephew the king and his family.

Eleanor had had her husband's blood transfused into her veins. This gave her the power of feeling what happened to him; when he died in 1644 she informed the king long before news of the event had reached him. Eleanor died in her seventy-first year. Her head reposes upon a cushion stuffed with her own gray hair—hair fallen off and carefully preserved during her long and wearisome incarceration.

Few convent churches are externally worth looking at, but here the interior vaulting is exquisite. The image of St. Bridget, too, has lately turned up after a retirement of three centuries; but to make up for her presence a youthful saint or bishop does duty as Martin Luther. Among the abbesses and burghers whose sepulchral slabs line the aisles, resting against the wall stands erect a stone of great beauty, date 1565, on which the Trinity is represented life-size. In Denmark alone the custom of portraying the Father Eternal in sculpture and painting survived the introduction of the Reformed Faith. Another instance occurs on the exterior of the church of Eckernfiorde.

I have elsewhere told you how the representation of the house of Ulfeld is now centred in the Austrian Counts of Walstein. When in Holland, Corfitz invited the representative of the States—Hogans Mogans—to the baptism of his new-born son, and later, a high compliment, to name the child. On the day of the christening the generous burghers arrived laden with cups and covered basins of pure gold, enamelled in blue and enriched with a "pavé" of cameos and incised gems—a triumph of goldsmith's work: you may still see them in the museum at Copenhagen. And they called the child "Leo Belgicus," to the amazement and consternation of poor Eleanor.

ENGESTOFTE.

We start for Saxkjöbing, halting on our way at Engestofte, the seat of M. de Wichfeld, where we pass some few hours. The house is not large, but the situation lovely: embowered in wood on the lake's side—such glorious limes too—now in full flower and perfume. Near the house stands a small chapel, admirably restored, carved altarpiece, repainted and regilded.

We crossed the lake in a punt to the small island where once stood the very castle given by King Valdemar to his son by Tove. The waters of the lake are now low and half-dried up; and lately amongst the weeds have been discovered numerous antiquities of the Stone Age—hammers, chisels, knives—many unfinished, with their chippings—showing there must have been a manufactory, and either that the lake was once dry land, or that the ancient Scandinavians made ducks and drakes of these weapons and household implements, throwing them into the water. Small boys, whose eyes are sharp and near the ground, came off triumphant with an unpolished chisel and a flint knife, to say nothing of chippings innumerable.

An agriculturist would rejoice in the farm-buildings of Engestofte lately constructed—so well built, so artistic; more spacious than required for an English establishment, where cows are not counted by hundreds, and housed, as well as sheep, during the winter season. In the cow-stable the name of each beast hangs over her stall—Jomfru Faust, Trina Smith. Twelve young heifers were named after the planets, but Georgium Sidus, Jupiter, and Saturn were words the Lolland milkmaid could never accustom her tongue to.

We take leave, pass through the town of Saxkjøbing, and on to Hardenberg, the seat of the counts of that name—"Hardenberg-Reventlow," and a great deal more.

HARDENBERG.

To Jutland and Funen we must give the palm for their châteaux of ancient date, their long, trim allées, their hedges, and gardens of by-gone centuries: but to flat, fertile Lolland the prize for her fair plaisaunces. Nothing can be more beautiful than this garden, a very wilderness of summer flowers, losing itself in the park-like field, backed by rich woods in the distance. Look, too, at the castle—what a fine old moated building!—. what a pity they have restored it "white," instead of its early red brick! But it stands grand and imposing, with its three capped towers—mark, there are only three, for thereby hangs a legend.

It was long long ago—not in the time of the Reventlows—though, had its possessor, the brother of the fair Sophia, treated her in the same way, she would only have met with her deserts—nor yet in that of the Rosenkrantz; all possessors of the place declare it was before their time—that the daughter of some noble owner of the domain loved a boy of low degree. Months ran on—it is an old tale, and one oft told—she bore a child, and was doomed by her enraged relatives to undergo the punishment allotted to her crime—to be immured, like the nuns of old, in a small chamber of the tower, and there, with the offspring of her love, to pine and die by a cruel death—starvation.

Years rolled by; the story was well-nigh forgotten, when one night, during a fearful storm, the lightning struck the fatal tower, rending it in twain; and there against the wall was discovered the skeleton of the luckless damsel, her mummy baby pressed against her breast. The destruction of this tower was looked upon as a judgment of Providence, an expression of its indignation against the authors of this foul deed. None have dared to rebuild it. The crumbling ruins were removed, and the foundations alone attest that it had once existed.

The interior of the castle is fitted up with a luxury almost unknown in Denmark. As we descended by the spiral staircase of the tower, which leads to the garden, its narrow window, now lighted with purple glass, cast a cool pleasant light on the small statuettes of Florence alabaster which are ranged on brackets down the open limaçon of the staircase. Matters have changed for the better since the sad tragedy occurred in the sister-tower. Talk of good old times—in books if you will: but let us thank our stars we didn't live in them!

It was dark when we arrived at the little sea-side town of Nysted. "Maribo and Saxkjøbing are pleasant places," says the proverb, "but Nysted surpasses them both." We shall see to-morrow.

NYSTED.

Nysted resembles other small Danish towns. When you gain the sea-side, a long double avenue of trees conducts you to the ancient château of Aalholm, a huge red brick pile of buildings, with massive square towers, dating from Queen Margaret's days, thanks to Marsk Stig and Skipper Clemens, a rarissima avis in Denmark. Here resided her brother—poor half-begotten little Christopher—Duke of Lolland, whose effigy in alabaster we have seen in Roeskilde cathedral, all broken to pieces, the Danish Government too poor or too stingy to afford the cement necessary for sticking him together. Some authors declare that he was poisoned at Queen Margaret's wedding, but there is no truth in the story: in those uncomfortable days no one was allowed to die peaceably without suspicion.

The castle—"over-rumplet" (taken by surprise) in 1534—is now the property of the Count of Raben, but is seldom inhabited: the gardens, kept in the true Lolland style, are well worthy of a visit.

Such black coal-scuttle bonnets as the women wear here! of carton, like the Fionese; not japanned, tea-tray fashion—sober black, ugly enough to frighten you. Now we make for Strandbye, the ferry-station to Falster, a five minutes' passage. Really Lolland and Falster so nearly join, it seems quite ridiculous their being separated.

CHAPTER LI.

Island of Falster — Queen Sophia and the parson's wife — How she rules her household — The lady who could not die — Molesworth's account of swan-shooting — Familiar spirits and other superstitions of the island — Island of Møen — The strong-minded Dorothea — The bathing-place of Liselund — The chalk klints and beauty of the scenery — The Klint King — Bacchanalian harvest-home.

ISLAND OF FALSTER.

NYKJØBING.

August 29.—WE land on the small pier of Nykjøbing, stop to breakfast, and then drive through the island on our way to Møen.

There is nothing to see in Falster—no herregaards. More exclusive than Lolland, the island, until some years since, was a royal possession, the usual jointure and residence of queens.

In the small town of Nykjøbing dwelt good Queen Sophia, the widowed mother of Christian IV., glad to retire from the court of her son, whose morals ill accorded with the principles of his right-thinking mother. Here too she died.

In the church hangs her pedigree—pedigree of the house of Mecklenburg, with portraits of each member from the earliest days.

When Queen Sophia ruled over the island she did much good, encouraging industry, and employing in her manufactures many hundred people. There still stands an oak between Vaalse and Nykjøbing which goes by the name of "Præste Kongen, from a wager laid by the parson's wife with the queen that she would spin a thread out of a pound of flax so fine it should reach from her parsonage to the palace gate. The lady proceeded on her way till her flax was expended at the house which bears her name. Queen Sophia was a good ménagère, and kept her maids as well as her men in order, not sparing the whip when they deserved correction:

"Linde Herre skal have Eege svenne,"
"A maitre de tilleul, domestique de chêne,"

was her motto. She died the richest queen in Europe; and though Christian IV. honoured and loved his mother, yet to judge from his correspondence he was quite alive to the advantages to be derived from his inheritance.

Scarcely is she on her death-bed when the king writes word "they must take care to look after her keys."* He writes to his sister Augusta to send down the jeweller to value the queen's effects; orders mourning for the children, who are to travel to Vordingborg to receive the "widowed queen's coffin:" they are to wait for the corpse and get something to eat at

---

* Many of good Queen Sophia's people lie buried in the church of Nykjøbing. Such a "maitresse femine" as was Queen Sophia! Such rules and regulations, such modesty and virtue among her maids! such propriety among her men! Mrs. Ollegaard Penz, her noble housekeeper—her place not then, as now, a sinecure—at the end of eleven years' service died, worn out by her troubles and domestic cares, and even now, after the lapse of two centuries and more, she can't rest quiet in her grave. She fidgets and fusses about the château of Fredskov, rattles the keys, opens and shuts the drawers, rings the bells, winds up the clocks, and dusts, dusts away, and will dust—so folks say—in sæcula sæculorum, so disgusted is she at the degeneracy of all Danish housemaids.

the ferry-house; the cook-boy can accompany them and take what is necessary. Christian appears to have been in good humour with his succession, for he presented his mother's maid who cooked his soup with ten rose nobles.

One letter, dated the latter end of the year 1631, is as follows:—" Apothecary Peter, fill your satchel full of rotulen, musk, and amber, and other spices, as good as you can get them, and bring it here at once.— Frederiksborg."

What could this be for? Nothing less than the necessary medicaments for the embalmment of Queen Sophia.

You will find many old acquaintances in these portraits; among them the queen of Christian I., here ungagged; old Joachim of Brandenburg, holding a drawn scimitar in hand, looking like some vindictive Blue beard, right in the face of poor Protestant Elizabeth. She was quite right to run away; by his very look, he'd have bricked her up. The palace of Queen Sophia has disappeared; gone most likely to build up something else. If a royal Danish brick could only speak, what tales it could tell of the sights it has witnessed from the days of Thyre Danebod downwards, picked out from the Danevirke for the erection of some château fort, and so handed down to the present century!

We leave to the left the village of Torkildstrup, named after the heathen Thorkild—the first man, say the Danes, who pretended the earth turned round.

We passed in the distance a church-spire, concerning which there runs a tale:—Many years ago dwelt in the island of Falster a rich and noble dowager, who had neither son nor daughter to inherit her golden treasures.

She resolved to build a very great and splendid church. When the building was finished she ordered the altar candles to be lighted; then proceeding in great state through the aisle to the high altar, she fell down upon her knees and prayed God, as a reward for her pious gift, to let her live as long as her church was standing. Her foolish prayer was granted. Her kinsmen and servants died, but she outlived them all. At length she had neither contemporary friends nor relations to speak to; she saw all their children become old and die, and then again their children after them sink under the weight of years,—still she lived on. By degrees she lost the use of almost all her senses, and at last she only recovered her power of speech once a year—each Christmas-eve, for one single hour. She begged one Christmas to be laid in an oaken coffin and placed in the church, to try if she could not die there. They did as she demanded, and her coffin was placed in the church, but she has not been allowed to die to this day. Every year at the appointed hour the parson comes to her, and lifts up the heavy lid of the coffin. She slowly raises herself till she sits erect in the coffin, when she asks, "Is my church still standing?" "Yes," answers the parson: " Would to God," she exclaims, " that my church were burnt, for then would my wail end!" Sighing, she once more sinks back upon her hard pillow, the parson shuts the coffin, and does not return until the Christmas following.

We drive to Corselitze, a small country house, half-farm, and then enter a lovely forest by the blue water's side. Midway between that small homestead and the ferry of Gronsund we pass the little inn of Solyst, a favourite place of Sunday resort to the badauds of

Nykjøbing. It stands on the water-side, and you might easily while away a week among the surrounding forest and its coasts. Herds of deer, wild chevreuils in number, and fawns of all sizes, as well as hares, cross our path. Chevreuil and roe-deer are not the only game which abound in this island. In the year 1692 Christian V., together with his queen and many illustrious personages, on their journey from Møen to Nykjøbing, enjoyed a goodly sport, slaughtering in one day four hundred and twenty wild swans by the village of Gjedsen. Battues of wild swans were a favourite diversion of the last century, for Molesworth writes, " These wild swans haunt a small island, about one mile distant from Copenhagen, and breed there. About this time of year the young ones are near as big as the old, before the feathers are grown long enough for them to fly. The king, queen, and the court ladies, with other nobles, are invited to take part in this sport. Every person of condition has a pinnace allotted to him, and when they come near the haunt surround the place, and a great multitude of swans—sometimes a thousand—are killed. The flesh is worthless, but the feathers and down are preserved."

Superstition thrives in Falster as elsewhere. The farmers have nisses, but cottagers are compelled to put up with " familiar spirits "—a preposterous fairy called Dragedukke, who not only supplies them with all manner of good things, but also gives them the power of transferring the good luck of others to themselves. A woman of Kragehave was possessed of a Dragedukke. In vain her neighbours tried to churn; she could take away all the butter from them, while she had plenty herself even in the worst weather: money, too, her husband had always at his command. A neighbour asked him for the loan of a hundred pounds: he went to a cupboard and took it at once from what appeared to be an empty hog's bladder; but the borrower heard groans issuing from the bladder, as though the fairy within was bewailing the loss of the money. When a corpse leaves the door, they cast a pail of water behind it, that the ghost may not reappear. On Christmas-eve those who wish their fruit-trees to bear an abundant crop go into the garden at midnight, and, taking the sticks from the bakers' ovens, strike each tree thrice, exclaiming, "Rejoice O tree,—rejoice, and be fruitful!'

We reach the ferry, leaving to the left the small town of Stubbekjöbing, and in a minute are landed on the opposite coast of Møen.

ISLAND OF MØEN.

A two hours' drive brought us to Stege. The small hotel was full of bathers, tea-drinking and eating their suppers in the garden overlooking the sea. A church with lofty massive tower and quaint old gate-house, a rarity in Denmark. The moats exist still, and are nicely laid out in promenades. The castle has long since disappeared, granted by King Erik, after the death of Queen Philippa, to a certain Dorothea, a strong-minded young woman, quite above the prejudices of this world, who bore inscribed upon her signet-ring the words "Dorothea, King Erik's concubine." We drove on, passed by two or three villages, having for ever a gray ridge of mountains before us—elsewhere you would have called them hillocks—and then came to a stone which by daylight indicates the way "To Liselund;"

here we turn off, after a time come to a gaard, and
drive in. It is nearly twelve o'clock, all the world
asleep, even the watch-dog. We halloo, bawl, crack
the whips, kick, for twenty minutes without success; at
last a sleepy head looks out from the stable-window,
later the farmer himself appears, yawning his very jaws
asunder.

September 1*st*.—We are now quietly settled, and perhaps you may like to know what Liselund really is.

Liselund is a country place, the property of M. de
Rosenkrantz; not a herregaard; a square court, three
sides of which are occupied by stalls, granaries, and
farm-buildings, the remaining side forms the abode of
the family. Our apartments consist of a large saloon
opening into the garden, with bed-rooms on the same
floor; to take our baths we pass down an avenue of
trees into a second garden, in which stands a small
villa-house: the whole is backed by woods, and as
pretty as gay flowers, orchard-trees, creeper-bedecked
summer-houses, water, swans, rock-work, boats, and
bridges can make it. Passing through the wood, you
arrive at the klint's edge, clothed with beech, juniper,
and the prickly sloe, covered with its purple-bloomed
fruit; turning into a narrow walk by the side of a
ruined chapel, with its sanctus bell, once used as
a bathing-house, you here gain the shore. This
beech-clothed descent is lovely, and peeps of the
verdure-famed Baltic most enjoyable; in the month
of May this small Alpine region must be a carpet of
spring flowers. Denmark is the country of spring par
excellence. The autumnal tints are so fine, people
say, in the forests! they may be, but somehow, when
in the autumn of life oneself, one admires more fer-

vently the spring and youth in others. White silver hairs are venerable, and there is a beauty in real green old age, but nothing to extacise about in gray stubbly whiskers. Autumn among the mountains is beautiful, but not in a flat prairie country; the beach is shingly and unpleasant to walk upon; when once immersed, however, you will find a sandy bottom, if you only watch the yellow lines on the water.

To gratify your eyes, as there is no boat nigh, you must swim out to sea. Look before you, to the left—did you ever see anything more striking, more grand, than that ragged, rugged white chalk cliff, boldly découpé, jutting out into the water? The Taleren it is called; the first of a long ridge of miniature white mountains, which rise like a succession of fortresses to defend the eastern coast of Møen.

Fossils of all kinds abound on the shore—echini, madrepores, chamæ, oysters, and sea anemones; and better specimens still may be dug from the pulverised chalk of the klint itself.

From Liselund there are two ways of visiting the Store klint; first by the narrow walks cut out along the edge of the precipice itself. You pass by a small cottage in the wood—a milk-white peacock spreads his tail, as much as to say "Look at me"—and then straight on. But all the world are not pedestrians; hire then the farmer's carriage, and drive through the beech-forest, now suffering from a plague of hairy caterpillars—a forest of many hundreds of acres leafless; up the trunks of each devoted tree they crawl in myriads—some yellow, some dark brown, of all sizes—Vor Herreds Hunds, our Lord's dogs, they are called. They covered the stems, they covered the branches to the very ends, and, what was worse still, they finished by covering us—tumbling down upon our hats, heads, clothes, my beard, and the ladies' faces. Two of the moths hung sticking to the trees, one of those brown leaf-like species. After passing through the unleafed forest, you suddenly turn into an open space cleared among the trees; to the left before you rises a small châlet with a rustic kitchen, a long table and benches spread out before it, where a decent woman and her pretty dark-eyed daughter keep a small restaurant. We embark in a small boat to view the klints from the sea. They rise up white against the pure blue sky, a range of miniature Apennines—peaks and ridges;—how chalk ever became so convulsed, so romantic, to me remains a mystery.

"And the Klint Konge," we inquire of the old boatman, "where does he live?" "He lives there," was the answer, pointing to a hole under the Queen's Stool. He came originally from Upsala—han har flyttet—to Stevnsklint. Why he abandoned Möen no one can say; but it is supposed he found it dull, and preferred the society of the Elf King, with whom he is also confounded.

You see the range of cliffs, dazzling in their whiteness with their trimmings of green, to full advantage from the wide open sea; but to judge well of their fantastic distorted forms, their sharp sugar-loafed pics, you must follow the greenwood path on the heights above. The highest eminence is that of the Queen's Stool, 450 feet above the level of the sea, a mile English in length to the right perhaps, and then gradually the range of coast descends in altitude, and near the lighthouse you again see table-ground.

With the klints you have exhausted the sights of Møen. The island is richly cultivated, and earlier in the year may have been more beautiful, for it undulates well; but we are now in the month of September; and, let it undulate for ever, there is no beauty in undulating stubble.

Herregaards of antiquity there are none. Møen was a royal property, sold up in the last century. Not far from the picturesque church of Magleby (the Møen churches are highly picturesque and unwhitewashed) is a fine dolmen of seven stones, standing erect on a height—a feature in the surrounding country. When I showed it to a small boy—an unbelieving generation is the present—and explained how it was the work of the ancient Scandinavians, same men who fashioned the knives and chisels he had picked up at Engelstofte,—he would give no credit to the truth of my assertion. "They move these great stones? nonsense! I'll never believe it: well, if they did build it a thousand years ago, the stones were then pebbles, and must have grown since." And he stuck to his opinion, looking all the while as stubborn as a young bull-dog. In ancient times, says tradition, Møen was governed by two giants: one, Grøn, after whom the Sound is christened; the other, like the Klint Konge, came from Upsala. Instead of fighting and beating each other's brains out, as giants mostly did, they lived together in amity; and when they died, were buried side by side in the same stone chamber under the høi surmounted by my favourite dolmen.

September 1st.—The harvest-home came off last evening. A cart drove into the court laden with sheaves of corn and peasants, male and female, shouting and singing to the full extent of their voice. Horses, men, women, all were decorated with garlands of leaves and flowers, the latter bearing in their hands large bouquets stuck upon the ends of long sticks, most Bacchanalian, like a picture of Jaques Jordaen's. Then later other carts, decorated and begarlanded like the first, followed in succession; and when all had duly arrived, a sort of rustic Silenus, more horrid-looking than can be imagined, approaches, according to ancient custom, the farmer and his wife, and, sickle in hand, exclaims—

"We have cut the corn; it is ripe; it is gathered in. Will you now that we cut the cabbages in the garden?"

"No, thank you," replied the huusbond and the hustru; "we had rather not."

"But we will: the corn is gathered in; we will now cut the cabbages in the garden."

"No," answers the master, "as the corn is ripened and is gathered into the barn, we will give you a festival."

The company are now satisfied; supper is furnished for them, and they pass an evening of innocent jollity. Beyond this little fête of the harvest-home, Liselund is all quiet and repose. The church-bells alone sound in the distance; they ring up (as the expression goes) the sun, and ring it down again; and then in the midst you hear nine distinct strokes—one, the first, clear and solemn, for the Pater Noster; seven for the seven separate petitions of the Lord's Prayer; and lastly you hear a loud booming ninth proclaiming Amen.*

---

* The twelve o'clock bell was first appointed in 1455, by Pope Nicholas V., who orders that the bells be rung every day at that hour, in order that the people, on hearing them, may offer up a prayer for the Christians fighting against the heathen in foreign lands.

CHAPTER LII.

The island of Bornholm; its reputation for salmon — A coachman from the diggings — Round churches of Ny and Ole — Church-pushers and hourglasses — The Trolles of Bornholm — Their tricks upon Bondevedde — Their patriotism — How they love butter — The three-legged cat — They man the cliffs to defend the island — Hammershuus, the prison of Corfitz and Eleanor Ulfeld.

ISLAND OF BORNHOLM.

September 13th.—Our boat is named the "Mercury," and to start at seven. Cowhides and mouse-traps are our cargo—the last hang suspended to the backs of two itinerant vendors, bound like myself for Rønne. Then we have a dozen odds and ends of passengers, the greater part for Ystad—Germans with dirty faces, the inevitable gold ring on the fore-finger, and long pipes. I fraternise with the mousetrap-vendors, and ask them where they are going? Two boys they are, making their "tour" as journeymen. From Bornholm they pass to Sweden; next year, they hope, to Germany, and so on till their three years are out. Would they not like to settle? I inquire. "Oh, no! they must see the world first. Quite right too they are; better sell mousetraps and see the world, even undergoing a few hardships, than be stuck down at once in some poky village your life's long day.

Wonderful the luggage people of the provinces travel with in Denmark. Only look at that huge chest, with antique lock and repoussé ornaments; the trunk too of those Zealand peasant-women in their lace caps, with silver crown and flowing ribbons. It is not unlike a cellaret—painted and picked out in various colours—two hearts united under a wreath, with initials—the wedding-chest of some happy pair long since gathered to the dust.

The coasts of Sweden are flat and uninteresting; after breakfast—breakfasts are excellent on board those steamers—such lobsters and dried fish!—I mount in time to admire the splendid old château of a Baron Stjermblad, flanked by two lofty spiral turrets — a Danish edifice built by the Danes when Skaane was their own; then further a building, bigger still—the summer residence of a Judge Sylvan; and then into the little harbour of Ysted. We unload our cow-skins, peasant-women in their quaint costume the porters. Swedish hussar officers in blue uniform and turned-up moustaches loiter and look on. We have exchanged our red-cross pennon for one of yellow on a purple ground, with a sort of hybrid union jack placed in the corner.

The town of Ysted, commercial in corn, is clean—at least it appears so after the dirty "Mercury;" but its pavement outdoes the Danish in its eccentricity—rock and pebble, pulverised tombstone, and yawning puddle, all coalesce in friendly neighbourhood. Then too it has a wide deserted look—not that "motherly appearance" of the dull island towns of its sister Denmark. We sail out again; the moon is up. Five hours' passage at least, for the boat, though seaworthy, is "meget langsom;" so I retire below. Towards half-past eleven in bounces the stewardess—"Coming strax to Rønne." On mounting, a flat, faint, dark line appears, so go down again and just get to sleep when the boat stops, and we really are safe arrived. We mount the cliff through the churchyard, behind which lies the haven of our journey, a primitive but clean inn, looking through the trees on the cemetery, and then, beyond, the sea and a little flotilla of fishers' boats—all very charming, only bed is preferable to moon-gazing.

September 14th.—Order breakfast when you may in Denmark, you have time to stroll and gain an appetite previous to its arrival—no one is ever punctual; this morning I had ample leisure to potter about and look around me before my coffee (coming strax since halfpast seven) was served and ready. A striped lowhoused town is Rønne, interspersed with trees, planted to shade the windows: the view from the churchyard, overlooking the harbour and its new-constructed jetty, is picturesque. A small martello tower stands on the cliffs to the left, dignified by the name of "Arsenal." The little flotilla of fishing boats possess a harbour of their own, and nestle comfortably together—they have just returned laden with whiting and brill. There is shipping to the right, shipping in dock, ships turned up on end undergoing a cleaning operation, ships on the stocks being built—altogether they present quite an imposing appearance.

Bornholm enjoys a reputation for the excellence of its salmon, which fetches a higher price in the market than even that of Randers. The salmon are taken with hooks at twelve English miles off shore. Every week a vessel sails for Prussia; there the fish is disembarked, and packed off as fast as express train can carry it to France, reappearing in the windows of Chevet and other restaurants of the Parisian capital. Rønne boasts another little commerce of her own, that of pottery—a manufacture of terracotta — statuettes, baskets, and other ornaments, well executed and in the best taste, such as you see exposed for sale in the galanterie shops of Copenhagen. Her wooden clocks, too, have a reputation of their own: in the last century a vessel was wrecked off the coast, and a small cuckoo clock saved among the cargo; a hidden genius pulled it to pieces, studied its works and movements, and before many weeks fabricated the first clock ever known in the island.

The English vice-consul has kindly engaged us a carriage, with a coachman speaking English, saving us a world of trouble, and at twelve we start on our adventures.

The country is flat in the neighbourhood of Rønne, but, like Jutland, undivided; a forest of birch and pines runs along the sea-side, planted wisely by the government some thirty years since, before which period, said my coachman, the road and fields adjoining were ruined by the flying sands, and he pointed out to me a line of dunes running along the centre of a field at some distance from the road. "I recollect," he continued, "when the land you see under cultivation was worthless—now it sells in lots for as good a price as in other localities." We passed on our way some Swedish peasant women in their picturesque red bodices, a striking contrast to the sober-clad, blue-eyed, fair-haired girls of Bornholm; they come over to dispose of their embroideries—she-pedlars—carrying their packs across their shoulders. If the Swedes, however, outdo the natives in the brilliancy of their costumes, the women of the island carry off the palm of comeliness.

As we drive along my guide points out on the coast not far from the little town of Hasle two separate coal-mines. "Coal in Denmark!" "Oh, yes; plenty in Bornholm—very good for houses and cookery purposes, but not for the blacksmiths." "Who works the mines?" "They are scarcely worked at all, the quality is not good enough." "But who ever heard of good coal at the top of a mine?—you have always to get rid of much rubbish before you arrive at the fine sort." "Very true, sir, but we Danes are not like you English—we have no enterprise; if a Dane does not find good coal at the top of his mine, he will never have energy to proceed. I know my own countrymen and yours too, sir. I was three years in Australia at the diggings." "No wonder you speak English so well: and did you succeed?" "Well enough, sir. My father was a farmer, with ten sons; when he died, we could not purchase his farm, but I had just enough to take me to Australia. I did well, till the fever seized me, and a large portion of my earnings were expended, so I returned to Bornholm after an absence of three years, with exactly 300*l*. in my pocket, a large sum for this little place, married, settled, and am now getting on very comfortably." I inquired "Did you go alone?" "No; and that's the curious part of the story. A young fellow, a schoolfellow of mine, had long ardently desired to accompany me, but had no money; he was very low in spirits, for I was to sail in the spring, and it was the month of February. Towards the latter end of the month he was engaged tilling the land, when, on turning over a large stone which impeded the plough's progress, he came upon a massive arm-ring; at first he believed it to be copper, but on taking it to the jeweller it was pronounced to be gold. The lad was well nigh mad for joy; he sent it to Copenhagen, and at the end of the fortnight received as his payment the sum of 350 rix-dollars. Well, sir, we sailed together, and he is still in Australia doing well, and will return some day, richer and better off than any of the farmers of the island. It's a curious history—is it not, sir?—his finding that gold ring; the people here believe it was all the Trolles' doings, but you look on that as nonsense, I have no doubt,"—and he shut up at once.

We stopped at the village of Nyker, where is the first of the four round churches for which Bornholm is celebrated.

NYKER.

The round churches of Nyker and Olsker* are, as regards the original edifices, built upon the same plan —a large* round tower, capped "en éteignoir," with scale-like slates, evidently constructed as "church militants," to serve as fortresses in time of need; that of Ole is pierced around with loopholes like a castle turret, while that of Ny appears to be incomplete. In the interior, which served for prayer, the roofs are round vaulted, supported in the centre by one circular massive column; small external turret staircases lead to the upper story, through the loopholes of which the archers and men-at-arms shot forth their arrows; these churches of Bornholm have a peculiar cachet, with their picturesque stone belfries apart from the building, a striped wood and brick upper story and slate pointed

---

* Ker—kirke, church : Ny-ker, Ols-ker, Lars-ker, &c.

cap, as well as the lich-gates, of which there are several to each cemetery. In the church of Ny, to the left of the pulpit hang suspended four hour-glasses, the gift of Margaret, wife of Peter Bemholt, the priest, date sixteen hundred and something: clocks at that period were not in general use in these remote parts.

> The glass is running,
> Time is going,
> We are tracking on.
> Jesus, dear Lord Jesus, help us," &c.

So runs the painted doggrel. The white-haired schoolmaster informed me how he had heard from his grandfather that Parson Bemholt preached most interminable sermons; so his wife out of her own pocket caused the hour-glasses to be placed. The early Lutheran clergy became so enamoured of their own discourses, that people went to church when the sermon was half over, in consequence of which "yawning stocks" were placed at the church-door, and he who arrived late' was placed therein. Folks now came early enough, but went to sleep instead, so in 1688 "Kirke-Gubber," or "Church-pushers," were appointed—officers whose duty it was to nudge the offenders and prevent them from indulging in a nap, for which service they received the sum of six dollars annually. After a time the clergy, in despair, finished where they should have begun—they limited the duration of the sermon to one hour, and, after the example of Parson Bemholt's wife, ordered hour-glasses* to be fixed by the side of every pulpit; but so popular

---

* No sooner were the hour-glasses established than the country appears to have been inundated with Sanduhrmachers (hour-glass makers) from Leipsig and elsewhere. Strange these Northerns never could run alone without foreign help!

was a certain preacher of Copenhagen, that one Sunday, when the sand was run out, the congregation exclaimed together in a body, "Turn it—turn it again!" In all the churches you enter hangs, surmounted by a skeleton mowing away for his very life, a statistical table of the deaths caused in the different parishes of the island by the pest of 1618, when 5185 persons fell victims to its rage in Bornholm alone.

OLSKER.

I have seldom come across a more picturesque church than that of Olsker, which we next visited; it has scarcely any excrescence attached to its solid round tower, supported by Cyclopean buttresses, one round-arch doorway, the weeest apse in the world; the little cemetery, surrounded by stone walls, possesses four lich-gates, one for each point of the compass; and the queerest of all queer striped belfries. Outside the cemetery walls are attached iron rings, some to the wall itself, others to posts, the larger ones with the name of the proprietor inscribed above, intended for securing the farmer's steed during his attendance at divine service. Loyal Bornholm proclaims on a painted board, with much respect, that in the year 1687 his —— (at least four lines of titles) Majesty Christian V. honoured the round church of Ole with a visit. Leaving the church, you have a fine view over the Baltic, with the fortress island of Christiansø, and two other little Ø's. On approaching the main road we find ourselves among the blue rocks of Bornholm, which rise among the fields, among the woods, everywhere, clothed with gray lichen. The cows are of a smaller race than those of Denmark, small and black streaked. We passed by one bog, where the men were engaged cutting turf; huge trunks of oak are here discovered, black as ebony, like the Irish—in the moors of Jutland, oak is unknown. We then turn down a descent, and drive into the little town of Allinge.

We had a long conversation about the Trolles, most important personages in this island of Bornholm. In the year 1624, about the very time Parson Bemholt was preaching his long-winded sermons, the clergyman of St. Peter's writes a statistical account of his parish to Copenhagen. Among sundry matters of no account, he proceeds to relate:—

"In a høi called Faalhøi the Trolles are said to reside, and there lives now a girl who has passed many years with them underground, and borne by them eight children. The girl's name is Karen."

The favourite hero of Trolledom is a certain Bondevedde, who inhabited the parish of St. Peter's about the year 1700. Tradition declares him to have been the offspring of a farmer and a mermaid. On taking leave of her lover, the mermaid desired him to return that day year to the same place, and he would find an infant, an infant who would be endowed with the gift of seeing and hearing what was said by the Trolles—a little people, invisible to the eyes of common mortals. So the farmer did as the mermaid bade him, and in one year's time repaired to the very same spot on the sea-shore, where he found a male child lying in a cradle delicately framed of seaweeds; not a pearl, not a coral did the haufrue suspend round the neck of her baby; he was a fine healthy blue-eyed child, nothing more. So the young farmer removed him to his own house, and he went by the name of Bondevedde. The boy grew stout and strong, and after his father's death inherited his farm. In course of time he married, and his wife gave promise of adding to the hopes of the family.

Now, if there is one thing the Trolles cannot abide, it is having a spy upon their actions, and they dwelt within a høi adjoining Bondevedde's farm; as regards privacy they might just as well have pitched their tents in the market-place of Aakirkeby; he was everlastingly watching their doings and overhearing their conversation, so they determined among themselves to punish him. One day as Bondevedde was passing by he observed a Trolle with the trunk of a tree in his hand, and heard him say to his companion, "Cut it, Snef; cut it as like Bondevedde's wife as two peas."

"You're after some mischief, my boys," says Bondevedde to himself, "but I'll be even with you yet:" so he kept watch and held his peace. In process of time his wife lay sick in childbed, and, according to custom, her room was crammed full of her female neighbours. Then came the Trolles along with the rest, invisible to all mortal eyes but Bondevedde's, bearing the image of his wife admirably carved, so like nature no one could mistake it. Laying this on the bed, they carried off the suffering woman, and passed her outside the window as they imagined to their companions; but Bondevedde, who was up to their tricks, waiting outside, received his wife in his arms, and laid her in a place of safety; then, entering the sick room, seized the wooden image with the Trolles into the bargain, and stuffed them all together into the baker's oven, where they burnt like faggots. The Trolles kicked and howled, and tried to get out; the women on their side screamed, for they fancied it was their neighbour who was burning; but Bondevedde took them aside, and showed them his wife safe in bed with a fine boy, born since she was moved out of window. So the farmer and his wife were left in peace for some time after. However, the Trolles recovered from the effects of their defeat, and one day as Bondevedde passed near the høi he overheard one of them say, "Bondevedde's wife will brew her ale to-morrow; let us go and steal it!" When the ale was brewed, Bondevedde took a kettle of boiling water, and, calling together all his farm-men, said to them, "Get your stoutest sticks, and wherever I pour the water there do you lay to lustily."

When the Trolles came, Bondevedde poured the scalding water on their heads, and the farm-men laid to with all their might and main; so they ran off, scalded and beaten, burrowing like moles underground, leaving behind them an iron hook they carried with them to hang the cask of ale upon. This iron hook Bondevedde gave to the church of Rø, and out of it was made the massive iron hinges on which the door hangs. The Trolles, now highly wroth, determined to make away with their enemy; so one day as he rode by he saw the Trolles dancing in a ring round the høi under which they dwelt. "Stop, Bondevedde," they cried, "stop and have something to drink." The farmer carried about him his own silver cup, and the Trolles filled it with a golden liquid like hydromel. Bondevedde held his cup high, making semblance to drink to their health, at the same time tossing the contents over his right shoulder: some of the liquid fell upon his horse's haunches, and the hair and skin frizzled and flamed as though burnt by a red-hot iron, leaving a deep wound in the flesh. From that time, seeing it was no go, the Trolles left Boudevedde and his wife in peace and quietness.

But the Trolles are not always mischievous. They are good patriots, and, in time of war, fight like demons in defence of their country. Some centuries since, when Bornholm was attacked by the English fleet (when was it?) the Trolles rose up in thousands to aid in repelling the invaders. Every hoi was covered with them, and they fired—bless you! they fired three shots in the time you would take in firing one. The invaders saw them from their ships, and, when repulsed, the English admiral, with his officers and men, having first taken their solemn Bible oath to the truth of the assertion, drew up a statement which they all signed, and forwarded to the English government, declaring (no doubt the document is still preserved in the Record Office) how they were vanquished, not by the inhabitants of Bornholm, but by the supernatural agency of the Trolles. The Trolles, however, are now quiet enough. One weakness they have, of which they never will be cured, and that is for butter. With a peculiar art of their own, they come out after nightfall and suck the butter from the cows, without disturbing either the milk or the cream. The milk is laid in the pan, the cream rises, and in its turn is placed in the churn: the farm-women churn away till their arms nearly fall off—no use, the butter is not there. Now, a farmer by Alminde, a friend of my coachman, suspecting what was the matter, lay in wait one night and watched the cows. Shortly after dark came one of the Trolles—incognito as Trolles always do appear—disguised under the form of a three-legged cat. Trolles, as well as the devil, can only transform themselves into maimed animals. His Satanic Majesty particularly affects the form of a rat, but always a rat without a tail; try as hard as he can, he never can produce even the stump of one. Whenever you come across a three-legged cat, shoot it if you have a gun by you; it's a Trolle in masquerade, and after some mischief. The farmer waited till the three-legged cat was hanging well to the cow's udder, sucking out the butter; then, slily approaching from behind, made him prisoner; and how did he catch him? that's the question. As much art is required in the catching of a Trolle as in the killing of a Norwegian salmon. Well, I will tell you how he acted; he went to the stable, and, removing the hempen halter from the neck of a coal-black stallion, passed it round the neck of the cat and fastened her to the manger. The next morning, when he came to look at his captive, what do you think he found? Not a three-legged cat, but an old woman. He let her go, for he dared not injure her; so the Trolle got off after all.

The last time the Trolles appeared in public was in the years '48, 9, 50, at the time of the Slesvig-Holstein rebellion. All united Germany was down upon Denmark, and she had lately suffered some reverses—men's hearts were sad—when one morning a ship arrived at the little town of Rönne. The sailors related how, as they passed by the cliffs of Bornholm by night, they had seen hundreds and thousands of the Trolles busy doing military exercise on the heights, already prepared to rise in the defence of their native country.

"Hurrah! hurrah!" exclaimed the people; "the Trolles are out—the Trolles are up—no fear of conquest now—the victory will be ours—hurrah! hurrah!" and they were at once wild with joy and delight.* Well, it turned out as they expected; the Germans were repulsed and kicked out of the country, though whether the Trolles had much to do with the matter is uncertain. Educate the people as you may—and an excellent education all the Danish nation receive, from highest to lowest—you will find it difficult to eradicate from the heads of the peasants the belief, handed down from father to son, in the existence of the Trolles, who dwell within the bois and heights of the sea-girt island of Bornholm.

"Well, sir," concluded the coachman, "I'm glad you don't laugh at the Trolles, for most of our people believe in them. I can't say I have ever seen them myself; but of a night, in the forest of Alminde and along the sea-coast, I have seen lights wandering about up and down among the woods and the rocks, and followed them, too; but where they came from, or where they went to, I never could tell. I fancy the Trolles must have had something to do with it." "No doubt," I replied. Was I wrong? Ought I to have unveiled to him the fallacies of igneous gases, of jack o' lanterns, &c.? May be I should; but I left him to his simple belief.

At the house of old Mrs. Kurts, in the sea-washed town of Allinge, we stayed but the time necessary to leave our portmanteau and order dinner to be ready for our return, then started on our way to Hammershuus, two miles distant.

The little town of Allinge straggles along by the sea-side. If it wished to extend, it must extend itself

---

* This anecdote was related to me by the Amtmaun.

lengthways—for it has rocks below and above, purple rocks clothed with moss, lichen, and delicate ferns, growing out from its clefts and interstices. Allinge possesses for its fishing-boats a little home-constructed harbour and basin, hewed out of the solid rock, without the aid of engineer, and there lay a flotilla of barques, protected behind the rubble jetties. There is something fresh and exciting, as we drive along, in the air and appearance of the country: fine green turf, like emerald velvet, and those rocks of purple marble—marble used in the construction of the noblest buildings of Denmark, but not the fashion, for in Bornholm stand only four churches composed of this material. Search where you like, you will not make them out; they are tastefully covered over with, at least, six inches of whitewash. We turn into a forest—not a Danish forest of beech, but scattered clumps of oak, elm, ash, and hawthorn, rising among monster boulders, mossy swards, and creeping junipers—drive up to a striped farm-house, sheltered from the blast by a protecting group of trees, pass through a wooden gate, and the ruins of Hammershuus stand before us.

Hammershuus was a château fort of early date. Some writers ascribe its erection to Valdemar the Great;[*] probably it was the handiwork of some Archbishop of Lund, of whose diocese Bornholm formed part and parcel, and whose authority here reigned supreme.

---

[*] Valdemar the Great was proud of the buildings he caused to be erected. On the plate found placed at the head of his coffin in the abbey church of Ringsted, it is expressly mentioned how he constructed the castle of Sprogø with burnt bricks; would he then have omitted to make mention of so much more important a work as the far-famed castle of Hammershuus?

Bornholm has never possessed any herregaards. So much the better for the peasants, as they have been always free. Many of her inhabitants had pretensions to birth, and the impudent prelates dared to ennoble their favourites without demanding the assent of the sovereign. First among the families of the island stood that of Hafod, or Hofad, descendants of that mighty Earl who in the ninth century, with his gallant band of Northmen, overran the fair provinces of England and France.

By a document, dated 1514, the then Archbishop of Lund, legate of the pope, proceeds to confer letters of nobility upon his trusty servant, "granting him for arms a silver buckle on a field gules, with a pair of horns to wear upon his helmet." In Popish days sovereigns winked at ecclesiastical impertinence so long as it did not interfere with their own personal interests; but their heyday over, down comes a thundering letter (one of his own peculiar) from King Frederic II. Understanding how certain inhabitants of the island of Bornholm look upon themselves as noble, he informs them that no patent conferred by foreign authority can be accepted, and they are for the future to consider themselves as "nobodies." In case of their again offending against the "allerhøieste" command, the lehnsmand has orders to conduct them to the castle of Hammershuus, and there treat them according to "law and right." The borrowed plumes were soon set aside, for people well knew that Frederic's "law and right" were matters not to be trifled with.

In later days Hammershuus became a state prison: Corfitz and Eleanor Ulfeld were here confined for the space of one year: they escaped, but were again taken at the town of Allinge, in the act of embarking on board a fishing-boat, by Governor Fuchs, who was afterwards stabbed by their son Christian, in the streets of Brussels, to revenge his father's imprisonment. When separated from her husband, Eleanor consoled him with these well-known lines—

> "Rebus in adversis, facile est contemnere mortem,
> Fortius ille facit, qui miser esse potest."

There is an old Danish proverb—as well as the French one*—when "qvinde taler Latin," &c.—when a woman talks Latin, no good will come of it; which in Eleanor's case was carried out. Later Hammershuus fell into decay, was not, for a wonder, blown up by the Swedes in the seventeenth century, but got half pulled down for its materials in the eighteenth, at the period when everything was destroyed, from a downright spirit of Vandalism. The beauty of a ruin consists not in its extent, but rather in the manner of its fall; and Hammershuus, like Julius Cæsar, and Iphigenia in Aulis, in the Greek play, has had the good taste to fall "gracefully." It stands on an isolated hill formed by nature. On one side it overlooks the waters of the Baltic—the Swedish coast for a background; on the opposite side a natural ravine, at the foot a stream of running water. At the period of its might and power this rivulet, dammed up, rendered approach by this side impossible. Whichever way the eye turns you gaze enraptured with the beauty of the site: the bright sparkling sea, and its long line of purple coast,

---

* Soleil qui luiserne au matin,
Enfant qui boit du vin,
Femme qui parle Latin,
Font toujours mauvaise fin.

rising in fantastic crags, like those of our own Channel islands; to the right again, across the fresh-water lake which almost touches the boundaries of the sea, rises another green and purple hill, on the opposite side of which you will find a ruined chapel, with a holy well, dedicated, of all queer dedications, to King Solomon.* But if the sea-side view is enchanting, the inland is no less so. Standing upon the walls' height, you look down into the green wooded ravine below: on the other side rises a lofty bankside, scattered with boulders, trees, turf, broom, heath, and cytisus, all mingling together in exquisite variety.

The square tower in which Eleanor Ulfeld passed her year's confinement; the ruined round tower of the outer side, fallen in varied and unstudied desolation, are grand and imposing: even the flora is unlike that of old castles in general; the wild convolvulus here leaps and trails itself like a vine along the crumbling ruins; the sea-pink perfumes the air with its fragrance, and tufts of the dark-blue dwarf veronica (ærenpriis) grow luxuriant among the fallen stones. A heavy stone, fined at the edge to a point, jutted out from the crumbling wall. After hard pulling it came out—strong cement that †—and there it lay in my hand, a massive hammer of the stone age, broken at the place of piercing, marks of the chisel still visible. What a pedigree has that hammer! In its early youth smashing the head and braining some Pagan Scandinavian, in

---

* King Solomon and the Siege of Troy were favourite subjects of the middle ages.

† Of home manufacture, too, for the cement-stone abounds in Bornholm, and great quantities of it, crushed ready for use, are exported in barrels to Copenhagen, Sweden, and other localities.

the twelfth century built into the fortress of Hammershuus, and now soon to be lodged with other stone-lumber of the sort in a Mechanics' Museum.

But before we quit Hammershuus, observe even in the remote island of Bornholm how much is done for the healthful enjoyment of the people. Look around how in every direction walks are cut out, trees planted, seats erected, everything turned to account—as it always is in Denmark—and where are people so happy and so respectable? As much is here done among the wild scenery of Hammershuus, and more too, than in the most populous towns of our native England.

CHAPTER LIII.

Farming in Bornholm — Village beacons — The rock scenery — The White Oven visited at Christmas secure from ghosts — Bornholm gold coined by Christian IV. — Its diamonds in favour with Queen Louisa — Round church of Øster Lars — Fastelavn at Shrovetide — —Forest of Alminde — The birds at the Cross — Tower of Christiansminde — Horse-fair — Font of Aakirkeby.

September 15*th*.—DAMM, the coachman—now, don't imagine I'm swearing: it's the man's own name—was round with his horses punctual as the clock struck seven, or, rather, as the hand pointed to the hour on his watch—very good gold watch too—won it as the chief prize for climbing up a greasy pole when in the land of nuggets. Old Mrs. Korts comes in with the bill at the very last moment, with a most determined look about her as though prepared for squalls. Bill just three times as much as elsewhere; but then she is not a regular gjæstgiver, but a lady who "takes people in" as a favour. I pay it tranquilly, and make no remark, having come to Bornholm to amuse myself, and not to get into a passion. We return as far as Olesker, and then make southwards. Fine bracing air. We pass through a succession of cultivated fields. Stubble days gone by, all is ploughed; many portions resown with rye. Farmers' carts, horses, and men, in full activity. In the background rises a ridge of purple rocks; while beyond these, towards the sea, among the thick protecting forests of ash and oaks, lie the farmhouses—small establishments when compared with those of Jutland. The farms here are seldom of more than 200 acres. Land has lately much increased in value. One farm, which some twenty-five years ago was valued at 2000 dollars, was lately sold for 12,000. The peasants are most careful cultivators. When the rye is sown, not one pebble is allowed to remain on the surface of the field. Were it a geranium-bed, it could not be more delicately raked or the ground finer; for this there is but one explanation—the peasant is here no tenant: the land is his own property; four or six horses are the extent of his possessions and a few farm-boys his labourers. The farm-buildings have a "cocky" appearance about them, unlike to sober Denmark. Each gable, be there ten of them, is surmounted by a vane.

We enter the parish of Rø. Perched upon a neighbouring høi stands what first appears a stork's nest on a pile of faggots within an open wooden frame: but it's no such thing; in each successive village you will come across the same—a beacon, always ready prepared, in time of peace as war, in case of a descent upon the island. No sooner does fire blaze up high into the sky than the church belfries send forth a peal. The alarm once given, a dozen others flame in the neighbouring parishes; more bells ring, and the inhabitants rise to arms.

Before arriving at the church of Rø, built by one Simon Rø and his twelve sons—all named, from some vagary of his own, Simon, after himself—we turn off the road to visit the rock scenery of Bornholm. Guide not quite sure of his way; we therefore halloo to a farmer busily sowing his wheat from an oblong basket. Farmer turns round, having first completed his furrow, and then sows his way down the adjoining ridge to our very carriage-wheel. We are all right; drive on to his farm, put up our horses there, and—he is too busy himself, but his grandfather will show us the way to the Holy Well; so we follow his directions, but he soon appears at the house himself, on hospitality bent. We must have a cup of coffee; we decline—then on our return. His hustru was to have shown us the way—but the coffee? Leave it to the pige (servant-girl). Impossible! she is so careless she will be sure to burn it. She consults her husband; first looks at us, then at the coffee, and hospitality has the best of it; so the pige is summoned, and off we set across some fields, more boulders than grass, and then, after more wood, we come to the cliff's side. A narrow winding path leads to the beach below. Fine bold rocks, divided into squares, rise like turrets from the sea which reaches their base. The pige can tell me nothing. She thinks more of her own pretty face—and small blame to her!—than all the saints of paradise; but I find out later that 150 years ago there existed a chapel dedicated to the Trinity, and how this little ravine was planted with stone and wooden crosses, and the chapel hung with votive offerings, long tresses of women's hair among the number. All this has long since disappeared; the poor-box alone remains, iron-bound and massive, nailed to a stake firmly planted in the ground, and, like Hogarth's, with a cobweb across the opening. "Tell the gentleman," laughs the pige, "not to put anything in; "better give the money to me to buy a ribbon." You may be sure I followed her advice. She knows nothing about the Holy Well, but the spring runs from the rock into a small basin touching the sea, into which it discharges itself.

A boat will meet you at the Holy Well by order, for you can better judge of this wild and beautiful coast from the water than from the cliffs above. First, you pass a wild frontier pile of rocks, called the Candles; one candle got, however, blown over during last winter's heavy storms: then close by in the cliff's side you may distinguish the moulds in which they were cast, which said candle-moulds are of great extent, and run, as these holes always do, as far as Hammershuus. Ten strokes of the oar bring us to the entrance of the "Black Oven," a dark, cold, slimy, tumble-down sort of place. When once in, and after sliding and slipping you sit on a damp, cold rock, the view of the sea, Candles, and picturesque line of cliffs extending towards Allinge—well encadré by the black limestone—does repay you for your trouble. Further on you pass the "White Oven," an oven not to be entered save in time of extreme cold, when the winter is at its full and the Baltic frozen around the island. Then towards Christmas-time, in the holy days, or rather nights, when the days are short and obscure—"som stympede lys der have kun oyne og ender"—like the stump of a candle, only the beginning and the end—the peasant girls and boys come down in large parties with torches and lanterns to explore its wonders. They slide and they slip along, and the girls fall down on the ice—quite by accident, not at all for the pleasure of being picked up again—till they come to the place where, on raising their heads, they can see through an aperture the moon shining and myriads of stars blazing in the bright firmament of heaven; strange to say, when above-ground no one has yet discovered where this aperture may lie—it is hid to mortal eyes. But they go no farther. No one would dare even this journey save on holy nights, when the angels protect all innocent pleasures, for the White Oven bears a bad reputation, and is generally supposed to be a private entrance to a certain place, to which bad Danes as well as other folks are allowed free access without giving themselves the unnecessary trouble of crossing over by long sea from Copenhagen to Bornholm. Having visited the finest scenery of the cliffs, we clamber again up the bank's side: a mercy old grandfather, whom we passed cutting wood and who must be eighty at the very least, did not accompany us; down he may have got, but it would have required all the virtues of the Holy Well to have dragged him up again. We return to the farm-house. A carpenter is occupied putting in the double windows; of course, he asks whether we use them in England. "Seldom;" they are not required in our mild climate; besides, in our old country houses the windows close hermetically; there is never any draught—none, with us, particularly on the northern aspects. Our windows never rattle, much less let in the air."

We are now under weigh again, pass by the church of Rø, on whose door you may still see the iron hinge formed out of the hook left by the Trolles,—iron smelted by themselves, no doubt, for Bornholm is said to abound in minerals, though they have been but little worked. In old books you read accounts of a gold-mine, such as existed once in Scotland and other localities. King Christian IV. caused ducats to be coined, but the foreign merchants would not allow the gold to be real; so the king, when a second quantity was discovered, issued a series of whole, half, and quarter ducats, on which were represented a pair of spectacles, with the inscription, "Vide mira Domini," indicating that those who doubted the fact might be in want of them. Kings liked to coin medals from gold out of their own possessions. In the days of swords and knee-breeches, of powder, hoops, and shoe-buckles, when all men liked to be smart and glitter, Bornholm, like Alençon and Bristol, bore quite a reputation for diamonds. Somehow or other, tradition relates not how, these crystals were brought before the notice of our English princess the good Queen Louisa. From the day of her marriage she became Danoise pur sang, and loved, as much as was in her power, to promote the manufactures of her adopted country. She recollected, may be, the Bristol stones of her own native land, then in full vogue and fashion, and one fine night, at a Court reception, she wore in her head a "bæve naal" of glittering stones.*

The courtiers greatly admired the new ornament now first worn by the queen. It was beautiful! what taste! "A present lately sent from England?" "On the contrary," replied somebody; "it had arrived only that very morning by the courier from Vienna." Queen Louisa kept her counsel till late in the evening, and then informed her ladies and the courtiers that it was composed of Bornholm diamonds. "Bornholm diamonds! impossible!" The whole assembly was aghast, above all the dowagers of the old régime. Why,

---

* Bæve naal is a sort of pin mounted as a star, a flower, or a rosette, hung with dangles. Queen Louisa is represented with one in her portrait.

Bornholm was in Denmark! Was it prudent, was it politic, of her Majesty to encourage anything Danish? If it had only come from Germany,—they were certain Queen Madalena——" but Madalena was now only queen dowager, and, like most dowagers, out of fashion. The mode took, and the following year the jewellers of Copenhagen sold 1080 ornaments, shoe-buckles, and headpins of the newly-introduced material.

But Bornholm diamonds, like Bristol stones and Alençon crystals, had their day, and died out together with knee-breeches, hoops, and powder; and in the present century ask a Copenhagener if he knows what a Bornholm diamond is, he will stare you in the face and look on you as demented.

The country is now intersected by a succession of ravines rugged and wild—one, termed the Devil's Creek. Our drive continues—more sylvan, more picturesque. We pass a second beacon, and, turning a few yards off the road, drive up to the little cemetery, wherein, shaded by an ancient gnarled ash, growth of centuries, stands the church of Øster Lars, largest of the round churches of Bornholm. Around the top of the building runs a line of pigeon-holes. The tower itself is supported by buttresses of immense strength; we mounted to its summit. A narrow gallery runs round within the outside walls, pierced by the above-mentioned pigeon-holes. Then comes a second wall, stronger, if anything, than the first, with loopholes, like in the church of Ole ; and within again a third wall, defended in a similar manner, though when once driven within for protection there could be no possible outlet. The same arrangement is found in the second story below. The earlier Christian inhabitants of the island, pirates and sea-robbers, lovers

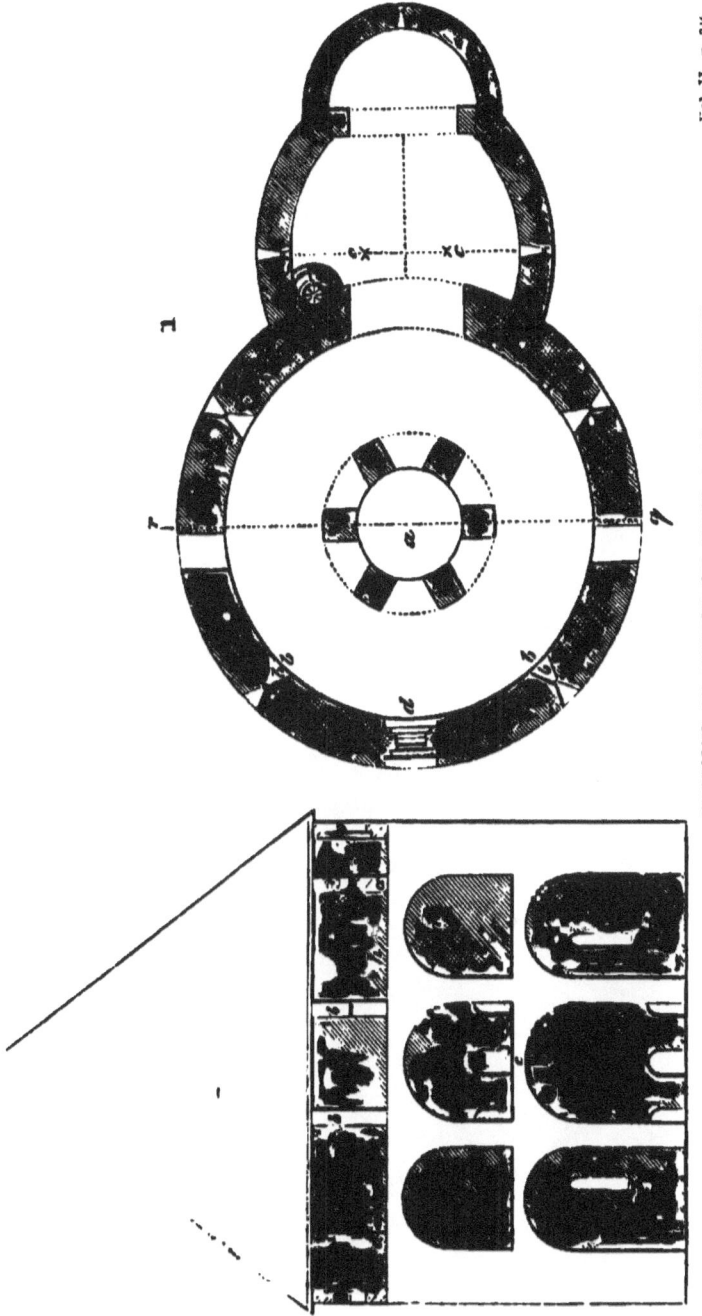

SECTIONS OF CHURCH OF OSTER LARS, BORNHOLM.

of booty, but at the same time anxious for the future safety of their souls, killed two birds with one stone— they founded churches and prayed to the saints. The church itself differs from the two preceding ones, which are supported by one solid pillar; here the centre is open and supported by six round arches. A broad cross spans the round-arch dome, resting on simple brackets. The arrangement is similar, on a smaller scale, to that of the Temple de Lanleff, in the neighbourhood of St. Brieuc, in Brittany. Unfortunately, these round churches are so defaced by galleries, pews, &c., it is difficult to judge of their proportions; and the apse here, which with the exterior is of fine old Norman work, is so bedaubed with whitewash as entirely to obscure the carvings with which it is decorated.

At the entrance without stands a Runic stone, dug out some years since from the bridge of the Devil's Creek,—dating from the Christian period, for in the centre is inscribed a cross. The signification of this I know not. Bornholm is rich in Runic stones, many of the Christian era. In the church of St. Clemens stand two of picturesque appearance under the shade of a walnut-tree, inscribed as follows. The first is of heathen times:—" Gobu Sven raised this stone to his son Bjørn, who was a mighty and a strong man. He had a wife named Godruna, and he was slain by the Jarl." The second: "Selfia raised this stone to her husband Gudbjørn. Christ help Gudbjørn Alerson's soul. Christ help the pious Selfia." Selfia appears to have had a good opinion of herself. These inscriptions mostly run in the same style; those of Pagan days merely stating who raised the stone and the manner of the death of the deceased, while the later ones for the most part terminate with the words, "God have mercy on his soul!"

We again proceeded on our way. The old customs of Bornholm differ little from those once prevalent in the rest of Denmark, though now gradually fading away. Christmas, as in other countries, is a season of universal rejoicing and merriment. "Gud signe eders Juul; Juul til Paaske"—May God bless your Christmas; may it last till Easter. The salt-cellar remains on the table during the festival of Juul; Christmas cake and the Juul tonne, which dates from Pagan days, to which all strangers are welcomed with "You shall not carry our Juul out of doors." From the 24th of December until the New Year no one works—neither man nor woman. The farmer drinks during that period of repose a considerable quantity of honey mixed with brandy—a sort of hydromel, the favourite beverage—and devours huge Christmas cakes; and the young people love the dance almost to frenzy. The New Year, however, is not danced in, as with us; it is "shot in" in Bornholm. Everybody who possesses or can shoulder a gun or discharge a pistol fires it off as the clock strikes twelve; large parties of the peasants mount their steeds, and, visiting the farms of their neighbours, fire against the window-panes, startling those slumbering within—a somewhat uproarious manner of wishing them "a happy New Year." On the festival of the Three Kings in every house is consumed a tallow candle with three wicks; then, at six weeks' distance from Christmas Day, the Bornholmers indulge in one week of fun and jollity, relics of the old Papistic carnival, termed "Fastelavn" (Shrovetide). They do their best to disguise and costume themselves, men as women, women as men, and, with masks on their faces, go round and visit the different houses. Sometimes there are cavalcades on horseback, horses decked out as well as their riders; but for this one week they dance from morning till night and from night till morning; and Damm, the coachman, who, among other accomplishments, plays the fiddle, assured me that by the time the Bornholm week's carnival is spent his arms are well-nigh played out of their sockets.* Another pastime of Fastelavn appears to me of a somewhat barbarous nature. An unfortunate cat is hung up, hermetically sealed, in a barrel, and each man tries his skill, with a wooden club, to smash the barrel to pieces. A prize, of course, is awarded to the victor. Fastelavn, too, is a season of grand fun for the children of the family in Denmark. Some days previous to its arrival, you will see the smaller cellars and shops filled with small rods, gilded and tied up with particoloured ribbons. The young ones of every house are up at earliest dawn, and, armed with these miniature implements of correction, proceed to belabour the bedclothes of the whole household—"Whip up, Fastelavn," as they call it—and exact, as their right and ransom, toys, sweetmeats, and such like.

* "Do everything by rule, as the tailor said when he killed his wife with a rule," is a vulgar—very vulgar—Danish proverb, but one which the island peasants adhere to strongly, more especially as regards the traditions of the Church of Rome. On Good Friday " they set their willows." They have an especial day for the planting of everything, and, as for signs and wonders, the life of a farmer must be a torment to him. If on Ascension Day the rye be not in ear, woe betide them; or again, should it rain on any one of the Sundays when the Gospels are read from St. Luke, it is a bad look-out for the harvest. A great festival, too, is Hellig Bonder's Day, the week after St. Volborg's, the time for sowing the corn and the week when people clean out their houses.

Turning off nearer to the coast, we descend a small hill, and drive into the little seaport town of Svaneke, a pretty little striped town, built up the ascent from the rocky coast, with a well-to-do look about it; each house has a large garden, gay with autumn flowers and fruit-laden trees and walnuts. Were lodgings to be procured, it would be a charming sojourn for sea-bathers.

At Carlsons, where we stopped to dine, the usual question—never-failing—was asked me. Was I the author whose books they loved so much, and who made them pass so many a pleasant evening in the long winter season? I believe Captain Marryat's books are still popular in his own country, but here, in the North of Europe, they excite a very furore; scarcely a farmer, scarcely a publican, no less than those of a higher class, in the remotest part of Denmark, but put to me invariably the same question; and when I, in my humility, have pleaded guilty—although I be no 'Naval Officer'—to being "own brother to 'Snarley Yow,'" I could not, were I the author himself, have met with greater civility and attention.

Here, at Svaneke, was I formally introduced to a sort of a *nephew*—qui valait bien sans doute mes autres—a large black and white setter puppy, dragged howling into the room by the scruff of his neck, christened "Japhet," in honour of that individual who set out over the wide world in search of his father.

A drive across a balmy, breezy moor brought us to the royal forest of Alminde. A mile further we land at the house of Mr. Rosen, the guardian, where we pass the night.

September 16th.—The forest of Alminde is a royal

possession. It is Swedish in its character; the ground undulating, the hills and dales strewn with purple rocks and boulders, tossed about and rising on all sides in most chaotic confusion. The pine, the oak, the ash, and the birch, wych-elm and dog-wood. September is set in, and the tints of autumn in their endless variety of colouring are most charming.

This morning we set off on an early walk, passing by an obelisk erected to commemorate the visit of his present Majesty, when a young man, to his loyal possession of Bornholm—a building open to the public on high days and holidays, and to-day all is motion and activity, for it is the annual cattle-show of the island, and prizes are awarded to bulls, bullocks, pigs, et hoc genus omne. Long tables are spread out under the trees, with coffee, tea, and smör bröd, to say nothing of schnapps; and while the judges are busy awarding the prizes the farmers and their families are occupied with their inward restoration. Very sturdy little bulls —small, like all island breeds—stand quiescent under inspection. A prize-ticket is fastened on to a dun-coloured animal with a white streak across his back; then we make our way on, up and down, down and up, till we come to the entrance of a huge encampment, surrounded by an earthen vallum, here termed Gamleborg. Nobody knows aught of its history; it is now studded over with trees, but it is worth while to climb on the opposite side merely to look down on the valley beneath.

In an opposite direction, remarkable alone for its site—for little of the castle remains—stands the sister fortress of Lilleborg, a stronghold of the Archbishop of Lund, built of Bornholm stone. Many ancient urns were here discovered some years since and forwarded to the Northern Museum at Copenhagen. Foxes abound in Alminde, chevreuil too, but the larger deer, though frequently imported, do not thrive. Many rare birds here build their nests which have been known to do so nowhere else among the islands of Denmark. The eggs of the peregrine falcon, as well as the larger woodcock, were both taken here last spring. Herons are plentiful in Bornholm, but the stork is more chary of its visits. When the swallow abounds in summer, the peasants and folks of the little towns can happily console themselves for the stork's absence, for the swallow is even more beloved of the two, and in old papistic times was supposed to live and fly under the special protection of Our Lady. There exists a charming old song—I have, however, never been able to procure a copy of it—sung still, sometimes, by the old crones of the island of Zealand, in which the swallow goes to the Virgin to beg the loan of a needle and thread to sew her nest together.

Then again there is an old Popish tradition, which may be known in other lands, but to me is new, so I may as well give it:—"It was on that fearful Friday when our Saviour hung in his agony upon the cross, when the sun was turned into blood, and darkness was upon all the earth, that three birds, flying from east to west, passed by the accursed hill of Golgotha. First came the lapwing; and when the bird saw the sight before him he flew round about the cross, crying, in his querulous tone, 'Piin ham! piin ham!—torment him! torment him!' For this reason the lapwing is for ever accursed, and can never be at rest; it flies round and round its nest, fluttering and uttering a plaintive cry; in the swamp its eggs are stolen. Then came the stork, and the stork cried in its sorrow and its grief for the ill deed done, 'Styrk ham! styrk ham!—Give him strength! give him strength!' Therefore is the stork blessed, and wherever it comes it is welcome, and the people love to see it build upon their houses; it is a sacred bird, and for ever unharmed. Lastly came the swallow, and when it saw what was done it cried, 'Sval ham! sval ham!—refresh him! cool him!' So the swallow is the most beloved of the three; he dwells and builds his nests under the very roofs of men's houses, he looks into their very windows and watches their doings, and no man disturbs him either on the palaces or the houses of the poorest peasants. For this reason, as you travel in Denmark, you will observe the swallows' nests remain undisturbed; no one would dream for a moment of scratching them down or destroying them as we do in England." To this tradition the Swedes add a fourth bird, the turtle-dove, who, perching on the cross in its anguish, cried, "Kurrie! kurrie! kurrie!" (kyrie—Lord!) Since that day the dove has never been glad, but flies through the forest still repeating its sad notes.

On our way home we visited the celebrated rokkesteen, or shaking stone, the largest in the North of Europe. It lies in the forest, almost surrounded with earth, unlike those of the Breton heath, which stand erect and lifted up on high.

Christiansminde, the lion of the island, is a square lofty tower of Bornholm stone, erected to commemorate the visit of the present king and the Countess Danner. The king is here popular; Bornholm is loyal and marble is cheap, and this edifice is an improvement on the old-fashioned useless obelisk, for you can here mount to the summit and enjoy the view over the bright sparkling sea as far as your eye can gaze.

On our return we found the horse-fair in full force: competition for a prize of one hundred dollars. The mares were arranged all in a line for inspection down by the Koldekilde, a once-celebrated spring, whose waters, if quaffed on St. John's Eve, cured all sorts of maladies that flesh is heir to, and the taste is said in old books to be at all times equal to brandy. Times are changed, and the waters with them. To-day, for every one farmer who drank of the limpid fountain, ninety-nine took a swig at the brandy-bottle. But the exhibition of horses had never been so bad as this year, all the better cattle having been sold off to Prussia during the war-fever in Germany. It must be from these islands of the North that Franconi and the travelling circuses recruit their studs; for among the numerous "café au lait," dun-coloured, flea-bitten, and other varieties, stood two geldings, as queer specimens of the equine race as ever mortals clapped eyes upon: black as the raven's wing, with four white legs — not stockings — white manes, with tails to correspond. It is said that somebody from the North presented four of these eccentric animals to Louis XIV., who was so much pleased with their appearance that he had them harnessed to his own particular private gilded caroche.

When we had exhausted the mares and the stallions, the three-year-olds, and the very small ponies, we returned to our carriage. Our first halt was at Aakirkeby — one of Bornholm's renowned blue marble churches, luxuriant in whitewash, a tumbledown concern filled

CHAPTER LIV.

Return to Zealand — Island of Bøgø — King Valdemar and the Hanse-atikers — The Goose Tower — Goose carried off by King Erik — Castigation of the fair Cecilia — Herlufsholm the Harrow of Denmark — Old Bridget and the missing title-deeds — The gallant Admiral Trolle — Hvitfeldt the chronicler's Dance of Death.

MØEN.

October 11.—THE autumn is now far advanced; the leaves, undevoured by caterpillars, hang thinly to the trees; a feeling of damp pervades the forest and the klint; the bathing bower smells like a fungus; even the mushrooms are saturated with wet—wood-mushrooms, large enough to form dinner-tables to a marriage-party of Trolles or Nisses; they have now all turned black, and are quite uneatable. So we yawn, abuse the weather, and, thanking our stars the month of October is at last arrived, pay a farewell visit to the Stor Klint, slide once more into the numerous giants' chambers, pack up our clothes, and start, inwardly rejoicing, for Copenhagen.

ISLAND OF BØGO.

We again embark upon the "Zampa," bound from Stege to Vordingborg. Two ferry-boats meet us in the centre of the strait, by Kallehave; we bend our course through a world of little islands. The coast of Zealand is richly wooded; we pass by Bøgo, or the Isle of Beeches, celebrated in the annals of old story, when every insil possessed her own rulers, and they each individually made war one against another; but we have had the same story elsewhere of the sowing of the beech-masts, so may pass it by: and then, suddenly, in the distance rises like a phare—though not half so useful—a tall, slender tower, the far-famed Goose Tower of the castle of Vordingborg.

VORDINGBORG.

We land at one English mile from the little town, once a city of note in the days of the Valdemerians, now a village, with its tower, its castle-site, alone remaining to test the truth of its earlier glories.

All the Valdemerians dwelt at Vordingborg Castle, and mightily affected it as a residence—it was the Windsor of the thirteenth and fourteenth centuries; in her own convent church, rich still in old carved altar-piece, was crowned King Christopher II.* It was the apanage of our Prince George; at his death returned to the Crown; and was afterwards burnt to the ground, as is usual in Denmark. But the fun of the history of this château fort took place in the days of Queen Margaret's father, that "roi farceur," old Valdemar Atterdag. You recollect the story of the "amulet" taken by the prying

---

* The sovereigns seem in the beginning to have been crowned anywhere and everywhere, and the earlier ones—Knud the Holy, Niels, &c. —not at all. Some of them—Magnus and Svend Grathe—received the crown of the German emperor. Valdemar I. is the first one crowned; some were crowned by the Archbishop of Lund. Knud was crowned at Ringsted; Christopher II. at Vordingborg, and Erik Glipping in Viborg. Erik of Pomerania was crowned at Calmar, and Christopher of Bavaria at Ribe. Generally on some Saint's day the coronation took place. First it was not customary to make knights, but Erik of Pomerania made one hundred and twenty-three on the occasion.

courtier from the breast of poor murdered Tove—how, driven well nigh demented by the affection of his sovereign, transferred from the corpse of the defunct mistress to himself, he flung the precious stone into a lake near Vordingborg, in which locality the affections of his master were henceforth concentrated.

It was in the period of their power and glory that the cities of the Hanseatic League, irritated at some real or imaginary injury, despatched each severally his envoy —seventy-seven they arrived together—to declare war against the Danish sovereign. Loud laughed King Valdemar when he was told of their arrival, and louder still when he heard that those of South Germany, fearing the inclemency of the Danish climate, had muffled up their persons in furs and skins, much after the manner of Greenlanders and Esquimaux. The king invites the embassy on the morrow to a state banquet in the riddersaal of the castle. The ambassadors arrive, seventy-seven in number, arranged according to precedence, and are conducted to the hall of state where the banquet is prepared. Sable and miniver, squirrel and humble catskin envelop the portly persons of the proud burghers of the important League. The king caused the stoves to be heaped with wood, and the hall to be heated like the fiery furnace of Shadrach, Meshach, and Abednego; have a carouse with his worthy envoys he would: the doors were locked, the wine-cup passed, the poor ambassadors in their heavy robes melt and suffocate, the king and his courtiers at their ease enjoy the fun; they drink, they revel, regardless of the sufferings of their guests, till nearly break of morn, when the envoys are released, with compliments, and orders to return the following day to a fresh banquet and receive the royal answer. On the morrow they come—not to be taken in this time; the day is cold, the snow falls, the wind bitter—never mind, the King's Grace keeps good fires; so the worthy envoys appear clad in garments of the lightest and thinnest textures, when, lo! to their horror, they find a banquet spread for them in the open air in the castle court. The king, well wrapped himself, receives them smiling, and, after a prolonged carouse under a falling snow, delivers to the indignant ambassadors his answer in "platt" German, a doggrel of his own composition—

Søven und søventig Hense.	Seventy-seven Hanseatikers.
Søven und søventig Gense.	Seventy-seven geese.
Bieten mich nicht die Genso	If the geese don't bite I don't care
So frag ich nicht cen Schit na die Hense.	a fig for the Hanseatic towns.

Very rude on the part of King Valdemar, but this sovereign was a free speaker and stuck at nothing. His religious opinions were undecided; at one time he appears an atheist, at another he makes a pilgrimage to the Holy Sepulchre; he pays a visit to the pope at Avignon, and later, when his Holiness advises him to reign mildly, as a father, and not like a tyrant, and threatens him with excommunication, Valdemar writes to him the following well-known epistle:—

"King Valdemar to the Roman Pontiff greeting. We have our nature from God, our kingdom from the inhabitants, our riches from our forefathers, and our faith from your predecessors; which faith, if you do not favour us, we return you by these presents. Farewell."[*]

---

[*] Waldemar Rex Pontifici Romano Salutem. Naturam habemus à Deo, Regnum ab Incolis, Divitias à Parentibus, Fidem a tuis Prædecessoribus, quam, si nobis non faves, per præsentes remittimus. Vale.

This is the most daring letter ever received by a pope, but, being composed with peculiar naïveté and openheartedness, the author was not called to account. The pope only said, "Valdé amarum est," it is very bitter.

In commemoration of the Hanseatic embassy, Valdemar caused to be constructed the celebrated Goose Tower, surmounted by a vane—a goose of fine gold. When, in after days, Erik the Pomeranian fled with the fair Cecilia to the island of Gothland, they carried off with them the crown jewels, and all valuables they could lay their hands upon, among which was numbered the golden goose—the weather-cock of the castle of Vordingborg. This fair Cecilia was own lady's-maid to our English Queen Philippa; beyond the fact that she accompanied Erik to Gothland and remained with him nine or ten years, little is recorded concerning her except the following anecdote. One day, a powerful noble, Sir Olaf Axelsen Thott* by name, when riding accompanied by his squires in the neighbourhood of Vordingborg, met a lady driving in great state in a queen's coach; so he got off his horse, and, taking off his hat, like a well-mannered gentleman, made her a low bow.

"Haw, haw!" laughed the squires. "Sirrahs, what do you mean by such insolence?" exclaimed the astonished noble. The attendants here explained who the lady was. "Stop the chariot!" roared Sir Olaf. "Pull the jade out!" His orders are promptly obeyed, and, seizing the unlucky Cecilia across his knees, he treats her just as nurses do refractory children, and gave her,

---

* He was one of the nine sons of Axel Thott, known under the name of Axelsønner.

as the author expresses it, "tre smæk paa rumpen," adding, "Take that to your lord, and tell him by your bad influence you will some day cause his separation from Denmark." The knight was right, for she did so.

We slept but one night at Vordingborg. The scenery over the water is soft and smiling, soothing to the nerves, like that of Denmark in general.

NESTVED.

October 3rd.—How the wind did blow, how the rain did pour, as we drove along the dull road on our way to Nestved! we had decidedly remained too late in Møen, and ought already to be lodged safe somewhere, and not wandering at this season over the wide, blowing country of the island of Zealand.

The little town of Nestved was of more importance in former days, and the "consul and proconsul" were treated with becoming respect by King Christian I., who summoned them to attend the wedding of Prince Hans with "his bride Christina of Saxony," in these terms :—" Christianus I., &c.—Further, dear friends, as we intend, with the will of God, to keep the wedding of our son on Sunday next after Bartholomew's day in Copenhagen, we invite you to come and enjoy yourselves, with your wives, and other friends who shall come,"—a more general invitation than is given to royal weddings in the present day.

We are lodged at the hotel and rather inclined to grumble, but the weather after noon-time clears up; the sun, wearied of staying at home within the black curtain-clouds, comes out for a gaze on this world below, and, dried and in the sweetest of tempers, we stroll out to visit Herlufsholm, the Eton—no! Sorø, a real royal foundation, is the Eton—the Harrow rather of the Danish dominions. A clear meandering trout-stream, through a leafy forest, guides us on our way; a stray professor, pale and unwholesome-looking, with the inevitable spectacles on nose, taking his daily constitutional, and then, further on a party of happy schoolboys, walking arm in arm, imparting to each other their little mutual confidences. Group after group passes by, all neatly dressed and walking with decorum, for it is Sunday, on which day alone the boys are permitted to go into the town of Nestved, and after four o'clock, the Lutheran Sabbath being over, to visit the "tuck-shops" of the city.

Two children look wistfully at us as we pass, and whisper something to each other; we look back, they turn, and then a small boy, more venturesome than his companion, runs up, capping us, and we recognise two small acquaintances whom we had met in the châteaux of their fathers during our wanderings in Jutland. They volunteer to do the honours, procure the keys, and initiate us into the academy of Herlufsholm, at which they are pursuing their elementary studies.

HERLUFSHOLM.

Herlufsholm, once a convent of Benedictines, resembles most of the red brick gaards of its period; much massacred, happily unwashed. It was founded in the 16th century by the celebrated Admiral Herluf Trolle and his wife Bridget Giøe.* Herluf exchanged

---

* The Giøe family date back to the thirteenth century. Mogens, father of Bridget, became a great advocate of the Reformation and corresponded with Luther. He was appointed to arrange the marriage of Christian II. with the Princess Elizabeth, whom he espoused by procuration. His brother Henry commanded the fleet sent to bring

the manor of Skovkloster with King Frederic II. for that of Hillerødsholm, now Frederiksborg.

It's a very pious act, no doubt, founding colleges and hospitals after you're dead with your money, but the proceeding is seldom approved of by your nearest heirs and relatives. It having come to the knowledge of "the disinherited" that the title-deeds of the college were mislaid, they forthwith brought an action against the foundation for the recovery of the manor and its dependencies. Most indefatigable search had been made into every cupboard, every mouse-hole of the manor, without effect; the lawsuit was going against the Academy; and the rector, worried and sad (as he himself relates), worn out with anxiety and useless racking of his brain, fell asleep one evening in his arm-chair in his homely bed-room of the old conventual building. The moon shone bright, and suddenly visible in her pale rays appeared before him the form of old Bridget Giøe, wife of the founder; angry and exceeding wrathful she looked, menacing with her hand, as much as to say, "What's the use of my founding academies if you spectacled fools go and lose the title-deeds?—ugh! you st-o-o-o-pid!" and down, in her wrath, she banged her clenched fist upon a small table by the fire-side, making the very chamber ring with the noise, and then disappeared. The tormented rector starts from his chair alarmed; suddenly a thought strikes him; he seizes the poker, and, following the example of the ghost, bangs away at the table, till it flies shivered to bits, and there, hidden in a secret drawer, lies forgotten

---

her to Denmark, and remained faithful to her fortunes to the last, for which his property was confiscated by Frederic I.

the very document whose loss had well-nigh caused the dissolution of the budding academy.

We visited the dormitories, each with its fifteen beds—boys arranged according to their ages and size—name on each bed—the washing-rooms, studies, gymnasium, and salle d'armes; many are the portraits of the worthy founders. Old Bridget looks well capable of smashing a table or a skull if she felt inclined—the last person in the world one would care to meet with on an excursion from the land of spirits. She was lady of honour to Queen Dorothea, and is said to have contributed more to the establishment of the Reformation than any one in Denmark, for, when Hans Tausen first preached the doctrines of Luther, she it was who induced Ronnøv, the Bishop of Zealand, not to treat the matter harshly. (Ronnøv was an admirer of Bridget before he entered into holy orders.) Lastly, we visit the chapel, where behind the altar lie the splendid black and white marble monuments of the founders; better kept they might be, and should be, for it is little to the credit of the authorities to allow them to be mutilated, and made resting-places for brooms and brushes.

Small boy brings us a cannon-ball, most uncomfortable affair, with a spike projecting from one end of it; he dragged it out from among some rubbish—the very ball from which the gallant old Admiral met his death-wound in a conflict with the Swedes in 1565.*

---

* When about to start on this last expedition, a friend remonstrated with him on again risking his life after such long service. Trolle replied, "If I lose this life, I enter another. Do you know why we are called gentlemen, and why we wear chains of gold; why we possess lordships, and expect more respect from others? It is because we have the satisfaction to see our peasants live in peace, while we, with our

But really the authorities—for we all know how immoveable learned corporations are all the world over—have made a move of late years; they have closed the coffin of Denmark's Lord Chancellor and historian, Hvitfeldt, who is here interred.* Old Herlufsholmians recollect the time when, in the heyday of their youth and spirits, though perhaps not grace, they —on mischief bent—uncovered the sarcophagus of the old chronicler, dragged him from his resting-place, and, each giving him a hand, waltzed him round and round the church—a living Dance of Death, not painted in the designs of Cranach, or Hans Hemling either—irreverent monkeys!

The evening is bright and autumnal; our young guides conduct us by a new way through the forest towards Nestved. We pass through their summer playground, a waving canopy of foliage overhead, not to be penetrated by the sun's rays. This forest is very charming, most enjoyable, doubly so to youth; and then, having taken leave of the little fellows with that mysterious pressure of the hand, a sort of freemasonry which makes a visit from "friends of home" extra acceptable, we dismiss them to their tuck-shop, bull's-eyes, hardbake, and toffy. May angels watch over their digestion!

One advantage have Sorø and Herlufsholm over our public schools of Eton and Harrow—recollect I speak

---

king, defend our country. If we wish for what is sweet, we must also taste the bitter." It was Herluf who commenced the collection of chronicles of which his nephew Hvitfeldt later made use.

* He died at Herlufsholm 1608. Hvitfeldt was sent ambassador to the Court of Queen Elizabeth to restore the insignia of the Garter at the death of King Frederic II. His History of the Danish Monarchy extends from Dan Mikillati to Frederic II., and was edited and continued by Resen.

as man, not with the feelings of a schoolboy, who prefers all that is wrong in this world to what is good for him. Being far removed from large towns, the boys are not encouraged to run into every kind of extravagance, and compelled to pay just three times the value of every article in which they invest their pocket-money—a system of robbery licensed, Heaven only knows why, by the authorities of the above-mentioned places. As regards learning, who ever learned anything useful at a public school in England except to be and conduct himself like a gentleman? with that we all rest satisfied: self-education will come later, somehow or other, when once a man feels the want of it.

CHAPTER LV.

Peter Thott and his høi — The Black Friis of Borreby — The enchanted bell of the Letter-room — Old Valdemar Daa the alchymist — The giant girl and the sandhills — The "Lady of the Morn" the curse of Zealand — Thorvaldsen at Nysø — The convent for noble ladies at Gisselfeld — Peter Oxe the minister of Frederic II. — The ladies of Vemmetofte — A starlight night — Spoliation of the goddess Freia.

GAUNØ.

October 4th.—THREE days' rain; it is over, and we have bright autumn weather again. We started this morning early, for the days close in fast, and it is well to have the daylight before you, to visit Gaunø, the sea-girt château of Baron Reedts Thott, at a mile's distance from the town of Nestved. A fine old place it is, and contains a great many pictures—heirlooms to the family — how many thousands I dare not affirm. The Thott family, say some, existed centuries before the Christian era. One Peter Thott is mentioned as having rendered good service to King Valdemar in his wars against the Wends. Pagan he remained though patriot, but his son Thor the Bearded was baptised and became Governor of Iceland and Skaane. He stuck however to the good old customs, and was buried like a true Scandinavian under a høi in Skaane, called Kiøling-høi. On this hill were many stones, one of which, called Lille Tulle, bore the following inscription :—

"Dalby mill and Kielby mead,
Beechen grove and Ringsø lake,
Give I to Bosie Kloster new;
But I myself lie under this høi."

A peasant once carried off the stone to repair his house, but the ghosts made such a hideous noise, his family were scared out of their wits, and resolved to depart bag and baggage, when a ghost appeared before them, saying, "Replace Lille Tulle." They did so, and the noises ceased. Later, however, the stone was carried off by Tage Thott to use in the construction of his château at Eriksholm, but he was one of the family, and the ghosts said nothing.

We had meant to extend our journey as far as Holstenborg and Skjelskør, the former the seat of the Counts of Holstein; Skjelskør a small town, remarkable for nothing except for the fact that no Danish king has ever visited within its walls since the days of Erik Menved. According to tradition, Skjelskør is one of the strongholds of the Elf King; and were a living monarch to attempt to cross the bridge which leads within its gates, the structure would straightway crumble down and immerse the royal party in the waters below.

But though Skjelskør is a town of little historic interest, not far from it stands the picturesque château of Borreby, built, it is said, with the stones from Marsk Stig's stronghold at Stigs Næs. Borreby is the herregaard of a branch of the Friis family—the "Black Friis" as they were styled, from their bearing three black squirrels[*] as their arms—one of whom, John Friis, was the

---

[*] The Friis, of Friisenborg, bear a red squirrel cracking a nut.

first Protestant High Chancellor of Denmark, the friend of Luther and Melancthon, who faithfully served his country for fifty years under four successive sovereigns. John died unmarried, and Borreby descended to his nephew Christian,* who likewise filled the office of Chancellor, and was minister plenipotentiary to the Court of Queen Elizabeth. Now, in the southern wing of the old mansion was a vaulted chamber called the "Letter-room," formerly full of old chests and manuscripts long since dispersed. From the ceiling hung suspended an enchanted bell; and when the Chancellor Christian Friis was at his last extremity, he told the Lady Mette Hardenberg, his wife, that, when she should hear the bell in the letter-chamber sound, she must prepare to follow him to the grave. And thus it occurred some years afterwards. One evening the lady was sitting at cards when the bell in the letter-chamber was heard to toll. Lady Mette laid down her cards, and said to her friends, "I have a good hand, but I shall not live to play it out—I am about to die." At the same time she expired.

The Daa family next became lords of the manor. Valdemar Daa laid waste a forest of oaks by cutting down the largest trees to build a costly man-of-war, which he expected the king, Frederic III., to purchase at an

---

* The Friis have given two Chancellors of the name of Christian. The other, great-nephew to the gallant old Bishop of Viborg, was one of the first eleven knights of the Armed Hand, whose names are perpetuated in a distich:—

"Friis, Lung, Skeel, Rantzau, Rantzau, tu Bildeque, Rantzau,
  Sinklar, Sparr, et Pens, Sandberg et Skeel, partis equestris."

Charles I. esteemed him so highly that, when Sir Thomas Roe was sent ambassador to Denmark, Charles gave him an autograph letter to Friis, recommending him to his especial notice.

exorbitant price. The king sent an admiral to inspect it, who admired a fine pair of black horses which Valdemar had in his stable. Valdemar would not take the hint and present them to the admiral, so the latter returned and gave a bad report of the ship; the king declined the purchase, and it was left to rot upon the strand. Later, Valdemar turned alchymist, and became so poor that one hard winter his three daughters remained months in bed because they could not afford fuel. At last he fancied he had discovered the great secret; but he let fall the precious vial; it broke, and his hopes were dashed to the ground. More poverty, mortgage foreclosed, &c., and the family had to leave Borreby. On foot, staff in hand, accompanied by his daughters, an alchymical vial in his bosom, he went forth a wanderer from his once princely home, to die in misery and obscurity. One day a large black dog arrived at Borreby, and entering the hall proceeded to the letter-room and pulled the bell with his teeth. The new possessor was alarmed, but afterwards found that at that very moment had expired at Viborg old Valdemar Daa, late lord of the manor of Borreby.

We returned to Nestved to breakfast, and again started on the road which leads towards Præsto. After leaving the town to the right, at some distance removed from the sea runs a lofty ridge of sand-banks, bakkere as they here call them. Splendid view from the top, says the postilion, finest in Zealand; we decline; much too windy; our energies, too, are well nigh exhausted. Geologists and wiseacres would be puzzled ever to know how this ridge of sand-hills got themselves here inland, where they have no business to be, were it not for Tradition, and she luckily knows everything. Once on a time in the neighbourhood of Nestved there lived a giant girl, a good girl enough, only she had long, bare legs, and the boys laughed at her, calling out "Long shanks! long shanks!" whenever she appeared. One day they worried and teased her beyond all bearing; in a fury she rushed down to the sea-shore, and, filling her apron with sand, was about to overwhelm the town of Nestved, and bury houses and inhabitants, rude boys and girls together; only there was a hole in her apron, and, as in her rage and haste she hurried along, the sand ran out, and when she arrived, quite out of breath, it was nearly all gone, so she plumped down the remainder just at the highest spot, turned tail, and was never seen again in the island of Zealand.

The way appeared to us somewhat long, varied only by occasional patches of beauty—untidy, stubbly fields—the yellow chrysanthemum, as noxious weeds always do in this world, growing and flowering in luxuriance. "Morgen frue," or lady of the morn,* as it is called by the simple and unsophisticated, a curse to the agriculturist, was until just two hundred years since unknown in the Danish dominions.

It was in the year 1659, when peace was proclaimed between Denmark and the Swedes, that the Brandenburghers and the Polacs were about to quit Jutland. Allies they were in name, but nothing more; they did greater harm by their ill deeds than the enemy themselves—destroyed, robbed, pillaged, and it is now said that the Jutlanders have never since recovered their prosperity. Before leaving the country they pur-

---

* Chrysanthemum segetum.

posed selling their supplies of corn and other provisions by auction. So the Jutlanders, ever true patriots, agreed they would none of them purchase the articles, and that the Polacs should derive no benefit from the disposal of their stores. The sale commenced, but no bidders appeared, save one aged peasant, a man who could not resist the temptation of the low prices, and, much to the disgust of his companions, he purchased the corn of the Polacs. "It will do you no good," they exclaimed; "recollect the old song:—

' When the Dane or the Swede
Sow German seed,
Ill luck will come to both Dane and to Swede.' "

But he laughed and went his way. Part of the corn he gave to his horses; they sickened at once and died, so he sowed the remainder; and when it came up, the fields were yellow as gold—it was two parts " morgen frue ;" the flowers seeded; the evil spread; and now you find this plant growing far and wide, to the injury of the crops of the Danish islands and Jutland south of the Liimfiorde.

PRÆSTO.

We approach the prettily-situated town of Præsto, or the Island of Priests—one Lutheran parson alone rules here supreme. We go to the little inn, where the landlord insists on preparing us a dinner which never can be ready before to-morrow morning. We first visit the banks of the lovely little fiorde—so blue, so wooded, so serene. Danish scenery is invented for the soothing of ruffled nerves. I highly recommend doctors to order thereunto all their hypochondriacal patients. Then we pass by an avenue of limes to Nysø, the manorial residence of the Baroness Stampe, whom we luckily find at home.

Nysø possesses another interest apart from its ancient buildings and its antique old-fashioned gardens; for in this manor-house Thorvaldsen, the honoured of kings and peasants, passed the last summers of his long and well-spent life. He had almost ceased to work, but the Baroness Stampe encouraged him to recommence his labours; and here, in the garden of clipped hedges, in a small kiosk, he held his studio, which is preserved as sacred, and where still exist many of his original bas-reliefs in plaster.

In the château hangs an admirable portrait of the great sculptor by his friend Horace Vernet—painted in his blouse; far superior to the Christmas-tree of Frederiksborg.

When we again returned to the inn, no chance of dinner; the pudding still boiling, so we waited till eight, and we waited till nine, and I had intentions of going dinnerless to bed; when, after the two-and-fortieth "strax," it did come, and very good it was; only we all had the nightmare, and I dreamt of the giant-girl of Nestved, who sat on my chest with a pudding, and throttled me, pouring sand through the hole in her apron. Nearly senseless, I awoke in an awful fright, and found myself almost buried alive under a hecatomb of duvet.

GISSELFELD.

October 5th.—Up betimes, and off early, as old Pepys would say, for we have a long day's sight-seeing before us—a day's sight-seeing which would have satisfied the worthy old gentleman himself. Very pretty is the road along the banks of the purple well-wooded fiorde after we pass Nysø; and then we get into the high road, like all other high roads odious, till we come to Kønnede kro, where we change horses, one mile's distance from Gisselfeld.

So, as the weather is bright and the bye-road dry, we continue our way on foot; the stately abbey, embowered in woods, is seen for a moment in the distance, and then disappears from our view. Gisselfeld was always somewhere, never where we expected it, till I almost fancied it to be like a plaisanterie of our Jutland friend, the fairy Morgana. At last, after turning off into a sort of park, mushroom bedecked, and richly timbered, we reach a lodge, mount the waggon, drive up to the gardener's house, and turn into the garden of the abbey. Nature has here done much, for she undulates well and supplies a lake of water; the slopes are clad with emerald turf and ornamental shrubs, sorbi and cratægi, in all the glory of their golden and blood-red fruit; art has furnished platebandes of gay autumn flowers, and the garden is well backed with beechen woods. Gisselfeld, of course, itself disappears from the scene. We were some time before we found the entrance to the fine old building—one of Denmark's best, but whitewashed. It was built in the days of the second Christian—perhaps a little earlier—by some member of the house of Oxe, of the same family as Torben Oxe; and later dwelt there the celebrated Peter Oxe, whose portrait hangs in the riddersaal. Minister to Frederic II., and Grand Master of Denmark, he contributed greatly to the advancement of his nephew Tycho Brahe, and it was he who first reformed the finances of the kingdom and diminished the expenses of the royal household—put the servants on board-wages, &c. Oxe introduced the crayfish, "Taske krabbe," into Denmark, as well as other sorts of fish, and a species of frog which went by the name of Peter Oxe's frog. He and his masculine wife Mette Rosenkrantz were interred in the Frue Kirke of Copenhagen, long since destroyed by fire. After passing into the female line, Gisselfeld was at last given or came into the possession of Christian Gyldenløve, son of Christian V. by Mrs. Moth, a brave and gallant man. He served in Italy under the Prince Eugene, commanding the Italian troops; but met with an early death, and by his will bequeathed the manor of Gisselfeld and its broad lands to found a convent for poor but noble maidens.

The head of the Danneskiold family enjoys the office of Administrator of Gisselfeld, and the eldest daughter of that house is born hereditary Abbess of the convent. As for the nuns, they are flitting about the world somewhere.

One half-hour's drive brings us to Bregentved, the princely residence of Count Moltke, the much respected ex-minister. If the approach were only freed from stables, outhouses, &c., it would be perfect. The gardens—prettily laid out in the French style, the long clipped allées with fountains and statues, staircases of marble and terraces—reminded me of Versailles without its stiff formality. Then, on the opposite side of the hedge, stand on the lake's bank two picturesque, creeper-embowered cottages, all stripes and gables. England, the country of garden, turf, and sward, could produce nothing prettier. On a height above an artificial cascade stands an obelisk to the memory of King

Frederic V., concerning whose visit to Bregentved tradition relates queer stories.

Frederic was, as you recollect, a gay and joyous youth, a little mauvais sujet—no wonder, bored to death by the hypocrisy of his father's court. He loved to run down to Bregentved, with a band of boon companions, to enjoy himself. They disguised themselves as peasants, and amused themselves among the villagers. One day, when at supper, the prince in a fit of jealousy drew his sword, and passed it through the body of his host and companion. The blood still stains the floor of the banqueting-hall; no scouring-drops, no soda, will remove the spot—indeed, the housekeeper declares the more you scrub the redder it becomes, like Rizzio's gore in the Palace of Holyrood.

VEMMETOFTE.

We are all among the nuns to-day, and hasten off as fast as horses will carry us towards the convent of Vemmetofte, anxious to catch the daylight. We were told to expect little beauty, but that the collection of royal portraits was interesting, as well as the interior of the building. The new courts lately erected—a fine series of gabled buildings in striped brickwork—are highly creditable to the "ladies" of the chapter: decidedly architecture is on the move in Denmark.

This chapter was founded in 1785 by Prince Charles, brother of King Frederic IV., and his sister the Princess Hedvig, who resided here until the day of her death. We were received by the priest of the establishment, who conducted us over the apartments, which have remained in statu quo since the death of the foundress, and contain many objects, embroidered screens, &c., of her handiwork. The portraits are good; none wanting save that of the Reventlow Queen, who seldom appears out of Jutland. Of Caroline Matilda there hangs a good specimen. Vemmetofte in its day was the property of the Brahe family, and in one of the reception-rooms there exists a fine old chimney-piece with the arms and device of Tycho carved thereon. In a small turret-chamber leading from the great saloon hang the portraits of the ten first-elected ladies of the chapter, attired in black, bearing on their breasts the badge and star of the order—ten prettier creatures I have seldom seen.

The convent of Vemmetofte is about to undergo a thorough restoration, rendered necessary by the contrast of its whitewashed walls with the admirable courts recently erected. Our reverend cicerone conducted us to the chapel — a low vaulted building, hung with numerous pictures, chiefly collected by Prince Charles when at Rome; some appeared to be of the Bolognese school, but light was insufficient. I can only retain a confused idea of a Last Judgment by Krock, of Flensborg—a miniature copy of the larger altarpiece consumed in the conflagration of Christiansborg Palace in 1794.

We had lingered so long over the tapestries and ancient furniture, the queer old gilded stones, the Chinese scent-bottles of the Princess Hedvig, the portraits, and various souvenirs of royalty treasured up and connected with the place, that daylight had fast closed in ere we quitted for our destination. We are still some ten or twelve miles' distance from the little town of Store Hedinge, where we purpose to pass the night. The evening is dark, but the stars shine brightly in the heavens; Karls Vogn—as is here called our Charles's Wain, or the Great Bear—with his companion, Qvinds Vogn, or our Lady's Waggon, the Little Bear, glitter and twinkle in the celestial hemisphere. The Pleiades too: and here ends my astronomical learning; for Orion is pale and indistinct; a month later he will come out bright in his full glory: old people in out-of-the-way parts of Jutland still term this brightest of constellations Freias Rok (distaff), the only possession Freia, Venus of the Scandinavian lands, still retains. Poor Freia! Never was spoliation more complete. They took from you everything—your stars, your flowers. That pretty golden vetch,* which grows creeping and trailing among the grass, known to every village child as ladies' shoes and stockings (our Lady's it should be), once Freia's, is now termed Maries Guldsko (gold shoes). Even the gossamer was taken from her, and became Jomfru traad—toile de la Vierge in France. What tears poor Freia must have shed at this spoliation of her belongings! and when she wept, as all men know, each briny drop as it trickled down became at once a nugget of the purest gold. May be it is the tears of this pagan goddess which lie scattered over the sheep-paths of our Australian colonies and California. Loki, the Genius of Evil, fared better; but then all his plants were rubbish, such as our English botany awards to the devil—flowers of poisonous or prickly nature, badly seeding; so nobody cared to have

---

* Lotus corniculatus.

them, and they still bear his name. Balder retains as his property one of the hawkweeds, termed Balders Braa (brow).*

---

* The god Balder is said by tradition to be buried at Funen, under a høi called Balder's Hill. Great treasures are, of course, concealed within. Some peasants many years since came there by night to dig for the gold. But no sooner did they turn the sod with the pickaxe than a rushing stream of water burst forth from the hill-top, washing peasants, pickaxe, shovel, and wheelbarrow, half across the isle of Zealand.

CHAPTER LVI.

The dominions of the Elf King — Hospitality at Store Hedinge — The Trolles and the church of Hpierup — Vallø, the Queen of Danish convents — The ancient house of Bille — Lucia the Flower of Denmark — The last of the Rosensparres — Ledreborg, the ancient Leira — Court etiquette of King Ring — Legend of King Skiold, founder of Leira.

STORE HEDINGE.

WE were tired and sick of star-gazing, when a light appears at the road's-end, faint at first, and later brighter, and then quick flits across the horizon a line of welcome stars: there is now no doubt we are at our journey's end, and before a few minutes have elapsed we drive into our haven, the town of Store Hedinge; we rattle down the street into the Place, where scarlet postilion stops and inquires, "Where shall I drive you to?" "Drive to?—to the hotel, of course." "There is none." "None? to the kro then." "No kro." "Nonsense! there must be." "The Gjæstgiver is in the churchyard, and the kro bankrupt." "Where can we sleep, then?" "At Kiøge, twelve miles further."

So we drive to the post-house, to order horses on to Kiøge. The postmaster was out, but we are ushered into a small, prettily furnished drawing-room, where we find his wife sitting working, together with her friends, round the table. How cosy and comfortable they did look! We tell our piteous tale, and the kind lady melts at our distress. Go on to Kiøge, impossible! such a cold night: she will send out and find us rooms in the town when her husband comes in. When did we dine? We own that we had eaten our smør brod at eleven o'clock at Rønnede kro, and had fasted ever since. Why, we must be faint! she will give us some tea, will take no denial (I can't say we did stand out vigorously), and off she goes to call her maid. In ten minutes' time we were ushered into the next room, not only to our tea, but to an excellent supper of cold meat, smør brod, compôte, and fruit, prettily arranged on old Danish china, fine linen, and bright silver; no fuss, no bother; we were kindly welcome. There is a refinement about the middle class of Danes in their household arrangements, seldom to be met with in other countries; and so we ate, drank, and refreshed ourselves, our kind hostess attending on us, watching and anticipating our wants; our spirits raised, we talked and chatted away, all about our travels, and then came in Postmaster Jaspersen himself with the news of rooms at an old lady's, who had turned her house upside down for our accommodation. When supper was finished we all sat and talked over the legends of the place; all about the Elf King, of whom you will hear more to-morrow; then, as a message arrived to say our rooms were ready, we departed—after many thanks on our side, and much pleasure on hers, lantern-lighted by the maid—to our resting-place, where we were received by our hostess, a jolly old dame, who could not do enough to make us comfortable. Such questions as she made about our breakfasts for to-morrow; such caresses to the dogs— Lina and Vic—who she felt certain were starving; they had already supped—no matter, they must sup again: a little milk at any rate. At last we got to bed, and slept like tops, till awakened by the market waggons rolling and rattling through the streets on the following morning.

October 6th.—We are in the dominions of the Elf King, a most important personage in these parts. Store Hedinge is his capital. According to the old tradition we mentioned at Skjelskør, no sovereign dares to plant his foot within the precincts of his kingdom—the Elf King would not allow it. "We'll soon see that," said King Christian IV.; so down he came in all the pomp and state of majesty, and made, after the manner of the day, a royal progress through the country. But the people did not believe in him a whit. "It's only," cried the peasants, "the Elf King, who, for good reasons known only to himself, has assumed the appearance of earthly royalty." A charming operetta, styled 'Elverhøi,' in which the best of the Danish national airs are introduced, has been composed on this subject. The Elf King was, however, affronted, quitted his residence at Stevns Klint, and took up his abode in the now deserted monks' prisons of the round church of Store Hedinge. We visited, as you may imagine, this celebrated edifice, but over its desecration let us drop a veil. What a deal of mischief well-intentioned ignorant people may and do do in this world. The sum of two thousand pounds English has been lately raised and expended on its restoration. It's too horrible to talk of; the architect deserves the fate of Marsyas. A pendent wooden roof of our own Henry VII.'s period; the character of the building entirely destroyed. On entering the churchyard my eyes first lighted on the stone cross erected to the memory of the defunct gjæstgiver, so vainly sought last night. He died some nine years ago, and has not since been replaced, speaking

SEA, SALINI AND CHURCH OF ΠΟΙΙΕΝΤ.

little for the commercial relations of the capital of Elfin Majesty.

We had just breakfasted and were about to start, when in comes our good-humoured hostess to ask would we receive the visit of Kammerherr ——, the chief gentleman of the town. Of course we are only too happy; and in he is ushered; is quite shocked to hear of our trouble of last night; has scolded the postmaster for not sending us to lodge with him, it would have given him and the Kammerherrinde such pleasure to receive us. She expects us to breakfast; we had only just concluded our own, but of course accept. So we accompany him to his house, and are kindly received by the lady and her daughters, and made to promise and vow if ever we come again to Store Hedinge we will make a long abode with them. The carriage is announced, and, after thanks and leave-taking, we drive off for Stevns Klint, a long ridge of chalk cliffs of no particular beauty or grandeur: but it would have been an insult to the island of Zealand had we omitted to see the queer old church of Høierup. Built in very early days—the fourteenth century—some say by a skipper, others by a pirate, a votive offering to heaven in gratitude for preservation from a fearful tempest, he constructed it near the klint's edge, to serve as a landmark to those at sea. It differs little from the old brick churches of this date. While the masons were engaged in building, probably they disturbed the Trolles, for as fast as they commenced it down it came; make the walls stand straight they could not. Ill-natured people accused the architect of not knowing his duty, most wrongfully, for it was all the Trolles. The masons were about to re-commence their task when they heard a loud deep voice from within the hill exclaim, in Swedish, "Høier up!"—higher up. They now knew how to act, and, following the advice of the voice, built their church on the summit of the cliff, calling it Høierup, and here it stands to the present day: but it would have toppled into the water long ago, only on each Christmas-eve the angels bear it back the footstep of a cock.

The Trolles became after a time so mischievous and insupportable in Zealand, that the parsons laid their heads together, and, by some method unknown, caught them and packed them all off in a boat to their cousins of the island of Bornholm.

VALLØ.

We hasten, as fast as Danish post-horses will carry us, to Vallø, the queen of all Danish convents, a right royal foundation; foundation of Queen Madalena the magnificent.

"Give me Vallø," asked Queen Madalena of her sovereign lord, "and I'll found a chapter there for noble ladies, and we'll have such a ceremony, and a medal struck with your head and mine; a princess (German of course)—somebody who ends in 'hausen'—shall be the Abbess, and the ladies shall have as many quarterings as Denmark possesses Syssels." Founded it was, and a fine ceremony too (see the Danish Vitruvius); and right royal looked Queen Madalena in her new gown. She didn't find a princess whose name ended in "hausen," but something better—a princess of the ducal house of Wurtemburg. The convent was opened in the year 1738, by the queen in person. An excellent foundation it proves to be: a pity we have none such in England. Do not fancy these convents have anything papistical about them, nothing at all: quarterings, too, are now no longer required; gentle birth alone is sufficient. The Hereditary Princess Caroline of Denmark is Abbess of the Institution. A Danish gentleman, who wishes his daughter to be entered upon the list of the ladies, intimates his desire to Count Moltke, after the baptism of the infant. On paying two thousand rix-dollars the name of his child is inscribed upon the books of the establishment, and from that day she receives a certain annual sum, the interest of the money: after that it becomes an affair of time. As the older ladies die off, the younger ones mount up. Of the Dames de Vallø, whom we see dancing and waltzing about the world in white tarletan, with grand cordon and badge of the order, most of them receive from about sixty to seventy pounds; then later, as they get old and high on the list, from one hundred and twenty to one hundred and thirty pounds yearly. The prioress receives an income of about six hundred pounds English. If any member dies or marries, she forfeits her entrance-money. The ten sisters highest on the list have apartments assigned to them in the convent: they have, of course, their own private room; but the drawing-rooms are lighted up of an evening, and they dine together, enjoy their own parson, own doctor, own equipages; a beautiful garden, with greenhouses and a deer-park;—live among their own people. Each lady of the first class is obliged to undertake the education of some orphan child at her own expense. On the whole it is a very happy institution, and the old ladies pass the autumn of their lives in good fellowship and social comfort. The ladies of Vallø, too, hold high rank in the tables of precedence of women, coming after countesses, and before the wives of counts' eldest sons. Those of Vemmetofte, however, rank only in the third class, along with the adjutant-generals and justices of the West India islands. Of these foundations there exist in the kingdom of Denmark, for unmarried ladies of birth, some twelve or thirteen, independent of others too numerous to mention for widows or maidens of a lower rank of life; many, indeed most, of these have been established from the economies of some dowager queen.

In England such establishments would be scarcely possible; people are too apt to care only for the sufferings of the lower classes, forgetful that those who have been reared in plenty and luxury are often more to be pitied in the time of adversity than those who have struggled against want from their youth upwards: added to this, there is a tendency with us to debase and degrade all our charities. How few foundations can be found in England, after a lapse of years, conducted according to the wishes of the founder! Establish an almshouse for the benefit of poor housekeepers—not people who have possessed houses of their own, but the old women who keep the keys and lock up the tea and sugar—why, before ten years have run by it will be swamped by dilapidated charwomen. No; establishments of this kind would never be popular in England, there would be a radical outcry against them: here, in Denmark, they are looked up to and respected; and why? simply because the population is not over-abundant, and all classes are here amply cared for.

It is a fine old building, Vallø, flanked by two lofty towers, one square, the other round; brick, encircled with stone medallions; its fine old gateway, rich in sandstone carvings, reminding me much of Voer Gaard; built it was (as, indeed, was Vemmetofte) by a Rosenkrantz, having first belonged to old Ellen Marsviin. On the bridge which spans the moat stand massive lions, bearing shields emblazoned with their arms. Mette Rosenkrantz, wife of Peter Oxe, who built the castle —a pious and virtuous lady, who, says her epitaph, in all affairs combined the mien and gesture of a real cavalier under the garments of a woman. What an awful creature she must have been! We visited the interior; the portraits—Madalena among the rest, in all her glory; the chapel, where the ladies say their prayers, in a sort of peeresses' pew, with the retainers of the establishment,—a second pew under the pulpit being set apart for the deaf ones; mounted the tower to admire the view; then, having been introduced to the original document of the foundation, gorgeously emblazoned, drove off on our way. In the parish church of Vallø hang the pedigrees of the house of Bille, dating from the seventh century. Bille is one of the most ancient of the few remaining Danish families, though perhaps the genealogy may be a little apocryphal. Of this family was Lucia Bille, Danmarks Blomster, the Flower of Denmark—la belle des belles—who lived in 1445 at the court of the Queen Dorothea, and who, to the despair of all young and gallant men, retired to a convent and became a nun. The manor of Billesborg lies hard by.

Before arriving at the town of Kiøge, where we stopped to feed and change horses, we passed the village of Herfølge, site of the engagement between Wellesley and Castenskiold in the early part of the present century. In the church lies interred the last of the noble house of Rosensparre, killed in a battle against the Swedes in Skaane in 1612. "You are the sole surviving member of your house, the last of an old stock; do not expose your life recklessly," advised his friends, when the battle raged at its utmost fury. "A good name before everything," was the reply. He threw himself into the thickest of the fight, and fell pierced by a hundred wounds. We continued our course, and arrived amidst a blaze of starlight at our old quarters of last year—hostel of the Prindsen at Roeskilde.

LEDREBORG.

October 7th.—The dull cathedral town of Roeskilde is in a state of unusual excitement, on account of the sitting of a rix or rath something—one of the endless innumerable assemblies which Denmark has the ill luck to be cursed with. The Prindsen is wonderfully smartened up since last year—hardly recognisable. Breakfast over, we start on an expedition to Ledreborg, the country seat of Count Holstein, some five or six miles distant.

Ledreborg, planted on a height overlooking a deep valley, is a fine specimen of the residence of a Danish nobleman. In the engravings of Pontoppidan there existed a fine old French garden of terraces, statues, and fountains, most in character with the architecture of the château. This was unfortunately destroyed some thirty years since, and replaced by a jardin Anglais, very beautiful in its way. The family were unluckily absent; but we visited the interior of the house, rich in pictures and works of art; the gorgeous chapel, where hangs a curious picture, a portrait group of the early reformers, Luther, Calvin, &c., and among them an Englishman named Perkins.* Independent of its princely mansion, its hanging gardens, and its beechen woods, Ledreborg possesses a deep historic interest, for it stands on the site of the ancient Leira—stronghold of pagan worship in the island of Zealand—rival to Viborg and Sigtuna.

Even in the days of the first Valdemar it was a city of some importance. To the south runs a long ridge of sand-hills, called Dan Mikillati's grave. Not far distant lies the valley of Hertha, still called the Holy Wood, where once stood the principal temple of that goddess in the Danish isles. Here, too, King Ring held his court. His wife, Queen Hvita, was a sorceress, and by her art changed her stepson, Prince Björn, into a bear, for which she afterwards suffered a cruel death. The etiquette of the Leiran court appears to have been at a low ebb; for we read that, after dinner, the royal party pelted one another with the bones they had picked clean during the repast.

The town of Leira was founded by King Skiold, son of Odin, though other traditions say he was offspring of Skeff, the Englishman, fourth son of Noah, born in the ark, concerning whose existence the Books of Moses are silent. He arrived in a ship from afar. At this time all Denmark was sad, for the king had no son, and the Danes knew not whom they should choose as a successor, when one day, as they flocked down to the sea-shore, they observed in the distance a sail which approached the land: it was evidently a ship royal; the mast was of gold; it had silken sails, and was laden with

---

* He was English envoy from Queen Elizabeth, put in, out of compliment, together with the devil and the monks.

great riches of gold and silver. Upon the deck of the vessel lay a beautiful child—a little boy—reposing upon a shield, while his head rested upon a sheaf of wheat. When the people beheld him they cried, "Behold the son of Odin, who comes to be our king!" So they took the child, and sowed the corn, which came up in plenty. each ear bearing more than any ear had before borne in this country; the boy was proclaimed king of Denmark. When only twelve years old he caught a bear and bound it fast in thongs, and at eighteen became king and assumed the reins of government. Courageous and just was King Skiold: in victory he declared "honour is the share of the king, but booty is for the soldiers." Long did he reign over Denmark, and, when an aged man and about to die, he caused himself to be placed in his old ship by his weeping servants, and, when the sails were set, the sun shone bright, and the wind arose, the ship sailed forth; all men wept, and no one knew where he went to. Such is the legend of King Skiold.

CHAPTER LVII.

DESTRUCTION OF THE PALACE OF FREDERIKSBORG BY FIRE.

December 17th.—OUR wanderings were over; and I little thought again to resume my pen to record so sad an event—a national misfortune to the history-loving people of Denmark.

I was sitting in my room at the Oresund, in Elsinore, busily and happily immersed in my books, when the chambermaid, bouncing into my room, announced, "Slot brander in Frederiksborg!"—"the castle's on fire!" On crossing over to the police-office the telegraphic despatch displayed before my eyes left no doubt that the story was, alas! too true. Engines—such engines, too—squirts, and the members of the fire-brigade, were hurrying off (I say so by courtesy) to lend their aid and assistance. In three quarters of an hour's time I was myself en route, fast as Danish post-horses and a highly-booted postilion could carry me.

The day was cold, foggy; the snow lay thick upon the ground. We really did rattle on at a good pace; but the way to me appeared interminable. As we rolled along, never had my recollection of that admirable gallery appeared so vivid as on that day: each figure seemed to start out in chronological order from its frame —singly and separately, one after the other. As we descended the hill, from behind the woods to the left, which obscure the palace from view, rose volumes of black cloudy smoke, curling and dispersing itself in the misty atmosphere. Those glorious minaret-like spires, capping the castle turrets—in vain I strained my eyes—they were not. The gate-house stood before us intact, and then in one moment the whole building lay discovered before us, rising from its very bed—roofless, blackened, still burning—a ruin. It was a sad sight. There was the council-chamber, which spanned the waters—now a red Bridge of Sighs—gutted; those glorious towers, triumphs of the northern Renaissance, were there no longer — the last had fallen at eleven o'clock, shaking the very earth as it fell; of Caroline Matilda's window, too, not one vestige remaining; the fire still rising from time to time, licking away the woodwork around the stone-mullioned windows, as though it were grease: never was devastation more complete. Then, as we passed the gateway, there stood the chapel half consumed—the riddersaal, that gem of art, all fallen in—and, turning into the outer court beyond the moat, oh! what a sight it was! that splendid palace — unique in its style in Europe — a tottering, blackened ruin, and all around frozen. The mischief was complete—all need of exertion now over; men walked up and down sad and astounded. The court was heaped with furniture, pictures, and hundreds of objects besides, snatched from the fury of the devouring element; and what rubbish had been saved! what pots and pans, commodes and chairs, shields of the Elephant, shields of the Dannebrog. My first inquiry was after the fate of the gallery: all gave a different answer. The pictures from the riddersaal had been saved: strange fate those portraits—they alone escaped the conflagration of Christiansborg in 1796. But the billiard-room?—

All lost. Queen Sophia?—Gone. I bowed my head. That triumph of portrait-painting—that chef-d'œuvre of Jacob von Dort. I asked no more questions: time would show the extent of the evil.

In a country like Denmark—fallen from its high estate among the powers of Europe—this calamity will be deeply felt; for they live in the past, in the memory of their own glorious history. Still I fear many of the Danes really do not know the extent of the loss they have sustained—not in the castle of Frederiksborg itself—that was their pride, their glory—but in the splendid historic gallery, of which so few pictures will be again seen.

The fire had burst out early in the morning in the room lately restored by the king for his own private collection—a room on the upper story adjoining the tower, towards the riddersaal. The workmen were occupied in repairs. Whether it was a flue—whether a misplaced stove—in which the evil originated, matters little: the result is the same. The lake was frozen over —this had added to the difficulties; the pipes of the engines, themselves far too short, were frozen, and could not at first be worked; and the fire, which at five o'clock was scarcely looked upon as dangerous, in the space of a few hours had reduced this beautiful monument of Christian IV.'s taste to its present sad condition.

Towards three o'clock the royal carriages were ordered round to convey the court to Copenhagen. The king had retired to one of the buildings of the outer court when all was over, having remained at his post till the very last, superintending the removal of the valuables. As his Majesty descended the steps on his way to the carriage he stayed for one moment to greet me, and, as

I expressed to him my sympathy at the terrible misfortune which had overwhelmed him, he kindly pressed my hand. He could only utter the words "Quel malheur irréparable—quel malheur irréparable!" And it was so indeed, for Frederiksborg can never be again what it once was: it was his pride, his hobby, and he had done, by judicious reparation, much to restore it to its pristine condition.

Accompanied by my friend M. Gyllick, the castellan, I crept through an outer door into the church, the further end of which had alone been injured. The organ, that gem of art, and the royal closet, enriched with its ceiling of ebony and ivory pendants, its paintings by the Dutch masters, were all gone; a heap of burning, smoking timbers still flamed at the further end: and when I saw that ceiling, cracking from the heat, come falling on the pavement below—that fretwork ceiling, the toning down of whose brilliant colours into one perfect harmony had so often excited my admiration and wonder at the superiority of art in days gone by—Heaven forgive me if in my sadness I forgot that under those smoking ruins lay buried four of my fellow creatures, called unprepared into eternity, crushed by the falling roof whilst in the execution of their duty.

Before leaving I again sought out my good friend Gyllick—he who, during the last twenty years, had, as castellan, done more towards the restoration of Frederiksborg than any human being alive. "I wish you good bye for ever, Gyllick; I shall never return. I have passed too many happy days in that dear old gallery, studying the history of Denmark in the portraits of her rulers, ever to bear the sight of its desolation. I have visited Frederiksborg in its glory —I have seen it under the excitement of its flames— I can never again look on it as a ruin." "But," he replied, "do not say that: come again in the spring-time; we may again build up the church, and perhaps some of your old friends may still be spared to us."

As we drove by the castle on our return to Elsinore it was already dark, and the whole building shone bright, illuminated by a lurid glowering of its still-burning flames—a Rembrandt effect of light and shade an artist would have gazed at for hours. I turned away my head —to me it was too painful.

Do not imagine I slept that night: no—I lay tossing on my bed; the spectre of that gallery was for ever before my eyes. Good Queen Sophia with her pale blue eyes; Christian IV. with his marlok, and frail Christina Munk; the splendid family of Gyldenløves; Adolf of Holstein, garter on knee, and his giant race; then, too, our house of Stuart—Prince Henry, with his transparent hand and saddened brow; our Winter Queen— first as a joyful girl with her dog, then that exquisite picture as a widow, so sad, so beautiful—later again a discontented woman; Charles I. or Buckingham— which it was, matters but little now; Henrietta of Orleans, and Eleanor Ulfeld, both alike unfortunate; my Carlyle room, too, where are they?

Frederiksborg, Monday.—I have again visited Frederiksborg on my way to Copenhagen, for the steamer no longer runs, on account of the ice. Professor Worsaae was already there, about to catalogue and inspect the pictures saved from the fire; so I remained, to know the worst. We stood at the entrance of the building where they were stowed away, and saw them brought out one by one, battered, singed, but few uninjured. At the first glance my mind misgave me; and when a Gyldenløve—gallant young son of Christian IV., slain at the siege of Copenhagen—first came forth, I felt at once the whole of the earlier portraits of the house of Oldenborg were doomed. Of that splendid series of two hundred years and upwards, from Christian I. downwards, not one remained—portraits by Lucas Cranach, by John of Cleves, Carl van Mander, Wuchter, Jacob van Dort: of our house of Stuart not one. The Northmen had been more fortunate; but the sole existing portrait of Tycho Brahe had perished. Of modern atrocities, copies, bad and worthless; of living celebrities, and those scarcely dead, there were enough, and more. , James II. and his brother, in their orange surcoats, came out one by one; but few portraits of any merit. My Carlyle room fared better. George II. and his glorious queen, the fair Princess of Hesse, and other old acquaintances, sadly bemired; and when Wilhelmina of Baireuth—the witty she of the memoirs—appeared, she looked so sprightly, so true to life, in her want of feeling, as though she thought it such fun being saved from the fire, I could have boxed her ears with as great a gusto as her plethoric old father ever did in his lifetime.

Of poor Caroline Matilda one portrait alone escaped, and that the ugly one. Strange fate hers, to be always burnt as a beauty and preserved as a fright!

CONCLUSION.

Palais Schimmelmann, April 16*th,* 1860.—My journal is at an end, for to-morrow we leave Copenhagen. I have faithfully transcribed what I have seen, what I have visited, and my impressions thereon. My wanderings through the kingdom of Denmark have to me been of great interest. Still, recollect, I do not recommend this tour to every one. The boy in the Blues—à moustache naissante—the youth late escaped from college, with leave of absence, and a life of hard military duty, or the prospect of a country parish before his eyes—may far better employ his time. Let him stop his two days at Copenhagen, fish his way up Norway, shoot it down Sweden, quaff the champagne of the "mère Cliquot" at St. Petersburg—he'll get it nowhere else—buy turquoises of the Tartars at Moscow (they'll all turn green a week after), on to Constantinople, poke his nose in a harem garden and get shot at, or say he did—ten to one if he's believed, if its true—and then on, on, avoiding all the interstices of travel, seeing what is best worth visiting in the world, sowing his wild oats, liberally, not wantonly—anything better than a later crop—and return to his own country and "do his duty in that state of life to which it has pleased God to call him." But for those more advanced in life—who have been everywhere and have done everything—who abominate being whirled for pleasure across the fair face of Europe by a locomotive—who detest German baths and their wickednesses—who, feeling they really know and are judges of what is grand and beautiful in this world, can afford, without losing their dignity, to be pleased with what is not perhaps first-rate—who like to drive through a country, to study its history, its customs, and its legends—who are content to take people as they find them—who prefer civil and kind treatment, with moderate prices, to fawning obsequiousness and robbery—to such people I can conscientiously promise much pleasure, much interest—especially if in spring-time—in their travels through the ancient province of Jutland and the fertile sea-girt islands of the Danish Archipelago.

THE END.

www.ingramcontent.com/pod-product-compliance
Lightning Source LLC
Chambersburg PA
CBHW030546300426
44111CB00009B/877